HE 87
D0646152

SATIRE *and* DISSENT

SATIRE and DISSENT

Interventions in Contemporary Political Debate

Amber Day

INDIANA UNIVERSITY PRESS

Bloomington & Indianapolis

This book is a publication of

Indiana University Press
601 North Morton Street
Bloomington, Indiana 47404-3797 USA

iupress.indiana.edu

Telephone orders 800-842-6796
Fax orders 812-855-7931
Orders by e-mail iuporder@indiana.edu

© 2011 by Amber Day
All rights reserved

Parts of chapter 3 previously appeared as "And Now . . . the News? Mimesis and the Real in *The Daily Show,*" in *Satire TV: Politics and Comedy in the Post-Network Era,* edited by Jonathan Gray, Jeffrey P. Jones, and Ethan Thompson (New York: New York University Press, 2009). Reprinted with permission of New York University Press. Parts of chapter 5 previously appeared as "Are They for Real? Activism and Ironic Identities," *Electronic Journal of Communication* 18.2–4 (2008). Reprinted with permission.

No part of this book may be reproduced or utilized in any form or by any means, electronic or mechanical, including photocopying and recording, or by any information storage and retrieval system, without permission in writing from the publisher. The Association of American University Presses' Resolution on Permissions constitutes the only exception to this prohibition.

∞ The paper used in this publication meets the minimum requirements of the American National Standard for Information Sciences—Permanence of Paper for Printed Library Materials, ANSI Z39.48-1992.

Manufactured in the United States of America

Library of Congress Cataloging-in-Publication Data

Day, Amber.
Satire and dissent : interventions in contemporary political debate / Amber Day.
p. cm.
Includes bibliographical references and index.
ISBN 978-0-253-35588-1 (cloth : alk. paper) — ISBN 978-0-253-22281-7 (pbk. : alk. paper) 1. Television in politics—United States. 2. Television talk shows—United States. 3. Documentary films—Political aspects—United States. 4. Irony—Political aspects. 5. Political satire, American—History and criticism. I. Title.
HE8700.76.U6D39 2011
791.45'65810973—dc22

2010033161

1 2 3 4 5 16 15 14 13 12 11

For AUDEN DAY MCEVOY

CONTENTS

ACKNOWLEDGMENTS

I have never managed to do anything without thoroughly mulling, debating, philosophizing, and kibitzing about the details with a team of advisors, and this book is no exception. I owe a special debt of gratitude to Jonathan Gray, who allowed me to tap his advice at many stages along the way and whose guidance was of enormous importance to me. Jeffrey Jones also provided valuable counsel and encouragement. Thanks, too, to Indiana University Press's readers for helping to mold the project into shape and to the staff at the press for shepherding it along. My colleagues at Bryant University have also been immensely supportive, particularly my chair, Mary Prescott, and the other members of the English and Cultural Studies department.

This project has gone through several incarnations, and its beginnings were significantly shaped by my coaches, Susan Manning, Jeffrey Sconce, and Tracy C. Davis, who provided patient mentoring and wise counsel. Robert Hariman and Chuck Kleinhans read chapters in the early stages, offering their time and their invaluable expertise, while Dilip Gaonkar ensured that I kept my head above water. Thanks also to some of my earliest readers, Iona Szeman, Ann Folino White, Stefka Mihaylova, Jesse Nijus, Dan Smith, and Christina McMahon, who supplied much-needed camaraderie along with their detailed feedback.

Finally, I could not have done this without my family, particularly without the help of Patrick McEvoy, my confidant, editor, advisor, and friend, who is an endless source of patience, enthusiasm, and love. And thanks to Auden, whose gestation roughly coincided with that of this book, supplying a non-negotiable deadline. Though he has yet to discover satire, this book is dedicated to him.

SATIRE *and* DISSENT

INTRODUCTION

Poking Holes in the Spectacle

While voter apathy may be a perpetual problem, interest in traditional news coverage may be on the wane, and professional political dialogue may be merely a repetition of partisan talking points, there is nevertheless a renaissance taking place in the realm of political satire. Turn on the television in any number of countries around the world, and you are bound to find at least one highly topical news-parody show providing its own take on contemporary events. As you forward choice clips from those shows, you will also likely encounter the newest satirical internet video. A trip to the multiplex offers you a slew of fiercely political documentaries which embody a striking blend of polemic and satire. Meanwhile, a multitude of activist groups is looking to capture your attention by staging elaborately ironic stunts or satirically impersonating their enemies. The political discourse taking place in the satiric register currently appears far more vibrant than any of the traditional outlets for serious political dialogue. And this is not something that has gone unnoticed. In the late twentieth and early twenty-first centuries, political satire has been attracting renewed attention, as various media from hard news to talk shows speculate about the impact of Michael Moore's *Fahrenheit 9/11* on a presidential election, loudly bemoan the rumor that American youth get more information from fake news programs like *The Daily Show* than from "legitimate" newscasts, and include prankster satirists in their roster of talking heads. Whether or not satire has become verifiably more popular, satiric media texts have become a part of (and a preoccupation of) mainstream political coverage, thereby making satirists legitimate players in serious political dialogue.

A number of new forms—or emergent genres—seem to have exploded in popularity almost simultaneously, all markedly political, all incorporating the real into the mimetic in striking ways, and all straddling the line between satire and serious political dialogue. This book focuses primarily on three of the most prevalent forms: the satiric documentary, the parodic news show, and ironic, media-savvy activism. These emergent genres are notable for their relative lack of fictionalized material and impersonations, relying instead on deconstructions of real news events, improvisational pranks, and ambushes of public figures. All share a uniquely performative form of parody and satire that injects the satirist's body into the traditional political world, as he or she physically engages, interrogates, and interacts with the real. They thereby cultivate a blurring of the traditional categories of entertainment and news, art and activism, satire and political dialogue. The question is, why? What does this simultaneous emergence tell us about contemporary media? Political dialogue? Publics and counterpublics? Notably, these forms have generated strong affective communities, capturing the interest of many in a way that organized politics has often struggled to do, as viewers look to the parodists to voice their opinions within the public arena. The fact that this mode has become so popular (not simply in audience numbers, but in increased legitimacy as a form of political speech) makes answering these questions particularly important.

Throughout what follows, I draw on the terms *irony, satire,* and *parody*. While I describe the documentaries, for the most part, as "satiric," refer to the fake news programs as "parodic," and use the more general "ironic" for the activist stunts, all three modes overlap to a significant degree. I have brought them together precisely because I see them as collectively making up the larger phenomenon I am describing. I will offer definitions of each mode when appropriate, but I also intentionally allow these concepts to bleed into one another to some extent, as I am less interested in formalism or a dissection of aesthetics than I am in analyzing the satiric/ironic/parodic register as a particular discursive strategy within the context of the larger media playing field. Similarly, while it would be possible to write a book about any one of the individual films, television programs, or activist groups profiled here (and, in a few cases, theorists already have), my intention is to provide a broad overview of the historical moment, connecting the dots to describe and analyze a large shift in both entertainment and political dialogue.

While I will argue against theories of satire and political humor that depict these modes as inevitably functioning conservatively, I do not wish to replace such theories with the impression that this humor is inherently subversive. Rather, I concur with Simon Dentith's assessment of parody when he argues that "there is no general politics of parody,"[1] as its workings are integrally dependent on the particular social and historical circumstances of its deployment. That said, I do believe that political satire may have more popular resonance and traction at particular moments in history than others. Part of the impetus for exploring this material is my feeling that political parody, irony, and satire have not only surged in popularity since the 1990s, but they have become complexly intertwined with serious political dialogue. In other words, these modes seem to offer a particularly attractive method of political communication at this moment, one that continues to gain traction.

This pull toward the ironic, this book contends, is directly related to the manufactured quality of contemporary public life. We live our lives interacting with virtual worlds as we play our video games, surf the web, and engage in virtual social networking—all of which may feel relatively comfortable. Importantly, though, when we tune back in to the here and now, the public discourse available to us is overwhelmingly designed as spectacle, though it rarely acknowledges itself as such. Political actors and corporate spokespeople are carefully staged, groomed, and scripted, and their armies of handlers are experts at getting their talking points on television. Everyone is fully aware that the "candid" moment of exchange between politician and citizen at a folksy roundtable has been assiduously preframed for us, but the news media rarely point this out. In a highly stage-managed, mediatized discursive landscape, then, earnestness can seem suspect. It is the very quality that politicians and other overproduced public figures bend over backward attempting to convey, while there is something about the unabashedly personal, ironic, tongue-in-cheek perspective that appears refreshingly authentic. This has, no doubt, contributed a great deal to the public's attraction to personalities such as Jon Stewart, Rick Mercer, Stephen Colbert, Michael Moore, Morgan Spurlock, and others who have all, as entertainers, slid into the role of semi-legitimate political pundits, while political activists craft spectacularly ironic stunts, similarly sliding into roles as entertainers. As this book will make clear, the satiric barb and the humorous political ambush are becoming more and more popular as means of momentarily gaining control of the conversational ball within political discourse.

Many commentators have noted that much of the exponential growth in satiric offerings in the United States in particular roughly coincided with the eight years of George W. Bush's tenure as president. That is not merely a coincidence. His administration greatly expanded presidential power while simultaneously limiting transparency and access. As a result, his staff became particularly skilled at using political doublespeak designed to obscure. At the same time, the terrorist attacks of September 11, 2001, produced an atmosphere in which the mainstream press was reticent to appear adversarial, meaning that much official language and policies went unchallenged, particularly in the lead-up to the Iraq war. The uninterrogated discourse of the Bush administration was then rife for deconstruction by ironists of all stripes, who moved in to fill the critical void (both inside and outside the United States). In acknowledgment of the boon that President Bush and his staff had been for political satirists, when Barack Obama won the election in 2008, there was a great deal of public discussion about whether figures like Jon Stewart of *The Daily Show* would be able to maintain their popularity and relevance. Since Obama had repeatedly pledged greater transparency, and since his ascendancy was surrounded by such rapturous, earnest excitement, there were predictions about the coming end of ironic humor. The *New York Times* reported, for instance, that in a public talk, Joan Didion had complained that "the United States in the era of Barack Obama had become an 'irony-free zone,' a vast Kool-Aid tank where 'naivete,' translated into 'hope,' was now 'in' and where 'innocence, even when looked at like ignorance, was now prized.'"[2]

This premature concern for the state of irony, though, now seems vastly overstated. Putting aside whatever naïveté someone like Didion sees in the character of excited Obama supporters, critiques such as these tend to assume that irony and earnestness are diametrically opposed, meaning that the presence of one negates the possibility of the other existing simultaneously. This is an assumption that I believe needs rethinking, and I will discuss it in much greater detail in the next chapter. Indeed, one of the consistent hallmarks of the newer forms of irony, parody, and satire collected here is their striking seriousness of purpose, where irony is put to use in the service of real political aims, pointing to flaws in the existing political discussion and gesturing toward possible solutions. Moreover, moving back to the specific assertion that the end of the Bush presidency or the start of the Obama era would somehow spell an end to the appeal of political satirists, this naïvely assumed that the characteristics of public debate would be instantly transformed due to the election (or deposition) of one man. While Obama may indeed live up to his promise of promoting greater openness about the actions of his administration, we will still have a system in which realities tend to be infinitely more complicated than the made-for-TV performances of those realities; in which public-relations-ese is the second language of most pundits, politicians, and corporate spokespeople; and in which public political discussion tends to be a difficult realm for anyone but industry insiders to break into. In other words, while the Bush administration did act as a catalyst for many of these tendencies, it nevertheless seems unlikely that the circumstances propelling the surge in political satire will all suddenly evaporate. And as long as these circumstances endure, so too will the desire to poke holes in the spectacle and to challenge the truth value of statements made by elites.

It should be acknowledged that the vast majority of the satiric forms collected here originate from the political left. While this may be somewhat a function of authorial selection, it is primarily because they far outnumber the opposition, particularly if we are focusing on the newly developing genres of performative satire. There are likely several reasons that this is the case. The most obvious is that, as has been noted, in the United States the government in power as these forms exploded was a conservative one, which generated frustration and resentment on the left and a desire to hear more liberal views expressed in the public discussion. In addition, there is likely also an issue of taste publics at play. Though I am wary of subscribing to facile descriptions of what, in the United States, is referred to as the red state/blue state divide, there are certainly some demographic factors that play a role in media tastes and attitudes. In North America, among younger, urban, liberal populations, there is some distrust of black-and-white morality and a related gravitation toward a more savvy, detached view of the world, which easily incorporates a knowingly ironic sense of humor and in which the affect of someone like Jon Stewart seems welcome and at home.

Despite these taste clusters, however, it is not the case that the ironic mode is universally embraced by those with liberal leanings. As we will explore in the next chapter, there are plenty of commentators from all points on the political spectrum who distrust irony. Equally, we should not assume that this form of ironic critique is the exclusive property of the political left. When satirists on the political right make use of it, they often do so for very similar reasons, out of belief that the mainstream political conversation is shutting out valid perspectives and that the media are not fulfilling their investigative function: the ironic salvo is intended to shift that discussion (see, for instance, my discussion of the Ben Stein documentary *Expelled* in chapter 4). In the early twenty-first century, there has undoubtedly been an enormous upsurge in the use of satire's edge to draw attention to hypocrisies and ironies in the supposedly serious world of political discourse and to advocate for alternative formulations of the issues of the day. It is thus inadequate to treat satire as mere commentary on the political landscape; rather, it seems crucial to understand it (along with other forms of discourse) as productive of that landscape.

This book's analysis of each of the genres involves several components: a historical review that traces how each genre developed out of earlier forms; a performance analysis of all aspects of the mise-en-scène, including the interactions between satirist and target, and the narrative framing of the subsequent text; and a discourse analysis that examines how the texts are situated within public debate, how they are framed by other media, and how they address potential spectators. I provide a general survey of the mushrooming field of satiric offerings on the internet, including the continuities in strategies between amateur and professional web videos and the productions of entertainers and activists working in other media, but I break the primary case studies into three main groupings. I see them as three fairly distinct genres that, while linked to previous forms, have all developed in their current incarnations quite recently. There is some cross-pollination between them, as several of the satirists have worked in multiple media, but the texts themselves can be clearly grouped by category.

By "parodic news show," I refer to a television show that is framed as if it were a straight news or current affairs program, but is understood by its audience to be a comedic send-up of the format. Though fake news has long been a successful comedic scenario within variety and sketch shows, in the twenty-first century a number of programs developed exclusively in this form have appeared in several countries. Though I touch on others,

I will concentrate primarily on *The Daily Show* and *The Colbert Report* in the United States and *This Hour Has 22 Minutes* and *The Rick Mercer Report* in Canada. Most of these shows have multiple rotating cast members, but there are a few people who have become particularly famous in the genre and whom I examine as celebrity figureheads: Jon Stewart, Stephen Colbert, and Rick Mercer.

The second genre is one I refer to as the "satiric documentary." The films in this category are politically motivated documentary exposés that are created in a comedic, tongue-in-cheek tone. The vast majority of these films are structured around a first-person narrator/protagonist who places himself in front of the camera as the everyman stand-in for the audience, the one who is willing to explore the issues firsthand and offer his own quirky personal account of the proceedings. The master of this form is filmmaker Michael Moore, on whose work I concentrate heavily. He has, however, popularized the genre to such an extent that others have followed in his footsteps, including Morgan Spurlock, whose work I also examine at some length.

Finally, I refer to "ironic activist groups" as a means of pointing to a particularly popular contemporary mode of political agitation. In this genre, groups that have a political issue they want publicly addressed attempt to capture media attention through spectacular stunts and jarringly ironic public happenings. One of the techniques I focus on in particular is one I refer to as "identity nabbing," in which members of the groups publicly pose as people they are not, often even attempting to stand in for their political enemies. I will also profile the more general practice of "culture jamming," which involves the ironic inversion of advertisements and other official texts, but I will concentrate most heavily on Billionaires for Bush, the Yes Men, and Reverend Billy. Billionaires for Bush attended protests and other events around the United States as exaggerated caricatures of the ultra-rich, ostensibly in support of President Bush and the Republican Party. The Yes Men have engineered multiple large-scale public stunts in which they attend conferences and even do television interviews as officials from companies to which they do not actually belong, speaking what they believe to be the real intent of these organizations. Meanwhile, Reverend Billy is a persona created by performance artist Bill Talen, a televangelist-style preacher at the helm of the Church of Life after Shopping, who, along with his congregation, stages shopping interventions and revivals at various retail corporations.

All of these examples, not incidentally, are markedly different from the wholly textual examples normally used to formulate analyses of the satiric mode within literary theory. Rather than being confined to the page and, quite often, to the realm of fiction and fantasy, these films, television programs, and pranks incorporate the real into the satiric in a tangible way. This ability to manipulate and alienate the real gives the satire a great deal of power. Rather than just doing a critical impersonation of a public figure and making up exaggerated lines for them, for instance, Michael Moore ambushes real officials, cornering them into playing *themselves* within the satiric frame and providing the damning evidence for the thesis he has already set up. Similarly, when Jon Stewart juxtaposes real footage of a politician's statements on several different occasions to demonstrate his/her duplicity, the piece becomes evidence in a real political argument on a level that a fictionalized skit does not. In a sense, then, these hybrid satiric genres become performative: they create that which they name/enact in the moment. This book theorizes specific instances of performative irony and satire in the belief that they function differently than the purely textual examples more commonly analyzed. For the same reason, exclusively text-centered theory also misses much of what is happening in these examples, as it cannot speak to the particularities of the interactions between players, including the specific dynamics that particular bodies bring to the encounters. Furthermore, literary-based theories can obscure the fact that parody/satire does not reside solely in narrative, but also in a singular act, such as the throwing of a pie at a public figure. The aim of this book, then, is to create cross-disciplinary dialogue around these hybrid case studies, allowing the material to both interrogate and be interrogated by theory within performance studies, media studies, communication studies, and literary studies.

The unique workings of these hybrid performative genres point up gaps both in the theories of parody/satire and in public sphere theory. The most common assumptions about political satire are that it is a mode which tends to be aesthetically detached from the problems it critiques and from any real desire for change, meaning that it is rarely treated as an example of substantive political speech (or is dismissed as the worst kind of negative, cynical politics). In a similar way, theorists of the public sphere have tended to focus on "rational" political debate, ignoring any discursive engagement that might take place in other registers. It seems crucial, however, to examine these texts as instances of political discourse and to take seriously their contributions to public dialogue.

While I clearly advocate understanding many of these examples as successful in directing public debate, it is still crucially important to note who is able to say what to whom and in what context. Here, the specificities of the embodied players are particularly salient. The vast majority of the individual satirists profiled here are both white and male. This is certainly not a coincidence. Each is able to poke fun at his own authority and at others' because he has some to begin with. As Michael Warner argues, the ability to abstract oneself into a universal public and to make the materiality of one's particular body seemingly irrelevant has always been the privilege of white, male, propertied bodies. This is why, Warner argues, at the height of the AIDS crisis, Ronald Reagan was able to argue that the disease had not spread to the "general public," since its primary victims were either homosexual or visible minorities but largely not straight, white males.[3] Similarly, Iris Marion Young explains that the widespread conception of the public which assumes that reason stands opposed to desire, affectivity, and the body "forces homogeneity upon the civic public, excluding from the public those individuals and groups that do not fit the model of the rational citizen capable of transcending body and sentiment."[4] White women and all people of color are still regrettably seen as the particular rather than as generalizable representatives of the public at large.

This becomes especially important in these examples of political satire, as the majority of the satirists are aiming to project an everyman quality. While Dustin Griffen holds that satire (meaning, primarily, classical literary satire) has always been an aristocratic art—disdainful and imperious, conscious of style, and suspicious of the mob[5]—I would argue that contemporary, mediatized political satire is being mobilized in a fairly populist register, as seemingly average Joes attempt to take down the mighty. But the figures who have achieved the most fame and popularity in this role are overwhelmingly white and male, both hypervisible and invisible in their material ordinariness. That said, most of these entertainers are still one step removed from the dominant, which allows them to play up their outsiders' eye for absurdity. Jon Stewart, for example, regularly references his Jewishness, while Rick Mercer and the entire original cast of *22 Minutes* are from Newfoundland, a poor and culturally marginalized province of Canada that is frequently the butt of national jokes. Rick Mercer also happens to be gay, though he does not make explicit reference to this fact on his program. And then there is Michael Moore, who is originally from the working class, a factor that he continues to allude to in his dress and demeanor (and that attracts a great deal of ire from his critics). Each draws on his distinction as a means of fueling his wry commentary on the social problems he sees around him, while still producing that commentary as the audience's everyman stand-in, who can display his disgust and amusement on our behalf. And it is absolutely because he is white and male that he can easily assume that privilege. The exceptions to this rule in the case studies profiled here are some of the activist groups, particularly the all-female Guerrilla Girls, who are already much more marginal than someone like Stewart or Moore, and whose members also wear gorilla masks in order to abstract themselves into an anonymous collective. Thus, while I am interested in tracking the successes of these genres in shifting public dialogue and influencing debate, it is also important to note the limitations on who has been granted the platforms from which to publicly speak up.

For those who have the ability, there are, of course, many advantages to attempting to stand in for a generalized public. The commentary, for instance, often avoids appearing whiny, too like a tirade, or dangerously transgressive. Instead, figures like Jon Stewart, Rick Mercer, and Morgan Spurlock act as if they are responding as anyone would to the crazy situations at hand, speaking out loud what we are all thinking, if perhaps in a somewhat wittier manner than we are able to do. In reality, of course, the views of these satirists are not actually what *everyone* is thinking. To a great extent, they interrogate and critique dominant perceptions and official policies, often articulating a perspective that is somewhat outside of the mainstream (some on a more radical level than others). I argue that, in so doing, they produce television programs, documentaries, and activist stunts which provide a focal point for many who already hold similar opinions, allowing people to identify through the consumption of and interaction with particular popular culture texts, while providing an easily shared reference. The effect, then, is that types of counterpublics are coalescing around these forms, as people look to the satirists as representatives who will push their particular worldview into the wider public sphere. Though it may seem odd that comedians, entertainers, and pranksters are garnering so much authority, it is precisely the blend of satire with the real in these emergent genres that accounts for their success; they function as a primary tool of alienation, posing questions that others might not, and, perhaps most important, attracting audiences, creating widely viewed popular culture texts, and insinuating their subject matter into broader discussions.

* * *

In classic literary theory on satire and political humor, there is an extensive tradition of criticism that links these modes unequivocally with the status quo and the shoring up of dominant norms. Much of this theory takes as its objects of study verse and prose satire written during the so-called age of satire in Western Europe from 1660 to 1800.[6] As Linda Hutcheon articulates, during the eighteenth century in particular, "most accounts—whether approving or disapproving—see satire and its irony as siding with authority in this period."[7] The assumption is that satirists ridicule non-normative behavior, thereby reinforcing existing attitudes. It is a theory that has continued to have widespread prominence to this day, with countless thinkers arguing that satirists typically ridicule particular personalities, going after character flaws and other weaknesses, but that they rarely critique the more crucial economic and political structures of their societies. The implication is that, while satire and political humor may appear transgressive, they are "essentially conservative in thought and impact,"[8] serving to assure us that, while particular individuals are fallible, the system itself works as it should. Many theorists take it as a given that satire, in all its forms and in all cultures, functions conservatively.

One particular incarnation of the satire-as-conservative-force view is the safety-valve theory, which builds on the theory of humor as a sublimation of aggression popularized by Sigmund Freud, asserting that, even if the satirist's intent is radical, she translates her anger and resentment into a satirical attack, purging both herself and her audience of the need for direct action.[9] As Leonard Feinberg puts it, "satire offers the reader the pleasures of superiority and safe release of aggressions."[10] He goes on to argue that satire is enjoyable *because* we know that it is only entertainment, that we get more pleasure from satire than from a sermon, even when they are making the exact same point, because we suspect the minister wants us to take action, while "we enjoy the satire because we know that nobody really expects us to do anything about it, and that we have no real intention of ever doing anything about it."[11] In short, satire would not be pleasurable if it actually pushed for political change; rather, it is entertainment, and entertainment only.

There are, on the other hand, theories of satire that take a more idealistic view of satire's function and intent. As Hutcheon puts it, this view holds that satire and irony have "the potential to offer a challenge to the hierarchy of the very 'sites' of discourse, a hierarchy based in social relations of dominance."[12] Satire is looked to, here, for its ability to unmask and to deconstruct, pointing us toward the flaws and the posturings of official policy.[13] The image of physically unveiling something or someone is one that recurs again and again in discussions of satire. Lillian and Edward Bloom argue further that, due to its ability to reveal our wrongs to us, great satire implies that "sensitivity to moral stumbling makes rectification a hope and preservation of the good possible."[14] However, they go on to explain, as do most theorists of satire, that despite its ability to reveal, satire ultimately has little political *effect* because it does not in itself initiate change and, in fact, rarely encourages it. Dustin Griffen, citing a study by Bertrand Goldgar on the relationship between satirists and politicians during the politically volatile period of Walpole's rule in Great Britain, concludes that since the writers of the time played no direct role in pressing measures in Parliament, it seems unlikely that their satire had any influence on politics itself.[15] The summation, time and again, is that satire is generally removed from the real machinations of the political world and thus has negligible political power.

The problem with these pat conclusions is that they are meant to explain all genres of satire in all cultures and periods. While it might be possible to make a strong argument about satire's remove from the political in a great many satiric texts, including some classical literary satire and the late-night talk-show monologues of today, the same argument does not seem to hold for the contemporary hybrid genres of satiric documentary, parodic news, and ironic activism. The clear separation between safely detached satire and real political life is often not as neatly identifiable in these genres, as individuals like Michael Moore like the Yes Men use their own bodies as primary compone stunts, physically interacting with the public figures in questi ing their impromptu reactions. These forms of performative satire are typically engaged, improvisatory, and embodied, often combining the deconstructive abilities of satire with the more visceral, carnivalesque qualities of political protest and street theater. Additionally, many of the satirists profiled here do actively remind their audiences that there are alternatives to the social problems portrayed and do entreat viewers to take action. This occurs to differing degrees in the various genres. The news shows, of course, are firmly rooted in the institutionalized environment of television, meaning they are usually less overtly political in the ways in which they exhort their audiences. In the cases of the documentarians and activists, however, all of them deliberately try to project the feeling of a community in opposition, presenting their viewers/readers with suggestions for political action and resources for further research, along with the sense that they are part of a larger group of people with shared goals. This becomes possible due to the networking of multiple media (websites, books, speaking tours), which extends the political efficacy beyond the reach of a singular text. Because the satirists are physically present in the works, there is also a tangible, recognizable person who is accountable for the views presented and who stands in as the audience's representative in pushing those views.

While the vast majority of theorists argue that satire can have little real political effect, this assertion rests on a conceptualization of political effect as a one-to-one relationship between the consumption of satire and action. As the Blooms lament, for example, "even the best intended satire does not readily convert desire into action."[16] They give little consideration, however, to either the slow process of shifting perceptions or the crucial work of creating a unified opposition to offending policies. In their dismissals of satire's political efficacy, both Griffen and Feinberg offhandedly concede, in Feinberg's words, that "when people already hold the opinions which satire expresses, those opinions are reinforced,"[17] but neither attributes much political significance to this process. I argue, however, that affirmation and reinforcement fulfill an integral community-building function, and that this function is a particularly important one when considering political discourse. For this reason, the other theoretical tradition in which this book intervenes is the discussion of the public sphere and oppositional counterpublics, which focuses on the circulation of public discourse and the competition of different worldviews within public culture.

All current debates about the concept of the "public sphere" must grapple with the original theory developed by Jürgen Habermas in his text *The Structural Transformation of the Public Sphere.* Habermas defines the "bourgeois public sphere" as "the sphere of private people come together as a public."[18] He pinpoints its development in the eighteenth-century coffeehouses of England, France, and Germany where individuals gathered for debate. In theory, all participants ignored the class and social backgrounds of the other speakers and concentrated on the relative rationality of the debate. According to Habermas, initial discussions around art and literature (newly accessible to the bourgeoisie) widened out to critiques of formerly unquestioned institutions (the monarchy in particular) and eventually "undercut the principle on which existing rule was based."[19] In the coffeehouses, "moral weeklies," which discussed literature and philosophy, began to be read and discussed, and gradually the press came to take on a critical responsibility. According to his description, public dialogue allowed the bourgeoisie to develop a powerful political consciousness. In other words, public forums for democratic debate led to the organic development of true public opinion.

Noting the significant exclusions that existed in the bourgeois public sphere, Habermas nevertheless holds up its basic principles as ideals to be contrasted with its debased contemporary counterpart. He describes a gradual transformation from a world of letters to one of cultural consumption, arguing that the bourgeois public sphere had initially been independent of the cycle of production and consumption, but once this threshold was crossed, rational/critical debate began to disappear as "the web of public communication unraveled into acts of individuated reception."[20] He targets the broadcast media of radio, television, and film in particular, explaining that they enthrall their audience, but "deprive it of the opportunity to say something and to disagree,"[21] meaning that the public sphere, according to Habermas, now exists in appearance only, as discussion is carefully controlled, assuming the form of a consumer item itself.

Both a widespread feeling that contemporary political discussion (particularly in the mass media) is inaccessible and remote, and the attractiveness of Habermas's ideal public sphere have contributed to the enduring popularity of his model, and the concept of the public sphere has continued to inspire and intrigue theorists from a wide variety of fields. The problem, however, is that there is good reason to believe that Habermas's bourgeois public sphere never actually existed as he described it, that it was (and is) impossible to bracket status differentials from deliberations, that there was never simply one unitary public sphere, and that his description of the contemporary public sphere is overly narrow and pessimistic. Most theorists now take these caveats as given and assume that one cannot speak unequivocally about *the* public.

Numerous thinkers have demonstrated that there are normally a multitude of different publics functioning simultaneously in any society. Nancy Fraser's insights are the most widely circulated. She argues that the bourgeois men involved in the coffeehouse culture in France deliberately developed elitist codes of conduct in order to distinguish themselves from other existing spheres, especially the more feminine salon culture. Thus, to conclude simply that women and the lower classes were regretfully excluded from the only functioning public sphere is misleading. Rather, contemporaneous with the coffeehouses, there existed counterpublics "elaborating alternative styles of political behavior and alternative norms of public speech."[22] She likewise interrogates the assumption that it is possible for interlocutors to bracket status and to deliberate as if they were social equals, arguing that, in stratified societies, "unequally empowered social groups tend to develop unequally valued cultural styles,"[23] and therefore informal pressures give the dominant group a significant advantage. For this reason, both historically and currently, it has been necessary for subordinated social groups to develop their own "counterpublic spheres," enabling them to "invent and circulate counterdiscourses to formulate oppositional interpretations of their identities, interests, and needs."[24]

While Fraser demonstrated that there are a number of different publics and counterpublics existing simultaneously in any society, others have refined the concept. Michael Warner, for instance, specifies that both publics and counterpublics are not just congeries of people or particular demographic groups. Rather, they are "intertextual frameworks for understanding texts against an organized background of the circulation of other texts, all interwoven not just by citational references but by the incorporation of a reflexive circulatory field in the mode of address and consumption."[25] In other words, publics are imaginary relationships between strangers, created and sustained through the circulation of discourse, requiring participation (or at least attention) for membership. Warner also explains that individuals inevitably belong to many different publics simultaneously. This is an idea I wish to explore further. For politicized publics and counterpublics, in particular, it seems especially important to be able to privilege one public over others in a particular moment and to make members feel as if they are actively part of a community. As Warner explains, each act of public discourse commits itself to the possible participation of any stranger, but it also entails a world-making function, as "public discourse says not only 'Let a public exist' but 'Let it have this character, speak this way, see the world in this way.' It then goes in search of confirmation that such a public exists."[26] Or, alternatively, as I argue, it then sets out to *convince* the world that such a public exists, while making a case for the importance of its outlook.

I conceptualize of the organization and relationship among publics as a constantly shifting Venn diagram. Some of the circles are undeniably closer to some sort of center (though none makes up a center in its entirety), with others that overlap in significant areas, and still others that are quite far removed. But all are pushing and shoving to a certain extent in order to obtain a better position, resulting in gradual, slow-moving shifts in cultural assumptions and norms. While some would argue that the multiplicity of publics combined with the lack of an ideally functioning democratic public forum render the very concept of the public sphere theoretically useless, I hold that it remains an important idea. The term allows us to speak both of the various intersecting realms of public debate that do in fact exist (however imperfectly) and of those we might wish to exist. Most important, if we expand the definition of what constitutes a public sphere, the concept provides a framework for thinking about the competition of multiple voices in multiple, overlapping publics, for taking up the project Fraser later suggests of theorizing "both the multiplicity of public spheres in contemporary late capitalist societies and also the power differentials among them."[27]

However, in order to analyze competing discourses within a mediatized world, one cannot simply dismiss the content carried by the mass media. Though the mass media do not account for the entirety of public dialogue, they do clearly have an enormous role in the circulation of discourse. One of the most problematic elements of Habermas's original work on the public sphere is the wholesale endorsement of a culture-industry model of media communication. (Habermas was a student of Theodor Adorno, one of the major thinkers associated with the critique of the "culture industry.") According to this view, the meanings of mass media texts are entirely created by their producers and then imposed on audiences. The assumption is that the majority of spectators passively receive the messages created by the industry, which inevitably shore up the position of the ruling elite. The problem with such a model, however, is that it implies, first, that all viewers receive and interpret texts the same way, leaving no room for the agency and diversity of individual spectators, and second, that all mass media texts have roughly the same cultural positioning and power. To subscribe to such a view, then, makes it impossible to attend to the various voices and positions vying for attention from across the media playing field and ignores the distinct currents of opinion within public discourse that are constantly pushing against one another—what Raymond Williams, for instance, labeled the "dominant," "residual," and "emergent" currents in social relations, which he understood as always dynamic and in flux.[28]

It is too easy to set up a binary between an idealized sphere of rational debate and a debased one of pure media consumption. As Craig Calhoun points out, Habermas looks to the major thinkers of the eighteenth and nineteenth centuries and compares them to the soap operas of the twentieth century, completely ignoring contemporary poets, philosophers, and avant-garde artists. I would add that he is also uninterested in the effects that eighteenth-century "low culture" had on discourse. Latent in this omission is the assumption that the forms of communication most popular in the eighteenth century were all linked to "high culture," discussions about art and literature eventually leading to reasoned critiques of political philosophy and policy. In contrast, he assumes that the most popular forms of communication in contemporary times are, by definition, lowbrow media that can only numb minds. The contrast is clearly slanted from the outset, already determining the conclusions. Instead, as Bruce Robbins argues, rather than looking backward to a hazily mythic lost public, we should attend to the "actual multiplicity of distinct and overlapping public discourses, public spheres, and scenes of evaluation that already exist, but that the usual idealizations have screened from view."[29] Without a doubt, that includes public discourse anchored in mass media communication.

This project seeks to take seriously the narratives circulating within popular culture, many of which are disseminated via the mass media. That means avoiding the tendencies of two (admittedly caricatured) extremes within media studies: on one hand, assuming that meaningful discourse is almost impossible within the existing mass media because of its unidirectional flow and emphasis on spectacle, and, on the other hand, fetishizing the power of the individual viewer to radically subvert the intended meaning of all mass media texts, resulting in unfettered, liberatory play. Instead, it is important to remain aware of the vested interests, distortions, and markedly unequal territories of the media, while insisting that it would be absurd to give up on the possibilities for speech and exchange. Since the mass media are clearly not going away any time soon, it is crucial to understand the circulation of varied voices within them and especially to track how narratives and worldviews that are at all different from the dominant manage to insinuate themselves into mainstream channels of communication and to influence the direction of public dialogue.

I will trace the tactics and trajectories of those who are successful in negotiating the realities of the system. Most of my examples are, to varying degrees, considered "alternative," often speaking to relatively small publics or espousing views outside the mainstream, though all are aiming for media amplification. They include the more institutionalized, less overtly activist television programs, the avowedly partisan documentaries, and the public stunts of the more fringe and deeply politicized activist groups. All have achieved some success in attracting attention and somehow influencing the tenor of public discussion, whether or not they have been ultimately successful in achieving their end goals. Each is important in any consideration of the realities of competing voices within twenty-first-century political discourse.

It is important to note that, while these satirists clearly seek to reach as wide an audience as possible, either through their own media productions or through news coverage and publicity, the goal is no longer to simply get media coverage as an end in itself, as it was for some of the '60s era political and countercultural groups that were enamored with the newfound power of the mass media. As Todd Gitlin points out, many of those earlier groups were consigned to marginality through mass media framing devices of trivialization, polarization, and emphasis on internal tensions.[30] The goal of the contemporary groups, however, tends to be to actually gain some control over the larger framing process. Fake news anchor Jon Stewart, for instance, has built his reputation on his ability to critique the straight news media, mercilessly ridiculing what he perceives as its reliance on formulas, appetite for sensationalism, and herd mentality. Meanwhile, Michael Moore creates seemingly absurd stunts and interactions with his targets in order to then shape the footage into his own carefully controlled narrative. Finally, a group such as the Yes Men convincingly impersonates and embodies authority so that it may then deconstruct it. All of them attempt to gain some control over the way in which particular issues are publicly discussed. Though the temptation is to view these examples as "only entertainment," consisting of amusing quips about contemporary political arguments, it is important to examine their attempts to actively reframe those arguments.

One of the shortcomings in the theorizing around the concept of public spheres is the exclusive focus, inherited from Habermas, on "rational discourse." In other words, if one discusses political discourse within the mass media, emphasis should gravitate almost exclusively to straight news and current affairs programs. As Jonathan Gray explains, "Entertainment is embarrassingly misunderstood and undervalued by too many who write of the public sphere, and it is long overdue that media and cultural studies reappraise the value of entertainment to the average citizen."[31] If we conceptualize of public discourse as existing only in the socially sanctioned outlets of serious debate, we miss a plethora of concurrent political, meaning-making sites, some of which have much more resonance and appeal for a great number of people. As these examples demonstrate, there is plenty of discursive exchange that takes place in the form of the seemingly "irrational"—in the registers of parody, satire, fiction, and nonsense. While political theorists tend to define the public sphere(s) fairly narrowly as the realm of outward-directed, specifically political organizing and discussion, I would describe the concept more broadly as social communication about all matters of collective concern, discursive spaces in which social narratives are created, sustained, dispersed, and challenged. Rather than restrict the scope of where such exchanges take place (even if we expand the list of media forums that make the cut), I concur with Noëlle McAfee's description of public spheres as consisting of the grids and flows of communication "through the mass media, through dinner table conversation, web logs, cable access television, the local paper, the art world, PTA meetings, letters to the editor, the chattering on the playground and in the classroom."[32] Much of that communication occurs not as serious, rational argument, but in every other register of exchange, including sarcasm, irony, parody, and satire, all of which afford the opportunity to say things one otherwise might not in "serious" debate.

Many of the satirists profiled here are attempting to challenge the taken-for-granted attribution of rationality to straight news and current affairs programs and other outlets of serious political discussion. *The Daily Show*'s host, Jon Stewart, goes to great lengths to demonstrate the flaws and biases of straight news coverage, while the parodic persona Stephen Colbert has created of a right-wing talk-show host regularly brags about how irrelevant he believes facts to be and how much more important his own opinions are. The implicit argument is that rationality is simply impossible when the gatekeepers of political discourse are so clearly enmeshed in ideology (and ego). Similarly, the Yes Men brazenly impersonate officials of the World Trade Organization, operating under the beliefs that public relations rhetoric has obscured the rational discussion of world trade and global inequities and that drastic (even duplicitous) steps are warranted in order to insert different language into the discussion. While the forms of these television programs, movies, and stunts may be more deliberately absurd and playful than what is typically included in notions of rational political debate, the subject matter discussed is often remarkably similar. And, as Gray explains about the parodic television program *The Simpsons,* the critique—here, too, embedded in the language of the irrational—"acknowledges that much of the media is failing to create a public sphere, but the talk *about* that failure builds its own public sphere."[33] Indeed, the eager fandom surrounding each of the examples surveyed here indicates that there is a desire to continue circulating these critiques and that there is pleasure in that shared circulation.

Of course, it is more difficult to pry apart competing voices and ideologies when we stray from the more cut-and-dried world of straight political argument and into the messier realm of entertainment and popular culture However, it is through the more diffuse background and widely shared world of popular culture that we absorb the majority of our beliefs, ideologies, and cultural narratives. Though perhaps less spectacular than a fiery parliamentary-style debate, it is in the everyday iterations of popular culture where the battle over hegemony is continuously waged. As described by Gramsci, hegemony is never a fixed, unchanging set of norms but is, rather, in constant flux. With that in mind, Stuart Hall explains that popular culture "is the arena of consent and resistance. It is partly where hegemony arises, and where it is secured."[34] Within our mediatized popular culture, there is a continuous push and pull as various social groups and ideologies engage in discursive struggle. John Fiske gives a particularly good account of this process, arguing that most (if not all) contemporary societies are multi-discursive, not mono-discursive, and so it is particularly important to uncover "the processes of discursive contestation by which discourses work to repress, marginalize, and invalidate others; by which they struggle for audibility and for access to the technologies of social circulation; and by which they fight to promote and defend the interests of their respective social formations."[35] This is certainly not an even fight by any stretch of the imagination, but there is never such a thing as total consensus or blanket discursive control. Even within the jittery, play-it-safe confines of the mainstream broadcast media, one can almost always locate competing voices.

This project, then, will examine several examples of those working against the grain, those who use the license afforded to parodists and satirists to push the direction of public dialogue. I am not making any claims about the ability of these television programs, films, and public stunts to single-handedly cause tangible political change. I think that any attempt to attribute that sort of causality to one isolated text—or, conversely, to *expect* a political text to unilaterally start a revolution—is absurd. Instead of holding out for monumental change, I am more interested in incremental shifts in influencing public debate and in creating or mobilizing political communities. Part of the function of shifting and influencing discourse involves, on a basic level, pushing particular narratives or worldviews that may be peripheral (and even totally foreign) to the dominant into the mainstream. It also can involve what Carol Burbank refers to as "reiterative resignification,"[36] gradually changing the pictures and associations that we have of particular people, concepts, or ideologies.

Much of the time, however, neither is possible without some sort of coherent oppositional position, which is why it is equally important to create the feeling of community in resistance and to mobilize those who may already share similar assumptions. Larry Bogad, writing about the function of "guerrilla electioneering" (when parodic political candidates enter real political races), explains their appeal through Bakhtin's concept of the carnivalesque. He observes that, while the primary function of these campaigns may be to degrade and to alienate, the secondary function is regenerative, which for Bakhtin is a necessary aspect of any carnivalesque endeavor. This function is to "echo, entertain and energize the performer's base community(ies), and communicate grievances from that marginal position to the center through parody and irony."[37] Likewise, the political satirists and activists profiled here largely seek both to strip down and to build back up, to shame and to inspire. It is through work at both poles that change can then occur.

* * *

This book begins with a discussion of the controversies and accusations that have dogged the ironic mode and a focus on the upsurge in politically engaged, earnestly sincere forms of irony. Narrowing into more specific examples, it then examines parodic news shows, satiric documentaries, and ironic forms of political activism. Importantly, while it is commonly assumed that irony is a mode of disengagement, that ironists make dismissive quips from the sidelines rather than committing to or advocating for anything sincere, in much of this material there is a striking blend of both irony and earnestness. It is the assumption of disengagement that has led many critics to assume that irony and satire contribute to cynicism. This becomes particularly apparent in discussions of the parodic news shows, which, due to their high profile, have attracted a great deal of hand-wringing over the belief that they must engender cynicism about the political process. However, closer analysis reveals that, far from treating politicians and policies with detached amusement, these shows often offer sustained dissections of political problems and demonstrate an engaged commitment to the development of solutions, creating a vibrant space for critique of the inadequacies of contemporary political discourse.

In providing a platform for political analysis and debate, all of the examples surveyed here have succeeded in becoming objects of identification for those who already share similar ideas. As I will explore in detail in discussing the documentary filmmakers, this frequently results in the attraction of political counterpublics around them, as fans look to the television personalities, filmmakers, and activists to articulate their views in public forums. And, in the case of the activist groups, which are most explicitly attempting to motivate action, the ultimate aim is to spur observers to actively identify with the importance of the issue at hand and to continue circulating the critique. None of these satirists is aiming for revolutionary change; rather, they are committed to the importance of incremental effects, of getting people engaged, and of slowly shifting debate.

All of the distinct genres, I argue, are linked by several important characteristics, including a desire to challenge the standard formulas and narratives within the mainstream press, a choice to do so by highlighting absurdities and inconsistencies through the use of irony, and a reliance on impromptu personal interactions and engagement in an attempt to reveal, trip up, or sabotage. And though each has somewhat different aims (they strive for differing combinations of efficacy and entertainment), they have all become popular culture phenomena to some extent, functioning as cultural reference points and attracting affective communities around them, thereby heightening the sense of community in opposition.

Across the board, the examples surveyed here are designed as directed salvos against the cynicism of manufactured political debate. They offer a method of influencing the political discussion, even just in minor ways, by poking holes in the preframed narratives, talking points, and public relations screens; and by providing to legions of fans relief, satisfaction, a sense of purpose, and connection with others. Ultimately, the realm of the satiric is one of the most vibrant arenas of public debate in operation today.

TWO

Ironic Authenticity

There is something synergistic about the relationship between new technologies and the emergent forms of irony, satire, and parody. The way in which contemporary irony has developed is intimately tied to the creation of digital technologies. As discussed in the introduction, the manufactured quality of public life has made expressions of serious earnestness somewhat suspect. One could argue that new technologies have been central to provoking this situation by helping to turn public life into highly managed spectacle; however, these technologies are equally being mobilized as means of critiquing and deconstructing that spectacle. The internet, in particular, has played a central role in the rapid dissemination and widespread popularity of many of these forms, while the digital technologies that enable easy access to video footage and provide accessible tools for editing and repurposing that footage or for easily mimicking existing media have had an enormous influence on the modes of engagement used by contemporary satirists. In short, the technology has made ironic critique easy; it is relatively simple to create a variety of pointed ironic commentaries on media discourse as it unfolds. Though many worry that the presence of irony must signal a lack of real engagement or sincerity, there has, in fact, been a flowering of irony wielded for earnest political aims.

Nowhere is the current pervasiveness of ironic/satiric humor more noticeable than in email inboxes and Facebook updates. The internet is a crucial component of the success of the majority of satirists examined here. At the most basic level, almost all of them are featured heavily on video-sharing sites such as YouTube and Google Video. There is no doubt that their popularity is at least partially due to their success as viral phenomena, with short clips from, say, *The Daily Show* forwarded widely among friends, transcending television schedules and national borders (though, in the case of the Comedy Central programs, Viacom keeps attempting to exert proprietary control over this internet replication). Communication over the internet has also been key to sustaining communities around these forms, particularly for those created with a clearly activist agenda. Michael Moore, for instance, maintains an enormous email list, sending missives about the topics covered in his films and about many others that are not, attempting to mobilize fans into action. The Billionaires for Bush post instruction manuals online, knowing that, given the blueprints, new Billionaires chapters will spring up across the country, while the Yes Men make use of an extensive email network to raise money for their latest pranks.

Beyond these more large-scale examples, though, there are also millions of individuals and small start-up companies making their own videos for web distribution (as well as much larger companies and conglomerates mimicking the genre). These are created at every level of production quality, from shaky camera-phone footage to sophisticated animation. An enormous number of these draw on irony, parody, and satire as the means through which to hook their audiences. And as the popularity of this sort of user-generated content has exploded, many sites, such as FunnyOrDie.com and CollegeHumor.com, have sprung up specifically to distribute it. The tactics of communication popular in these videos are also common to each of the satirists profiled in this book: editing to create ironic juxtapositions, the crafting of mashups that meld familiar snippets of popular culture with one another to generate unexpected moments of resonance, the creation of sophisticated parodies, and the shaming of public figures through collections of contradictory or duplicitous statements. Henry Jenkins and Stephen Duncombe point to practices such as these as making up a large-scale shift in communication, arguing, "this is how we tell our stories now—we quote from the media and the culture around us."[1] In making this point, they also explicitly critique the long-cherished model of the media consumer as a passive receiver, arguing that people act as "citizen-consumers" all the time, speaking back to and through the media field around them. This is a hallmark of the developing media age, which Jenkins refers to as a "convergence culture," a terrain where "old and new media collide, where grassroots and corporate media intersect, where the power of the media producer and the power of the media consumer interact in unpredictable ways."[2]

This relationship between large-scale producers and consumers, or industry and individuals is, of course, nowhere near an equal one, but there is nevertheless a robust level of engagement and imbrication, as people interact with their favorite texts, create their own paratexts, and craft their own social commentaries, often drawing on irony to do so. And all of it is similar to what the professional satirists and activists do on a larger scale. Though I focus heavily on the improvisatory, performative dimensions of their work, this type of performance is tailored to this new media universe and makes use of the new technologies as tools of critique and commentary. As literary theorist Linda Hutcheon describes it, irony is made of both a said and an unsaid meaning, along with an attitude or judgment about both.[3] *The Daily Show*'s Jon Stewart stages a conversation between himself and stopped and started newsclips as a way of interrogating their contents, while Michael Moore draws on old film footage and music to set the mood and to set up expectations in which his unwitting targets must play their part. Each uses a savvy form of irony as a tool for investigating, critiquing, and shaping the wider field of mediated discourse. Despite this widespread use of irony, though, or more likely *because* of it, irony is not a universally respected mode of communication. Worries about its ubiquity and speculations about its effects constantly swirl around irony, particularly when it is mixed with the political. Though much of this debate now centers around popular programs like *The Daily Show* and the mushrooming offerings on the web, the anxiety around irony is not new. Literary theorists have been arguing about the effects of irony for centuries, but its perceived prevalence as a cultural dominant since the 1990s has made it a particularly prominent contemporary preoccupation in both academic and journalistic criticism. It is worth briefly retracing some of these conversations and noting the recurring themes that bubble to the surface regardless of the specific object under discussion.

IRONY AS FRIEND OR FOE?

In the 1990s, *irony* was the catchall term that gestured toward the sensibilities of postmodernism, used as both description and explanation of the contemporary North American landscape, but its prevalence also created a backlash of sorts, with numerous voices speaking out about the dangers posed by this mode of discourse, a critique that reached a fever pitch at the end of the decade and culminated in the publication of Jedediah Purdy's *For Common Things.* Purdy's book and the subsequent discussion around it offer a good summation of the persistent suspicions and debates that surround irony. Purdy describes the contemporary culture as one inhabited by people who are "exquisitely self-aware"[4] and simultaneously terrified of appearing naïve. He sees the ironic pose as one motivated by "a fear of betrayal, disappointment, and humiliation, and a suspicion that believing, hoping, or caring too much will open us to these."[5] Instead, we, particularly the younger and more media-savvy among us, revel in the clever ironic quip, looking to Jerry Seinfeld (this being the late '90s) as our patron saint. In Purdy's description, the majority of us finds it difficult to speak earnestly about personal matters, while speaking earnestly about public issues is almost impossible, since we all know better than that. Everything we could say, we presume to already be a cliché. This protective layer of irony has had profound effects on public life in the United States, he argues, since "one of the defining features of the current generation's experience is the disappearance of credible public crusades, or the belief that politics can bring about an elementally different and better world. Instead of inspiration, contemporary irony finds in public life a proliferation of cant that reinforces ironic skepticism."[6]

It is a damning prognostication, and Purdy was both lionized and ridiculed within public discussion, as he was immediately seized on by commentators on all sides of the issue as the anti-irony poster boy. The media excitement over his book can be partially explained by his almost too-perfect accompanying personal narrative, as revealed in detail in a *New York Times* magazine feature: a 24-year-old boy wonder, he was home-schooled on a farm in West Virginia before attending a prestigious private school, followed by Harvard and then Yale law school. But the topic also seemed to strike a nerve, with both *Time* magazine and the *Christian Science Monitor,* among others, weighing in. Some praised him his insight and wisdom while many more dismissed him as a self-righteous scold. What most were reacting to, not surprisingly, was Purdy's treatment of irony, though he later expressed confusion over this focus. He mused, "I am somewhat frustrated that the attention paid to the book has concentrated so much on irony, which I intend[ed] as a way into a broader argument about indifference."[7] But this is precisely the problem. Purdy uses the word *irony* as a sort of open-ended container for an imprecise range of qualities, ultimately gesturing toward a generalized disengagement from public life. As one commentator snarkily but presciently put it, "Purdy's 'irony' is a mishmash of cynicism, nastiness, selfishness, self-awareness, individualism, apathy: a catchall for every meretricious modern attitude that goes against the communitarian world-view of the Appalachian back-to-the-land hamlet where he was (you guessed it) home-schooled."[8] Indeed, it seems that Purdy had a cluster of contemporary attitudes that he wanted to critique, and he worked backward to then choose the term *irony* to describe them.

Given that Purdy uses the term quite sloppily, we could simply dismiss his critique as actually having little to do with our discussion of irony. However, I believe that his usage of the concept is symptomatic of more widespread assumptions about the mode. There seems to be a commonly held belief that where there is irony, parody, or poking fun, there must be a smirking cynicism and, by extension, political disengagement. This is an accusation that consistently dogs irony in all of its forms. As discussed in the introduction, however, there are currently a growing number of artists and activists who are looking to irony as a prime tool with which to combat indifference, to advocate for change, and to get others riled up. In other words, the opposing camp sees irony as a potential *antidote* to cynicism and disengagement, precisely the opposite of its detractors. Again, this split does not necessarily break down along ideological lines. Though the more prominent twenty-first-century examples of North American political irony tend to be on the left, there are many on the right embracing irony and plenty of others on the left (like Purdy) condemning it. If anything, we can perhaps talk of a generational split, with younger generations taking to irony as a mode of political engagement in greater numbers, though that too may be overly simplistic. Ultimately, the two opposing viewpoints simply regard irony wildly differently, one seeing it as a mode of smug detachment signaling a lack of commitments and will, the other seeing it as a potentially powerful form of critique and mode of engagement.

This split was made apparent in an exchange between Purdy and *Slate* writer Michael Hirschorn shortly after the book's release. A portion of the discussion centers on a part of the book that most other reviewers ignored, in which Purdy refers to the flip-side of irony as an upsurge in belief in mythical figures like angels (also discussing the self-fulfillment philosophies of magazines like *Wired* and *Fast Company*). His argument is that the ironic view positions each individual as essentially alone, meaning that, despite our attempt to use irony as a guard against these emotions, sadness and disappointment creep into our lives. He points to the outpouring of novels and television shows involving angels as a form of compensation, though it is an ultimately fruitless one, as angels

> not only minister to us as isolated, needy bundles of wishes and fears, but paradoxically help us to stay that way. They provide a species of reassurance that we can have alone, in the privacy of our apartments and offices. Being at home in the world does not have to mean changing or reaching beyond ourselves, adjusting our habits and desires to our places and communities; instead, the world answers our wishes, just because they are ours.[9]

In his discussion with *Slate* magazine, he repeats these assertions, explaining that the two tendencies are part of the same phenomenon. If irony is one particularly popular pose, "so is a kind of spirituality, sincerity, and mawkishness that even those who utter it often can't seem to take seriously—for good reason." Hirschorn has a different perspective, however, arguing that the creeping sentimentality of the angel shows, like the programming on the WB network, the content of numerous pop songs, and a generalized "posey earnestness, protesting-too-much religiosity, and beyond–New Age solipsism" are, in fact, all arguments for the *necessity* of irony.[10] Hirschorn wants to hang on to irony as a particularly useful tool for cutting through all of that treacly posturing. Implicit in his position is the assumption that irony is a way of engaging with (even interrogating) the world rather than being a simple retreat from it. This premise is one that Purdy does not directly respond to, so the back-and-forth proceeds with each man painting a different picture of this thing called "irony."

This dispute replayed itself with a vengeance in the weeks immediately following the terrorist attacks of September 11, 2001. As columnists and commentators struggled to express what people were feeling and how the United States was to proceed, one of the pronouncements that started to echo through newspapers and magazines was that, if nothing else, irony would certainly now be put in its place. Graydon Carter, editor of *Vanity Fair,* announced the end of the age of irony, as did Roger Rosenblatt of *Time* magazine, who explained that, up until this moment, "the good folks in charge of America's intellectual life have insisted that nothing was to be believed in or taken seriously. Nothing was real. With a giggle and a smirk, our chattering classes—our columnists and pop culture makers—declared that detachment and personal whimsy were the necessary tools for an oh-so-cool life."[11] However, nothing is more real, he went on, than evil, something that now has to be taken seriously. Finally throwing off the tyranny of the ironists, he prophesied, people would "at last be ready to say what they wholeheartedly believe."[12] Many editorialists loudly concurred. There were, however, a few public voices of dissent.

Addressing these widespread pronouncements, David Beers of *Salon,* for instance, drew his readers' attention to the way in which irony was being defined, pointing out that, in contemporary public discourse, the term had somehow become associated with moral relativism and self-absorption, as the "nihilistic shrug of an irritatingly shallow smartass."[13] Though he expressed doubt that this type of irony was ever really as prevalent as its critics believed, he was comfortable with bidding it goodbye in the wake of 9/11. However, its demise, he hoped, would then open the way for a golden age of irony, the true, critically engaged kind that pays attention to contradictions and paradoxes, all the more important in times of crisis, when we may be too eager for moral certitudes. In what now seems a vaguely prophetic assessment, he went on to explain:

> That kind of irony would wonder if in this new battle on behalf of freedom, we may rush to strip away civil liberties. That kind of irony would wonder whether this new kind of war, waged to make us safe from terrorist attacks, might plunge the world into a far more dangerous conflagration. . . . To note these ironies is to engage yourself in the grave purpose at hand and take some responsibility for helping to think it through—and that's the opposite of ironic detachment.[14]

Indeed, many would now argue that a version of Beers's pessimistic policy prediction is exactly what happened in the years immediately following 9/11, though those years also saw the flowering of e irony. (Incidentally, Purdy also weighed in on the issue in an int directly after 9/11 in the *New York Times* and, like Beers, suggested that, as the mood got bellicose, it might actually be a good thing to inject some irony.)[15]

Looking back at the aftermath of 9/11, Jamie Warner points out that the Bush administration was a step ahead of Rosenblatt's call to seriousness, as it "immediately, forcefully, and repeatedly invoked an old, yet very useful and efficient emotional framework for making sense of the terrorist attack: the dichotomy of Good versus Evil."[16] This framework served as a powerful national unifier, but also severely restricted any form of dissent. As Warner explains, "[T]he either/or construction not only had the effect of demonizing the terrorists, it also worked to demonize anyone who questioned either side of the binary or even the construction of the binary itself. Any interpretation that differed from the official account of the attacks was labeled suspect, unpatriotic, even treasonous."[17] This included journalistic coverage. She goes on to enumerate studies of the news coverage of the time and subsequent interviews with journalists, which all indicate that the press felt obliged not only to repeat the terms of good versus evil used by the Bush administration, but to actively reaffirm that they, too, were on the correct side.

Warner's larger argument is that the satiric newspaper *The Onion* refused to be bound by this framework, instead using irony to introduce the terrain of ambiguity, thus prompting the reader to question the good versus evil dualism so dominant everywhere else. She asserts that the paper invited critical examination of the Bush administration's policies but "in a way not easily reappropriated and dismissed by the hegemonic frame."[18] While I would certainly agree with this claim, I think it is important to note that *The Onion* is not the only example we can point to. Rather, the lack of hard-hitting investigative reporting or substantive critique of the administration's actions in the mainstream press created a vacuum that was soon filled by a variety of ironic critiques. Though they certainly did not have the same frame-setting power as the mainstream media (and are widely variant in terms of cultural prominence), voices such as those of *The Daily Show*, Michael Moore, viral video makers, and numerous activist groups attempted to undermine the power of the dominant narrative, many drawing legions of fans eager to hear this critique made. Writing in

2008, Megan Boler and Ted Gournelos introduce an "Irony and Politics" edition of the *Electronic Journal of Communication* by suggesting, "it is not a coincidence that popularized satire has flourished during the past eight years of corporate media's all-too-frequent willingness to function as a mouthpiece for U.S. government interests."[19] Indeed, to combat frustration and rage over the lack of substantive political debate in the traditional outlets, many increasingly "adopted irony as a language of dissent."[20]

Like Boler and Gournelos and a number of other media and cultural studies researchers interested in these new forms of political satire (Gray, Jones, Baym, Duncombe), I clearly orient to irony as a mode of engagement rather than as a cynical dismissal of politics. This is not because I believe irony to be somehow inherently progressive, but because, in the contemporary moment, there has been such an enormous upsurge in its usage as a means of dialoging with the political sphere. There is no question that irony and self-referentiality have been pervasive for some years now, particularly for younger generations, and that some of it indeed takes the form of the distanced savvyness Purdy finds so off-putting. Can irony be used for the type of self-protection and apathy he references? Absolutely. But that does not mean we should elide all forms of irony with these modes. Perhaps because irony is such a lingua franca, there has been a movement to use the language of irony, the self-referentiality, the wit, and the bite, as political tools in the hope for change. The ironists discussed here are clearly anything but apathetic. They and their fans view themselves as actively engaging with the political world, and their popularity attests that they have struck a resonant chord.

It is again a case of divergent sensibilities. As touched on in the introduction, in a media-saturated world of manufactured emotion, earnestness itself is not always believable. Instead, for some, the personal and ironic can offer a more comfortable way of getting to authenticity, one that seems more transparent in its willingness to point to its own flaws and fakeries. Not incidentally, Purdy's book was released at almost the same time as *A Heartbreaking Work of Staggering Genius,* Dave Eggers's self-referential, cheeky memoir about raising his younger brother after the death of their parents. A number of reviewers explicitly contrasted the two, noting the way in which Eggers uses a clever, tongue-in-cheek approach as an effective way of imbuing the story with insight and genuine feeling. One commentator argued, for instance, that Eggers's book acts as a rebuttal to Purdy's assertions, as the self-consciousness is "trained on life's most unendurable experience, used to examine a memory too scorching to stare at, as one views an eclipse by projecting sunlight onto paper through a pinhole. This is not irony obscuring sincerity. It is, finally, irony in the service of sincerity."[21] Another commentator went so far as to coin the term "the Purdy-Eggers split"[22] as a way of pointing to the authors' widely divergent attitudes. Again, these attitudes involve implicit assumptions about whether irony is always diametrically opposed to authenticity or whether the two can productively be made to dovetail.

THE 2008 ELECTION AND VIRAL VIDEOS FOR ACTION

Despite the reservations that many, like Purdy, have about the ironic mode, there are many others making use of it for earnest displays of conviction. This became plainly evident in the viral video appeals produced by advocacy groups in the final months of the 2008 presidential election. With anticipation and engagement running high in the lead-up to the election, political organizations flooded inboxes with urgent email appeals to donate, to volunteer, and to speak to other voters. Particularly prevalent were short video segments meant to be forwarded. What was remarkable about a significant number of these videos was their striking combination of both irony and earnestness. As was plainly visible, the energy around Barack Obama's campaign produced a groundswell of idealism and earnest discussions of hope and change among his supporters, the type of profoundly uncynical political sentiment that Purdy longingly contrasts with irony. As discussed in the introduction, there was also much popular discussion about whether an Obama presidency would be the end of the contemporary renaissance in political satire precisely because of this perceived idealism and sincerity. However, that only follows if one believes irony and sincerity to be mutually exclusive, and it clearly has not turned out to be the case. If one takes a look at the popular cultural texts that swirled around the campaign as it surged to victory, it becomes apparent that many incorporated earnest optimism with a playful, self-conscious edge or parodic bite, putting irony to use for decidedly earnest appeals to action.

The most widely popular of these videos (and the one most widely covered in the news media) was "The Great Schlep," starring comedian

2.1. Sarah Silverman in "The Great Schlep" video informs viewers that, if Obama doesn't win the election, she is going to blame the Jews. *http://www.youtube.com/watch?v=AgHHX9R4Qtk*

Sarah Silverman. The video was put together by the nonprofit Jewish Council for Education and Research, which organized the Great Schlep project in the hopes of encouraging younger Jews to visit or call their grandparents in Florida in order to convince them to vote for Barack Obama (and to perhaps volunteer to talk to others in the retirement communities). The video, an instant hit, is narrated by Silverman, a comedian famous for her deadpan, potty-mouthed, sensitivity-steamrollering sense of humor. She tells us that if Obama doesn't become the next president of the United Sates, she is going to blame the Jews (who are visually represented by a cut-out of a giant nose), explaining that, though Jews may be known for their liberal, scrappy, civil-rightsy-ness, elderly Jews living in Florida are not necessarily of that persuasion. And since they could make or break the election, viewers need to get their "fat Jewish asses"[23] on a plane to Florida.

What is particularly interesting about the piece is that it simultaneously acts as a parody of typical advocacy advertisements while also earnestly functioning as one of these ads itself. So, the video opens with Silverman faux casually strolling into the frame and addressing the viewer in a measured, serious but warm tone, asking, "If you knew that visiting your grandparents could change the world, would you do it?"[24] In the

2.2. Silverman rhapsodizes on what elderly Jewish women and young black men have in common. *http://www.youtube.com/watch?v=AgHHX9R4Qtk*

same serious tone, she then answers her own question as if she were in a typical public service announcement, though her words comically signal to the audience that this appeal will be far different than a typical political ad; she emphatically states, "Of course you would. You would have to be a douche nozzle not to."[25] The rest of the video continues in this vein, with Silverman irreverently exceeding the boundaries of good taste and half-seriously poking fun at herself, her Jewish heritage, and the advocacy ad genre, while also sincerely reaching out to her audience. Silverman uses her sweet but obtusely naïve comedic persona to dive headlong into the issues of race and prejudice. Suddenly joined on her couch by an elderly Jewish woman and a young black man, she advises Jewish grandkids to explain to Nana that she actually has a lot in common with black men, including a love of track suits, Cadillacs, and bling. Here, she somehow manages to make us comically uncomfortable by her flippant use of racial stereotypes, while also communicating an earnest appeal for reconciliation across ethnic lines. It successfully reads as self-deprecation partially because the black actor is positioned as a foil, going from amused to uncomfortable as Silverman piles on the stereotypes, eventually getting up to leave in frustration when she explains that he and Jewish grandmothers are also linked by the fact that all of their friends are dying.

Throughout the ad, Silverman mixes real, persuasive details with more facetious ones. For instance, she lists "fun facts" about Obama that you can tell your grandparents, including both that his "foreign policy is much more stabilizing than John McCain's, and much better for Israel" and that "his brisket is beyond. It's beyond."[26] As a *New York Times* reporter puts it, the piece makes use of Silverman's particular comedic sensibility that "trusts her audience to know when she is totally kidding and when she is only sort of kidding."[27] While the video is hilarious in its parody, we also know that she is most emphatically *not* kidding when she tells us that our potential trip to Florida "can make the difference" in the election, and that Obama "is quite possibly this country's last hope of ending this country's reputation as the assholes of the universe."[28] Silverman and the organization behind the video were on a very real mission to get young Jews involved in Obama's campaign and to try to sway a potentially important demographic of elderly Jews in Florida. However, the video is definitely not aimed at Nana and Papa, but at their media-savvy, irony-loving, 20-something grandkids who are to be the eager volunteers in this mission.

Several other examples of viral videos in this vein were produced by the left-wing organization MoveOn, which sent them out to its sizable email list in the hopes that they would be widely passed along. Though these contained distinctly less potentially offensive jokes than "The Great Schlep," they made use of a similar self-conscious irony in the service of very earnest ends. One of them, titled "Talking to Your Parents about the Risks of John McCain Isn't as Hard as You Think," is likewise a parody of a public service announcement, specifically the ubiquitous real-life campaign urging parents to talk to their children about alcohol and drugs. In this spoof, a medley of teenage-looking actors (including two stars of the popular television program *Gossip Girl*) speak directly to the camera as if at a parent who has been caught engaging in inappropriate behavior. In the opening shot, one actor gravely says, "Mom, Dad, I found this in your room," holding up a cap emblazoned with the slogans "Drill Baby Drill" and "McCain Palin 2008."[29] The camera cuts from actor to actor, all gravely speaking parts of the same monologue, including sentiments like "voting Republican, even once, can have disastrous effects that last for years" and "just because other people your age are doing it doesn't make it cool."[30] The video then implores viewers to talk to their parents about

2.3. In "Talking to Your Parents about the Risks of John McCain Isn't as Hard as You Think," popular actors chastise off-screen parents for their risky behavior. *http://www.youtube.com/watch?v=yToy9mPDI2U*

John McCain. The ad concludes with a spot-on echo of the original anti-drug advertisements as the girl on camera assures her implied parent, "If you are ever out somewhere and you are considering voting McCain, just call me and I'll pick you up, no questions asked."[31] The ad works because it does such a good job of mimicking those anti-drug commercials, eliciting the pleasure of recognition, poking fun at the heavy-handedness of those ads, while also (heavy-handedly) driving home the point that voting for John McCain would be reckless. The video was linked to a website that was written with the same tongue-in-cheek premise that one's parents might be hooked on the Republican Party and may need to be slowly weaned off this habit, but it also contained real talking points and comebacks for young people to use when countering their parents' potential reservations about voting for Obama. Again, while the package is ironic and comedic, there is also a sincere embedded appeal to young Obama supporters to speak to their parents about their political beliefs.

A second MoveOn video was sent out to the group's supporters about two weeks before the election and quickly became a viral phenomenon. The original email message to which it was attached warned readers that there are all sorts of reasons that American citizens, even those who are intending to vote, won't actually get around to it, including oversleeping and getting the car fixed. That is because, the email goes on, they have not been reminded vividly enough, which is why MoveOn has made this funny, scary video about what could happen. Above the embedded video, the text reads, "Here's a version we prepared for you. You're in it—seriously, you. Check it out—and if you like it, send it to your friends."[32] And, indeed, you *are* in it, or at least your name is. The video, set a few days after the election, tells an exaggerated dystopic tale about how the election was lost because of *you*.

It is framed as a news report, in which a believable-looking anchor informs viewers that, while U.S. elections are often close, the nation was shocked Tuesday night to see John McCain defeat Barack Obama by a single vote. For many, he goes on, "shock soon turned to outrage as the *New York Times* revealed the identity of the particular nonvoter responsible for Obama's loss."[33] At this point, a faux newspaper clipping flashes on the screen with the viewer's name featured prominently, so that mine read "Non-Voter Identified: Amber Day. Investigation of Tallies Leads to Culprit."[34] The newscaster then explains that, in just a few days, this citizen has become a national pariah and has had to be taken into protective custody out of fear of retribution. The footage on-screen flashes from a graffiti-scrawled wall that reads "Amber = loser" to a sign outside a church that says "All God's Children Welcome except Amber Day"[35] to scenes of protesters demonstrating. Several protesters are interviewed, including an elderly woman who hilariously fumes that she "waited in line five hours to vote with an arthritic hip and this mother [bleep] [bleep] sucking [bleep] couldn't get out of bed in time to vote."[36] International reaction has apparently been just as intense, we are told, as a man herding goats in what appears to be a remote area in Central Asia speaks to the camera, a translation of his words appearing as "I can't believe Amber would allow this to happen."[37] The anchor reports, however, that the nonvoter has become a hero to one segment of the population, which is followed by an apparent thank you from George W. Bush and conservative pundit Bill O'Reilly. As the commercial closes, the newscaster transitions to another item, suggesting that the United States could start bombing Iran in a matter of days.

The comedic payoff of the piece resides in the thrill of seeing one's own name repeatedly positioned as the target of attention, and such negative attention at that. I laughed heartily at each new usage of my name as

2.4. The viewer of this video by MoveOn is identified as the sole cause of Obama's electoral defeat and is exposed as an object of international outrage. *http://www.cnnbcvideo.com/?combined=Amber%20Day&first=Amber&name_id=32749&last=Day&id=14590-577450-bYQdWrx&nid=cYI.GrbSBFdsQM73_4g8SDMyNzQ5*

a supposed object of international outrage. One could then forward the piece to friends, after inserting their names into the script, so that they could have the same experience, marveling at the programming trick that made it possible. As in all of these videos, the intended viewer is someone who is already an ardent Obama supporter. While the situation depicted is clearly somewhat absurd, the comedic irony resides in the viewer giggling over the idea of him- or herself—a staunch Obama advocate—as the cause of his electoral defeat. It also quite handily drives home the message that one should not be complacent at this stage of the election, and that every vote is going to be important.

Each of these videos manages to achieve a form of dialogism, like that described by Mikhail Bakhtin, who writes of literary genres (such as the novel) that incorporate a dialogue between diverse socio-ideological languages. Using the inherently double-voiced device of parody, these videos poke fun at and interrogate both the video itself and its viewer, while simultaneously driving home a serious message. The self-conscious irony reminds the viewer that this video is only playing at being a public service announcement or a news broadcast. And as it gleefully points out its own flaws and fakery, it thereby appears all the more sincere. Thus, the ironic mode is integral not just to the humor of the ads, but to their sincerity. We don't see them as suspiciously overproduced, or as trying too hard to be folksy or to convince us of something, because they are so clearly poking fun at themselves.

IRONY AS COMMUNAL GLUE

As we will explore in much greater detail in chapter 4, irony is a mode that functions successfully only when ironist and audience share particular assumptions and cultural cues, and for this same reason, it can serve to create a sense of community when those shared assumptions and senses of humor are highlighted. It is assumed, in the election-lost-because-of-you video, for instance, that the viewers would not relish the idea of being lauded by Bill O'Reilly and would chuckle in shared understanding that he is someone whose opinions are not to be valued. All of these pro-Obama videos were designed to appeal to those with shared political beliefs partially because of the sense of belonging and affirmation they were meant to impart. This is a crucial component for successful political movements, but one that is too easily dismissed as merely "preaching to the converted."

However, that component of shared meaning making among a sympathetic audience is also a slippery one, as it is sometimes impossible to delimit who will join that audience and with what preexisting ideas. This issue was at the root of the controversy surrounding another campaign text: the much-discussed *New Yorker* cover ironically depicting the Obamas as militants and terrorists in the run-up to the 2008 election. The illustration was intended as a satiric exaggeration of the worst sort of slurs that were being leveled at the candidate and his family as the campaign progressed, as a way of pointing to and ridiculing the nature of those slurs. However, many of the largely politically liberal readers of the magazine (including numerous supporters of Obama who were in agreement with the point the cartoonist was trying to make) were unhappy with the cover because they worried that the ironic intent was not unmistakable enough. The cover illustration was not accompanied by any sort of written commentary or ironic title, and since the *New Yorker* sits on newsstands across the country, visible to those who don't necessarily share the assumptions of its regular readers, they worried that others might simply take the illustration at face value, seeing it as confirmation of their existing racist beliefs. Though the letter writers professed to "getting" the joke, many expressed worry that others would not, betraying unease over what Linda Hutcheon refers to as irony's "instability,"[38] or the necessity of meaning making in two directions—from both author and audience—which inherently contains a possibility for misfire. Such is the danger of any form of satire or irony, particularly during something like a high-tension election, but I would also argue that, in our era of niche media, we are becoming more accustomed to the form of earnest irony (evidenced in the viral videos) that is targeted at a clearly demarcated audience, and so are less comfortable (as far as the political is concerned) with the type that is more potentially open to interpretation. What the viral videos succeeded in doing, and what the *New Yorker* cartoon was seen to have missed, was hailing their audience as members of a shared community, creating the pleasure of recognition, affirmation, and the empowering feeling of strength in numbers.

The downside to community-specific irony is, of course, that it can also function in an elitist manner. The understanding and appreciation of irony can frequently serve as a form of what Pierre Bourdieu refers to as "cultural capital." As Bourdieu explains, cultural capital, while distinct from economic capital, is a form of competency and knowledge that tends to go hand in hand with the economic. While cultural taste is entirely learned through education and exposure, it appears to be second nature, a "possession turned into being."[39] One's tastes function as a form of distinction, seeming to demonstrate something about one's person. There is no doubt that an understanding of irony and parody can function as a form of distinction in this way. As Jonathan Gray points out, being a knowing audience is something to be traded and performed publicly, as genre literacies in general "often serve as pass cards into many contemporary communities."[40]

With irony in particular, not only is there the desire to be part of the in-group, there is also the suspicion that if one doesn't appreciate the joke or implied meaning, one might in fact be the target of it. Purdy's skewering of irony contains an implicit critique of this elitism, which he seems to link to class entitlement, describing the mode as a form of sophisticated verbal wit employed by Ivy Leaguers. As he puts it, "The more time one has spent in school, and the more expensive the school, the greater the propensity to irony. This is not least among the reasons that New York and Hollywood, well populated with Ivy League–educated scriptwriters, produce a popular culture drenched in irony."[41] I would temper this concern somewhat by pointing out that the forms of irony surveyed here are those that tend to be mobilized in a fairly populist register, as the satirists in question position themselves as stand-ins for the everyday citizen frustrated at the dissembling of political figures or at the irresponsibility of the press corps. Nevertheless, it should be acknowledged that irony is not an inherently inclusive mode of discourse. As I will discuss in the activism chapter, it can easily serve to exacerbate existing polarization, particularly when used politically. This is certainly a limit to the use of irony as a form of political discourse. However, it is also particularly good at capturing attention, producing pleasure and engagement, and strengthening feelings of community and shared understanding, the importance of which we will explore in the coming chapters.

As developments in technology have made it easier to pick up and take apart pieces of the media field around us, while mainstream news and public affairs remain as insular as ever, amateurs and professionals alike are drawing on irony as a means of entering the public discussion. It is my strong conviction that as parody, satire, and irony are becoming increasingly popular as methods of political communication, they are being mobilized much of the time not as a form of retreat from substantive political issues, but as a deliberate way of engaging with them. It is a resurgence not of the detached, smirking form of irony that holds all politics to ultimately be laughable, but of the engaged, decidedly earnest form of irony. New technologies are enabling average citizens, professional entertainers, and political activists to respond to the political discourse around them, not necessarily to malign the political process or impugn the dignity of particular political actors, but often to make forceful political claims and to advocate action in the search for solutions to real problems. Perhaps more important, these modes seem to be succeeding in attracting and engaging numerous fans and building strong affective communities. Thus, irony is not inseparably linked to cynicism; instead, oddly perhaps, it appears that, for many, irony is becoming a new marker of sincerity.

THREE

Truthiness and Consequences in Parodic News

Since the 1990s, there has been an explosion of fake news and talk-show outlets in media markets around the world, including parodic newspapers in print and online and a growing number of television news-magazine send-ups. Rather than creating competition, each new entry seems to generate more attention and enthusiasm for the genre as a whole. The form is not entirely new, as faux news reports were incorporated into variety and sketch shows in the past. However, those segments were primarily featured as individual, recurring comedy sketches among many others. Now, as entire programs have developed around the conceit, a more fleshed-out genre has emerged. These newer programs involve far fewer impersonations, sketches based around politicians' personal foibles, and entirely made-up news items. Instead, they rely heavily on deconstructions of real news events, as well as interviews or ambushes of actual public figures, blending the mimetic and the real. In other words, they tread a much finer line between news and entertainment, satire and political argument. This hybridity, consequently, has served to thrust these programs into serious political debate, and well-known hosts of the format have begun to be treated as pundits in their own right, becoming legitimate players in the wider political dialogue. Due to these blurring boundaries, there is some cultural anxiety around the genre, with many observers accusing parodic news shows of fomenting cynicism and detachment from the political world. I argue quite the opposite: this blend of satire and political nonfiction enables and articulates a critique of the inadequacies of contemporary political discourse, while demonstrating an engaged commitment to the possibility of a more honest public debate. Though the popularity of these shows is at least partially the product of industry "narrowcasting"—appealing to a particular taste culture—they have nevertheless gained an entrée into wider publics and broader cultural discourses.

The genre that I am referring to as the "parodic news show" was not a naturally existing form just waiting to be accepted, nor will it necessarily become an enduring, universal genre. On the contrary, the work of theorists such as Jason Mittell and Rick Altman reminds us that genres are not static, preexisting classifications, but are cultural categories that evolve according to particular historical circumstances.[1] As Mittell argues, rather than asking what a genre means, "we need to ask what a genre means *for specific groups in a particular cultural instance.*"[2] Some questions to be posed about the emerging genre of parodic news coverage are: Why has it developed and become successful now? And what significance do these programs have at this moment for both fans and detractors?

Drawing on examples from four programs in particular (*The Daily Show* and *The Colbert Report* in the United States and *This Hour Has 22 Minutes* and *The Rick Mercer Report* in Canada), I will argue that this particular performative, hybrid form of satire and political discourse is having a much greater impact on serious political debate than most of its predecessors, as the comedian-commentators physically engage, interrogate, and interact with the real. Both the mimetic and the real are equally important components of these shows, as the mimetic frame allows the stolen fragments of the real to be satirically scrutinized, deconstructed, and even subsequently mobilized as a form of evidence in public debate, pointing up the flaws of contemporary political discourse. These shows then become focal points for existing dissatisfaction with the political sphere and its media coverage, while the high-profile hosts become viewers' surrogates who articulate that dissatisfaction through comedic transformations of the real. Though these programs are almost universally referred to as "fake news," that label obscures their more complicated relationship to "real" news programming, as well as the attraction they hold for fans frustrated with the compromised authenticity and relevance of straight news programming. Rather than being fictionalized imitations, the programs act as comedically critical filters through which to process the suspect real world of reportage and debate.

When relying on a term as seemingly transparent but as metaphysically complex as *real,* one runs the risk of implying either much more or much less than is intended. To clarify, on a basic level, I am using *real* to refer to nonfiction material: events and interactions that most would recognize as having a tangible existence outside of these programs. For instance, when I refer to the shows making use of real newsclips, I mean that the footage is of a real press conference, not professional actors pretending that they are at a press conference, but flesh-and-blood public figures, whose words and actions are likely to have a tangible effect on the lives of individuals around the world, talking to reporters. However, this is not to overlook the fact that the real officials at the press conference are also, in a sense, actors playing their roles, wearing the appropriate wardrobe, speaking in the expected tone of voice, and often mouthing memorized (or teleprompted) lines that have been scripted for them. Real most certainly does not refer to an essential authenticity or lack of artifice. Rather, it is precisely the importation of the real or nonfictional into the mimetic frame of these parodic programs that can serve to call attention to the way in which the real is itself constructed. One of the primary targets of many of these programs is the lack of substance behind much political discourse—the public relations spin tactics used by politicians and corporations and the lack of interrogation on the part of the news media. It is through this act of pointing out the artificiality of real newscasts, press conferences, and other forms of public discussion that, for many of their fans, these fake news shows actually come closer to embodying the characteristics—like authenticity and truth—that we would normally associate with the real.

PREDECESSORS

Though I argue that the parodic news show is an emergent genre that exploded in popularity starting in the mid- to late 1990s, the form is not without precedent. In general, most people would associate the birth of the televisual fake news form with variety shows of the late 1960s and early '70s, and I will certainly trace those connections. However, I think it is important to also flag two predecessors in the early 1960s that tackled the current affairs/news-magazine form: *That Was the Week That Was* in Britain (later copied in the United States) and *This Hour Has Seven Days* in Canada, each of which was actually much closer to the current parodic news form than the variety shows were. Both shows courted the genre-blending hybridity between satiric comedy and reportage that has now become more commonplace; both were extremely popular and controversial; and both met with early cancellations amid industry whisperings that they were ruffling too many feathers, leaving a wave of controversy and public debate in their wake.

That Was the Week That Was, or *TW3* as it came to be called, was developed in response to the sudden threat of competition the BBC faced with the creation of the more commercial ITV. As Paddy Scannell explains, the BBC set out to destroy its "maiden aunt image" through programs that "cocked an irreverent snook at authority, religion, and traditional values in general."[3] Premiering in 1962, *TW3* was one of the most popular and iconoclastic of the group. Much like the contemporary programs, the show was developed as a hybridized satiric news and current affairs program. Though the content consisted primarily of sketches, songs, and invented news items, many of the staff members were pulled from the serious broadcasting world. Producer and director Ned Sherrin, for instance, had previously worked on the BBC's news-magazine show *Tonight,* while among the many contributing writers were poets, critics, and one Labour MP, Gerald Kaufman.[4] In addition to skits, discussions, and monologues, one of the hosts regularly interviewed people in the news or those with strong views. Interestingly, it was housed within the current affairs division of the BBC rather than in light entertainment. In many ways, then, *TW3* encouraged some confusion between genres. Its presentation was also novel. The construction of the show was deliberately exposed so that viewers could see the set's scaffolding and the cameras moving in and out of shot, creating a newly informal feel. While the overall thrust of the program was certainly satiric, it did also have some serious journalistic moments, the most famous of which was the show broadcast the day after John F. Kennedy was killed. The entire program was devoted to a serious tribute to the president and was so well received that it was later read into the record of the U.S. Senate.[5] For the most part, however, the tone was irreverent, described by Dick Fiddy as "savage, unflinching in its devotion to highlight cant and hypocrisy and seemingly fearless in its near libelous accusations and innuendos."[6] Targets included the royal family, religion, and the hypocrisy of the ruling class.[7]

The show's run also happened to coincide with the Profumo affair, when MP John Profumo was revealed to have been in an extramarital relationship with a showgirl who had been simultaneously involved with an attaché at the Soviet embassy. The program mined the scandal for all of its comedic potential, further fanning the flames of controversy. Looking back, the BBC website now brags that the show had an enormous impact on its viewers, "most of whom had never realised that public figures could lead disreputable lives."[8] Despite *TW3*'s enormous popularity, the show was pulled at the end of 1963. Amid protestations, the BBC insisted that the program could have undue influence in the coming election year.

The *TW3* concept and name were briefly imported to the United States in 1964–1965, and the show initially debuted to critical and popular fanfare, with NBC reportedly receiving more than 12,000 letters, telegrams, and phone calls (the vast majority favorable) after the pilot aired.[9] As Stephen Kercher describes it, the content was erratic, veering from trenchant satire and scathing editorials to predictable one-liners and clichéd references. As it progressed, both its producer and the executives at NBC became more wary of offending and continually leaned on the show's writers to try to incorporate more popular cultural references as opposed to political ones. The show was then repeatedly preempted during the Republican and Democratic primaries. When it was finally returned to the air, it was moved from its prime Friday night slot to a Tuesday night one (despite the fact that it was designed to comment on the news of the week), opposite two extremely popular programs, allowing NBC to neutralize the potential risks of the show by allowing it to "die a slow, natural death."[10]

In Canada in 1964, *This Hour Has Seven Days* debuted on CBC television. According to Eric Koch, the British *TW3* was a major influence on producers Patrick Watson and Douglas Leiterman.[11] *Seven Days* was designed not as a spoof, but as a hard-hitting current affairs program. However, the aim was to "make reality every bit as fascinating and compelling as fiction,"[12] cutting across social barriers and appealing to everyone. It was the first time that public affairs television had made the conquest of a mass audience its highest priority. The show made a radical break from the established current affairs format, mixing together contentious subject matter, rapid-fire interviews on the studio's "hot seat," unpolished cinema verité footage, crusading documentaries, satirical sketches, and irreverent songs. As the producers had hoped, the show captured the imagination of the country, attracting substantial numbers of the university-educated as well as those without a high school diploma, endowing it with "almost half the total audience across Canada for all English television broadcast at that hour on Sunday evenings."[13] The show's success reportedly sparked interest in the United States and was the impetus for the eventual development of the current affairs program *60 Minutes*.[14]

From the beginning, however, the show was under fire for its journalistic techniques. In one notorious episode, two American Klansmen in full regalia were brought in for a hot-seat interview, but they were surprised midway through the interview when a black civil rights activist was invited to join them. The Klansmen eventually walked off the show after the host asked them to shake the activist's hand. Scenarios such as this led to charges of sensationalism. The staff also occasionally juxtaposed real interviews and reports with satiric sketches (often performed by the Second City comedy troupe). In a segment on the Vietnam War, for instance, actual footage of a southern U.S. senator arguing that the country should use all the weaponry available to it in the war was followed by a skit involving a similar but exaggerated character advocating the bombing of Asia, East Germany, and Harlem. As William O. Gilsdorf explains, "[T]he fast pace, the topicality of many of the segments, the portrayal and incitement of conflict, the irreverence of songs and skits, and the occasional emotionalism of the on-air team members all added to the popularity and the controversy that built around *Seven Days*."[15] Interestingly, much like *TW3*, the run of the show also coincided with the revelation of a high-level sex and security scandal referred to as the Munsinger affair. East German Greta Munsinger, a woman with questionable connections (possibly to espionage), was revealed to have had relationships with a number of the (married) members of Parliament in former prime minister John Diefenbaker's government. As the story was developing, *Seven Days* sent one of its reporters unannounced to the home of one of the former cabinet ministers (though no formal accusations had been made against him), inciting the politician to chase the reporter away with his cane. The footage was not aired, but CBC management was unhappy with the attempt.

Near the end of the program's second season, after a number of battles between the network's management and the staff of *Seven Days* and a great deal of friction between the show (in current affairs) and the CBC news division, management attempted to go over the producer's head to have co-hosts Patrick Watson and Laurier LaPierre fired, holding on to the show's popular name but gaining greater control over its content. The hosts retaliated by getting Parliament involved. The public outcry was enormous, galvanizing viewers to an extent unprecedented in Canadian broadcasting history and resulting in a strike threat by CBC producers, the formation of Save *Seven Days* committees across the country, and a number of parliamentary debates and investigations. Both sides dug in their heels, eventually resulting in the firing of the producer and the cancellation of the program. There is, to this day, an enormous amount of nostalgia for the show, which has led long-time CBC broadcaster and one-time adversary of the show Knowlton Nash to repeatedly reference the need to lay "to rest the ghost of *This Hour Has Seven Days*"[16] in his accounts of CBC news history.

Though *TW3* and *Seven Days* played out their respective lives in different national and industrial contexts, they were both created and destroyed by similar forces. Looking back, we can describe the mid-1960s as a period fraught with competing social currents. On one hand, there was a clear desire to question received truths, interrogate the powerful, and trouble authority. These shows accordingly offered the chance to view politics through an irreverent lens and to leach some of the status and power from traditional journalists and newsmakers. On the other hand, those same forces of change were considered destructive and threatening by many, particularly those in the traditional political and journalistic establishments. I would argue that, in the case of *TW3* and *Seven Days,* this threat was exacerbated by the instability posed by these slippery, hybrid programs, which were neither highbrow current affairs nor lowbrow vaudeville. In the end, the form was too potentially volatile for broadcasters to continue supporting.

After their demise, parodic news found a less contentious home in the variety show, programming that was clearly demarcated as comedic, light entertainment and largely removed from the political world. Though the news segment was deployed as only one comedic scenario among many on these shows, it nevertheless quickly became a popular premise. The program *Rowan and Martin's Laugh-In,* which aired on NBC in the United States from 1968 through 1973, was one of the first to make use of the format. *Laugh-In* was a fast-paced, frenetic show that Henry Jenkins describes as capturing the counterculture's "flamboyance, its anarchic energy, and its pop aesthetic, combining the black-out comedy of the vaudeville tradition with a 1960s-style 'happening.'"[17] One of the recurring segments was the "news of the present, news of the past, and news of the future," in which one of the hosts would read a variety of fabricated headlines. In at least one of the time periods, the performers would segue into a skit staged as an on-the-scene report. For instance, in one 1968 episode, the hosts appeared as sports commentators (in the present) supposedly broadcasting from a college campus. Rather than providing commentary on a football game, however, they announced play-by-plays of a college demonstration in progress, treating the students as one team and law enforcement as the other, quipping that the winners will head to Berkeley for the national championships.[18]

Another variety show on NBC, *The Flip Wilson Show,* premiered in 1970 and included a similar recurring skit called "The What's Happening Now News." As this type of segment became commonplace, guest performers would carry popular characters with them in appearances on different shows. George Carlin, for example, was well known for his character of the Hippie-Dippie Weatherman, who gave nonsensical, useless weather reports, and he showed up on a number of different programs. The conceit of many of these skits was to parody the way in which news broadcasting performs itself, often demonstrating its emptiness by distilling it down to exaggerated style without substance: a crisp suit, measured delivery, and a vapid smile.

Though the form was already fairly well established before *Saturday Night Live*'s premiere in 1975, that show's recurring "Weekend Update" sketch has become the most famous. The scenario was tested on the first episode of the program, with actor Chevy Chase as the news anchor. The skit became very popular and has remained a staple of the show to this day. Much like its predecessors, the original skit was conceived as a parody of the pomposity and predictability of the standard television news format. As Chase explains, "[T]here was a guy named Roger Grimsby in New York. He used to say, 'good evening, I'm Roger Grimsby, and here now the news.'—what the hell is that? Pretentious junk. . . . So I at some point—I usually winged these things—I went, 'I'm Chevy Chase and you're not.' I mean, I had nothing else to say."[19] Numerous other actors have played the news anchor role over the years, and many other segments were created involving a variety of characters as experts and talking heads. Jane Curtin and Dan Aykroyd, for instance developed a popular "Weekend Update" feature called "Point-Counterpoint" as a send-up of a running segment by the same name on the straight news magazine *60 Minutes.* The two would ostensibly debate an issue of topical concern, but would turn the conversation into an escalating contest of personal insults.

Beyond the broad parody of television news conventions, though, these programs have also been used as a platform for jokes about contemporary political events. The anchor typically runs through a list of the night's stories, including some that are completely fabricated but are based on the audience's preexisting knowledge of particular public figures and others that are roughly lifted from the real news but are followed up with the show's own fabricated punch line. For instance, in a 1980 *Saturday Night Live* episode, the anchor reported that Gerald Ford had announced that he had decided not to run for president in the upcoming election (a real news item), which was followed by the explanation that "Mr. Ford said, 'I believe that this country is in very grave danger, both at home and abroad, and I have decided that I am simply too stupid and inept to deal with the problems we face.'"[20] Due to the fast-paced nature of these headline segments, the political humor is often similar to that of contemporary late-night talk-show monologues. The jokes can be biting, but they are generally composed as one-liners, rather than as any sort of sustained critique. On *SNL* in particular, the cast also does impersonations of political figures. Leading up to an election, for instance, it is traditional for the show to stage faux debates between the candidates (played by actors). These segments allow for a lengthier development of the comedic premise, though they revolve primarily around send-ups of the politicians' personal foibles: George W. Bush was portrayed as a dim-witted frat boy, while Bill Clinton was a junk-food-loving skirt-chaser. But real political policy is rarely critiqued in any depth. As Jeffrey Jones explains, "[V]iewers are led to laugh but not disdain, to appreciate affectionately but not really criticize."[21]

A stark exception, of course, was Tina Fey's depiction of Alaska governor and vice presidential candidate Sarah Palin during the 2008 presidential campaign. This was an impression that probably did cause actual political damage because it moved beyond a simple impersonation of Palin's vocal or facial tics (though Fey clearly nailed those too). As Gray,

Jones, and Thompson have argued, "Fey's sketches bristled with judgment and aggression. This wasn't just mocking Gerald Ford for being clumsy or Hilary [*sic*] Clinton for wearing pantsuits; something important was being said."[22] And the skits were all the more damning because Fey was often repeating Palin's own statements practically verbatim, highlighting their absurdity. Finally, because Palin had previously been so carefully shielded from public scrutiny, Fey's version of her as an uninformed but dangerous beauty queen stuck.

With a few notable exceptions like these, however, an examination of the parodic news segments on shows like *SNL* largely supports the argument of many of the satire theorists surveyed in the introduction: that satire typically focuses on personalities rather than substantive policy. For the most part, over the years, the form has remained largely unchanged within the confines of the variety show. Beginning in the mid-'90s, however, satirical news programming underwent a sort of renaissance, as numerous programs devoted exclusively to the form started to crop up in varied national contexts. As parodic news and current affairs have begun to develop from support material into whole programs, the form has grown and changed, becoming its own emergent genre, one that often bears a greater resemblance to the earlier cancelled shows, *TW3* and *Seven Days,* in its highly hybridized format and that enters much deeper into the realm of serious political debate. The question is: Why has this particular genre been able to become so popular and successful at this moment, when the previous examples failed to receive the institutional support they needed?

CONTEMPORARY BROADCASTING

An important factor contributing to the viability of the parodic news genre at this moment is the changing face of the television industry itself. All across the world, television has undergone enormous transformations since the 1980s. The developments of cable, satellite, and digital technologies, combined with changes in regulation practices, have irrevocably altered the medium. As Lynn Spigel has argued, "[I]f TV refers to the technologies, industrial formations, government policies, and practices of looking that were associated with the medium in its classical public service and three-network age, it appears that we are entering a new phase of television—the phase that comes after 'TV.'"[23] These broad technological and industrial shifts have altered the way viewers watch television and, consequently, the way producers and advertisers conceptualize their target audiences, leading to the current industry practice of narrowcasting. As Jeffrey Sconce explains, "[C]able's fragmentation of the network audience, the growth of 'reality television,' and the concurrent reduction of more expensive narrative-based programming has created an environment of increasingly specialized narrative vehicles, allowing smaller audience groups the potential for targeted and intensive narrative investment."[24] Though he is referring specifically to fiction-based programming, the same is true across television genres, as niche cable networks that are focused on one highly specific subject (such as the Food Network, the History Channel, or Comedy Central) abound, and television programs that would never have been developed in a three-network system due to their selective appeal have become objects of adoration for devoted fans.

Most important, it means that the industry is more likely to develop potentially controversial material, as the program in question will inevitably be aimed specifically at an audience that will appreciate it and is unlikely to be viewed by those outside the taste culture who might find it offensive. Within this larger background, Spigel makes the argument that "the actual cultural styles in these new narrowcast media markets are increasingly based on irony, parody, skepticism, and 'TV-literate' critical reading protocols,"[25] in other words, this is television that is self-aware and that may reference or poke fun at other televisual formats. The parodic news show genre certainly fits within this larger pattern, providing an ironic outlet for many who are critical of the way public policy is debated and of the way the straight news is framed.

Many of the theorists who have written on the effects of narrowcasting reference in particular the American media, where these changes have been especially stark. However, they have had an analogous effect in other countries, though refracted through the particular domestic context. In Canada, broadcasting has, from the beginning, been influenced by the country's proximity to the United States and the two nations' population disparity. As Richard Collins observes, concern about the maintenance of the Canadian state and Canadian sovereignty has long manifested itself in a "fear of cultural domination via the broadcasting media by Canada's powerful southern neighbour, the USA."[26] The result has been the creation of a public broadcasting system (combined with the simultaneous existence of some private broadcasters), a series of Canadian content rules governing the percentage of Canadian-made programs that must be aired in a given time period, and rules for Canadian ownership of domestic networks. In a sense, Canadian content regulations have resulted in an institutionalized niche market for Canadian-focused media. However, this segment of the industry is under increased pressure to attract audiences as it is competing against the highly specialized and already popular narrowcast programs. Programs like *22 Minutes* and *The Rick Mercer Report,* both distributed by the CBC, are a boon for the broadcaster as they fulfill Canadian content and public service obligations by addressing Canadian political issues, while also drawing substantial audiences. As Serra Tinic explains, "[S]atirical sketch comedies have proven to be among the most popular genres on Canadian television, as well as one of the few domestic formats that regularly generates large audiences cross-nationally."[27]

Another factor affecting the viability of these programs is, of course, what contemporary technology itself allows. A television satirist is now able to literally incorporate pieces of the real to an unprecedented degree. Video and digital technologies make it relatively easy and inexpensive for the staff of *The Daily Show,* for example, to obtain and edit the day's newsclips, or for the cast of *This Hour Has 22 Minutes* to run after politicians. And, as John Caldwell points out, "[B]y 2000, widespread use of digital servers (allowing random and multiple access to image and sound) [made] the task of finding and incorporating archived file footage far less daunting."[28] As I will argue, one of the primary factors that sets these shows apart from other examples of political satire is this weaving of real news footage or the actions of real public figures into the satirist's narrative.

THE PROGRAMS

Beginning in the mid-1990s and continuing to the present, the melding of parody and satire with the discourses of news and current affairs has become so commonplace that it is now its own genre. In Britain, for example, 1994 saw the development of the parodic current affairs program *The Day Today,* which was adapted from a radio program called *On the Hour.* The cult hit ran for only six episodes, but writer and performer Christopher Morris then went on to create the hugely controversial faux news magazine *Brass Eye* in 1997. The latter show was made up of a series of fake reports which included some scripted material intermixed with footage of unwitting public figures responding seriously to a topic that viewers knew to be fictional, often giving impassioned pledges of support for the absurd causes. In 1998, the late-night comedy series *The 11 O'Clock Show* launched the career of Sacha Baron Cohen, who attracted enormous attention with his alter ego Ali G as a spectacularly uninformed interviewer. Two years later, he debuted his own program, *Da Ali G Show,* featuring several over-the-top characters, all played by Cohen, who interviewed high-level public officials and celebrities who believed that they were being featured on a straight current affairs and entertainment show and were goaded into reacting to the interviewer's stupidity or into agreeing with his absurd or offensive statements. The show then moved to the United States for several seasons, before Cohen began exporting the technique into feature films.

Meanwhile, in Canada, *This Hour Has 22 Minutes* debuted in 1993, becoming an instant hit. The show, whose title pays homage to the earlier show *This Hour Has Seven Days,* is framed as a news broadcast, combining satirical sketches, comedic political rants, parodies of Canadian popular culture, and ambush interviews with newsworthy public figures. Though the cast has continued to rotate, the show remains on the air to this day. The popularity of *22 Minutes* launched the career of political satirist Rick Mercer, who, after leaving the show, developed his own similar program called *Rick Mercer's Monday Report,* which began airing in 2004 and was then renamed *The Rick Mercer Report* the following year. His show is less reliant on sketches produced by a regular cast, but instead revolves around Mercer as a newsmagazine host, who travels the country investigating current events, profiling Canadian locales, interviewing celebrities and members of the public, and offering scathing editorials on political issues.

In the United States, Michael Moore debuted a show in 1994 called *TV Nation,* which was structured on the news-magazine format. His show did not focus on headlines or celebrities, but instead offered a satirical version of investigative journalism, usually focused on a company's abuses of power. After its demise, Moore repackaged the format in 1999 as *The Awful Truth.* Rather than taking potshots in the abstract, Moore and company consistently relied on public stunts designed pointedly to shame the socially irresponsible. These pretaped field segments were then sewn together by Moore's commentary as the host in front of a live audience. Meanwhile, in 1996, *The Daily Show* premiered on Comedy Central, originally hosted by Craig Kilborn. The format was a mixture of cheeky renditions of the day's news headlines, on-location reports on bizarre stories, and celebrity interviews. In 1999, Jon Stewart took over from Kilborn, at which point the show took on a more aggressively political edge. A spin-off centered around one of *The Daily Show*'s correspondents, *The Colbert Report* debuted in the fall of 2005. In the newer show, performer Stephen Colbert plays a pompous, conservative, blowhard journalist, who offers ironically absurd rants about current events and interviews real public figures who act as foils to his comedic worldview. The format uses parody to poke fun at the tendency among television pundits to value strong opinions and emotions over investigations of fact or reasonable debate.

This phenomenon is by no means limited to the English-speaking world. An Iraqi fake news program called *Hurry Up, He's Dead* aired in 2006 to enormous popularity, while programs featuring politicians played by puppets (inspired by the popular British program *Spitting Image*) have cropped up in countries as diverse as France, Chile, Russia, Israel, Mexico, and Serbia, among others. Part of this larger background also includes the popular parody newspaper *The Onion* in the United States and a growing number of similar online sources around the world. In 2007, *The Onion* also launched *The Onion News Network,* a faux news broadcast distributed online. Eager to stay relevant amid this growing appetite for news parody, some of the mainstream news shows have also begun experimenting with the incorporation of satirists or comedians into their programming. Surrounding the 2004 presidential election in the United States, the centrality of satiric campaign coverage became a major news story in itself in North America, generating numerous reports on the phenomenon. As one *New York Times* journalist put it, "[F]ake news is certainly the comic trope of the moment."[29] Later, though less successful, American programs included *The ½ Hour News Hour,* which was intended to be a specifically right-wing fake news program airing on Fox in 2007, and Comedy Central's *Chocolate News* and CNN's *D.L. Hughley*

Breaks the News, both of which began in 2008 and were pitched as satirical news from an African-American perspective. All three lasted only one season.

Out of this wide field of possible examples, I have chosen to focus primarily on four programs: *The Daily Show, The Colbert Report, This Hour Has 22 Minutes,* and *The Rick Mercer Report.* They are some of the most popular and/or long-running shows, and, even more important, they provide some of the best examples of the melding of satire with the world of serious political discourse. Beyond simply growing more popular and expanding to become its own genre, the fake news form has changed over the years, a factor that has undoubtedly contributed to its salience in political discourse. One of the major differences of these newer shows from their variety predecessors is a more developed incorporation of the real into the mimetic. The form has moved center stage as it has increasingly blurred the line between news and entertainment, satirizing real news footage as it unfolds and ambushing and interviewing real political figures. Integral to this melding is the specifically performative form of parody and satire that injects the comedian's body into the traditional political realm. These four shows and their lead performers provide excellent case studies of this engaged and embodied hybridity.

MIMESIS AND THE REAL

Clearly, as audience members, we are not to mistake the parodic newscasters for real newscasters, nor to view the shows as legitimate news broadcasts. None is vying to supplant traditional news. The structure and form of these programs remain squarely within the mimetic realm. *Mimesis,* the representation or imitation of something, is the primary function of theater, fictional film and television, and, of course, any form of parody. In Plato's foundational usage of the term, mimesis is to be viewed with suspicion, precisely because it is an (inferior) imitation of the real, though therein also lies its paradoxical appeal. As Tracy Davis argues in reference to theatrical mimesis, "a mimetic act refers to an ideal 'real' which can never quite be successfully invoked: theatre is doomed (or blessed) by this failure."[30] Similarly, much of the pleasure of the parodic news shows is derived precisely from this awareness of the mimetic act. Audiences are entertained by seeing actors create impressions of stereotypical television reporters on stereotypical news sets. All invoke the tropes of the news genre, including the prominent anchor's desk, a slick background, and a television monitor with iconic images and logos lurking over the reporters' shoulders. Some of the shows get a great deal of comedic momentum from inflated parodies of these tropes. For example, the opening sequence of *The Colbert Report* is an exaggerated send-up of the self-importance of many pundit-based shows, complete with the waving of an enormous American flag, a soaring computer-generated eagle, and the superimposition of absurdly pompous catchphrases, all of which appear humorously shallow and overwrought.

These parodied tropes often function as a critique of perceived flaws in the practices of broadcast news. Again, *The Colbert Report* provides a good example in its semi-regular "Threat-Down" segment. The joke is always reliant on the premise that, in their desire to attract interest and ratings, news programs frequently engage in a form of sensationalist fear-mongering, hooking their viewers before a commercial break, for instance, with the promise to reveal terrifying new information. Colbert accordingly prefaces these segments with statements like "Prepare to have the living shit scared out of you."[31] And, since his parody is frequently aimed at conservative pundits in particular, the items that follow are always absurdly innocuous products or developments, which he insists are threatening the American way of life, often because they are supposedly promoting a "gay lifestyle," or somehow insinuating a liberal agenda. This exaggerated incarnation of a broadcast style is intended to mimic a recognizable original.

In other respects, the parodied markers can function less as punch lines in themselves and more as a vehicle for the performers. On *The Daily Show,* for example, the set and its trappings are quite consistent with those of straight news programs. Anchor Jon Stewart plays a fairly believable news reporter, looking well-groomed but not overdone and using a predominantly well-measured tone. It is all the more pleasurable, then, when this respectable-looking newscaster throws a phrase like "douche bag" into his patter, reminding his viewers that he is only playing at respectability. Likewise, when Stewart segues to a report from a correspondent "on location," who is actually standing a few feet away on the set in front of a green screen that projects images behind him, the studio audience erupts in giggles every time. Much of the comedy, then, derives from the audience's awareness of mimesis and appreciation for the mimetic skills of the performers.

Within this parodic universe, however, the writers and performers actively poach from and draw in pieces of the real political world in a number of different ways. Most obviously, these programs rely heavily on real, evolving news stories. As opposed to simply making up fanciful fake events, all of them engage with and report on the day's news as it continues to unfold. Jon Stewart of *The Daily Show,* for example, has become well known for his extended deconstructions of current events. Rather than joking about what theoretically could have happened around a particular issue, Stewart spends several minutes of his opening monologue actively reporting an ongoing story, replaying footage seen on other news programs but coloring it with a decidedly comedic tone. As he explained in an interview with Bill Moyers, "[W]e don't make things up. We just distill it to, hopefully, its most humorous nugget."[32] The comedy most often lies in him uncovering what he believes to be the real story behind a particular issue, breaking down the official rhetoric and media sound-bites.

Stewart does this through strategies like highlighting particular statements within a longer exchange or speech, making faces of mock incredulity, or pretending that he believes the speaker is talking about something else as a means of throwing his/her logic or sincerity into question. For example, during the Terri Schiavo debacle, in early 2005, Stewart ran a clip of a senator grandiloquently announcing that a society's commitment to life is measured by the extent to which its laws honor and defend its most vulnerable citizens. He then paused the tape, joyfully shouting, "Oh my God, we are getting universal health care!" He prefaced the next clip by asking, "If you were wondering just how sick you have to be before Congress gives you health care . . . ?" and then segueing to footage of Bush getting off a plane in Washington. Stewart's answer was that, though he did not do so after the disastrous tsunami several months earlier, Bush had cut his vacation short so that he could sign a bill intended to prolong the life of the brain-dead Schiavo.[33] While the straight news world is supposed to simply report statements and developments, the cast of *The Daily Show* is free to satirically compare and contrast, interrogate, and mock, sometimes developing a deeper analysis of the story in question than the straight programs.

Though they are mining the same raw material as the major news broadcasters, drawing from congressional television, live feeds, and the other networks' reports, the way the parodic news shows engage with the footage is very different. As both Aaron McKain and Geoffrey Baym point out in articles on *The Daily Show,* these programs routinely seek out awkward and quiet moments in the footage they screen. Both are potentially revealing, "though the former is infrequently broadcast on News and the latter is television kryptonite, except for marked instances such as moments of silence."[34] On the straight news, officials are rarely shown to not have the answer to a question, to be unsure of themselves, or to be actively contradicting themselves. In parodic news shows, these moments are seized upon for the information they carry.

Within this humorous dissection of the day's news, many of these shows' performers also provide editorials on current events through pointed comedic tirades. Rick Mercer, in both *22 Minutes* and *The Rick Mercer Report,* is particularly well known for his political rants. These segments have been dubbed "streeters" as they are usually filmed while he is outside walking somewhere. As he tromps down the street or through a public park, he performs a monologue about some politically relevant topic. Since he is outside and not in the "newsroom," he does not have the visual aid of news footage, so the focus is more clearly on his own thoughts. These rants seem to be chosen exclusively based on Mercer's bone-to-pick of the moment rather than on comedic potential. Editorials first and foremost, they succeed as comedy only because he happens to be a witty performer. Interestingly, they are also often premised on the audience having a fairly sophisticated knowledge of ongoing Canadian party politics. In one 2005 segment, for example, he berates Jack Layton, the leader of the New Democratic Party (Canada's solidly left-wing party) for not doing anything noteworthy, instead slipping into obscurity among the opposition and drifting toward the center. He includes a joke about Layton's "parts" being shaved due to a recent appendix operation, but it is generally just a plea directed at Layton for him to stand up and get noticed. As far as the NDP goes, Mercer argues, the country "wants a pit-bull for a leader who is not afraid to go out there and make an arse out of himself in the name of social justice."[35]

One of Mercer's most famous rants took place during the federal election campaign in 2000–2001 and actually had a fairly serious impact

3.1. Rick Mercer engaged in one of his signature rants. *CBC, Mar. 23, 2010*

on one of the party platforms. Previously, Stockwell Day, the leader of the Canadian Alliance Party and potential prime minister, had announced that, as Canadian Alliance policy, he would institute a national referendum mechanism, which would automatically trigger a referendum on a particular issue if petitions were gathered from 3 percent of the electorate (roughly 400,000 people). Mercer ridiculed the policy in his rant, concluding with the request that viewers log on to the *22 Minutes* website and vote in support of the statement: "We demand that the government of Canada force Stockwell Day to change his first name to Doris."[36] The joke caught on fast, reportedly generating about a million signatures[37] and sparking a great deal of press. Though it was just a prank, it did serve to satirically demonstrate the flaws of the proposed law. As one reporter put it, "[W]hat began as a wickedly biting dissection of [Canadian] Alliance referendum policy became one of the most memorable aspects of the 2001 federal election."[38] Notably, Mercer has managed to make his editorials into successful comedy, while still allowing for extended deconstructions of political policy.

Though perhaps less explicitly didactic, Jon Stewart and the cast of *The Daily Show* also editorialize about the issues they cover. One of the topics they continuously return to, for instance, is the quality of reportage in serious broadcasting. Stewart becomes particularly incensed when journalists appear to line up behind one another, all repeating the same assertions without investigation or relying on "talking points" developed by politicians. One of the show's favored methods of disparaging this behavior is to create a montage sequence that both highlights and critiques the practice. In the lead-up to the 2004 election, for instance, Stewart did a piece ostensibly on how we arrive at conventional wisdom. In it, he focuses on the oft-quoted idea that presidential hopeful John Kerry and his running mate, John Edwards, are "out of touch with the mainstream." He muses over how it is that he remembers this piece of wisdom, remembering that TV drills it in. He then shows the audience a fast-paced montage of numerous commentators repeating phrases like "way outside the mainstream" and "second most liberal senator" over and over again, explaining that, though we have no idea how these rankings are arrived at or who compiles them, we do not like the sound of them. He closes with the epithet "Talking points: they're true because they're said a lot."[39] It is through this type of stinging commentary on the world of real news broadcasting and political debate that the show attempts to expose the artifice and scriptedness of that world.

While many segments are quite playful, all of the shows can take on a ruthless edge when a current event happens to strike a particularly sensitive chord for the writers and performers. During the 2008 U.S. presidential campaign, for instance, *The Daily Show* devoted an entire episode to responding to comments being made by members of the McCain campaign (including vice presidential candidate Sarah Palin) about the patriotic "real America," in reference to the small towns in which they supposedly had strong support. Stewart responds first by concluding that the big cities like Washington, D.C., and New York must then be the capitals of fake America, "the ground zero of fake America, if you will,"[40] meaning, he muses, that Osama bin Laden must feel pretty stupid knowing that he bombed the wrong America and that, if you were from fake America and signed up to fight in Iraq and died, then it doesn't count. He then comes up with a quiz that you can use to assess whether you are a real or a fake American, including questions like "Are you voting for McCain or the terrorist?"

Later in the program, Jason Jones, one of the show's correspondents, goes on location to Wasilla (Palin's Alaskan hometown) to investigate the "real America." The long segment includes an ironic commentary about the homey mom-and-pop-ness of the town coupled with footage

3.2. As a means of critiquing Sarah Palin's manipulative campaign rhetoric, Jon Stewart explains his quiz for discerning whether you are a real or a fake American. *Comedy Central, Oct. 20, 2008*

that depicts it as a wasteland of strip malls plagued by a thriving illicit drug trade, plus interviews with town residents showing off their obscene tattoos, drinking to belligerence, and generally displaying a great deal of ignorance. The segment also includes a comment Palin made belittling Obama's past experience as a community organizer by joking that being the mayor of Wasilla was kind of like that, except that she actually had responsibilities. Jones then segues to an interview with the current mayor of Wasilla, who seems painfully hard-pressed to list anything that she actually does. The piece closes with Jones's summation that he finally understands what real America is all about, while the on-screen images ironically undercut each statement. He intones, "It is about not having to lock your doors" (while the visual is of police officers kicking in the door of a home meth lab), "it's letting kids be kids" (accompanied by a shot of a pregnant teenager), "a place where no means maybe" (pointing to a newspaper headline listing Alaska as having the highest reported rapes in the country), "where strangers are just people you haven't had a chance to throw up on yet." The piece finally fades to an image of a New York fireman on September 11 as Jones concludes, "It is an example we big-city elitists could learn from." The extended segment was undeniably fueled by real emotion and a palpable anger. Stewart and the cast were not merely making quips about the unfolding election campaign, but passionately editorializing about the language and assumptions surrounding the campaign that had remained largely unchallenged.

In addition to the incorporation of real news footage and commentary, these programs also interact with the real political world in another important way: via interviews with politicians and other newsmakers. One of the forms this takes is the ambush interview, in which the individual in question is caught by surprise by the show's cameras and a persistent "reporter." *22 Minutes* is particularly known for this technique, frequently using public figures as live props for a type of targeted political editorial. The show long included a popular recurring character named Marg Delahunty (played by program creator Mary Walsh) who, on occasion, would turn into "Marg, Princess Warrior." Marg is a frumpy, middle-aged woman who dons a ridiculous-looking breastplate and sword in order to hunt down politicians in need of a good tongue-lashing. Once she catches one, she latches on like an eccentric auntie, offering her personal advice on their policies. Walsh strategically lectures at such a rapid pace and with such confidence that it is impossible for her victim to get a word in edgewise. Instead, he or she is usually left trying to appear good-natured for the camera while listening to the sometimes biting critique. In one 2002 episode, for instance, Marg managed to ambush British Columbia premier Gordon Campbell and urged him to take a break from his recent wave of cost cutting, advising him that "selling out the public good to the private sector, that's really soul-sucking exhausting work. . . . Go home, for God's sake, and put your head down and have a little rest. Nobody wants you to keep up this pace, my darling. Campbell: that's not the Campbell's soup is it? I know there is a heck of a lot of people in this province who'd like to see you canned."[41]

Just as Marg targets the politically powerful, there is another, differently powerful group that was regularly brought in for a drubbing on the show. While performer Rick Mercer was on the program, he developed an enormously popular recurring segment called "Talking to Americans," which eventually developed into its own hour-long comedy special. In it,

U.S. residents (often found on the campuses of prestigious universities) are goaded into displaying their ignorance of Canada. Canadians have long had a fraught psychological relationship with their southern neighbors, as it is impossible for them not to acquire an intimate knowledge of American culture—indeed, they are often elided with Americans—while Americans typically know very little about them. Further, Canada, which is a fragmented country regionally, culturally, and linguistically, has long agonized over its identity, often defining itself as what it is not, most commonly in opposition to the United States. As Tinic explains, "[S]atire resonates profoundly with the negative sense of identity that defines the Canadian national self-consciousness."[42] Referencing the "Talking to Americans" segment, Jody Berland argues that "the expression of ambivalence bordering on self-erasure most frequently takes the form of irony, as Mercer ably demonstrates on a weekly basis."[43] To get the incriminating footage, Mercer introduces himself as a reporter from the Canadian Broadcasting Corporation. The victims are seen congratulating Canada on its first mile of paved road or on legalizing insulin (which a Canadian discovered), offering their condemnations of the Toronto polar bear hunt, begging the Canadian government to legalize VCRs, and sending various messages to Prime Minister "Tim Horton" (the name of a Canadian coffee-shop chain). The high point came in 2000 when Mercer and crew, among a pack of real reporters, told presidential hopeful George W. Bush that Canada's prime minister, Jean "Poutine" (a popular Quebecois snack of fried potatoes and gravy), was supporting his candidacy. (For the record, Prime Minister Jean Chrétien was doing no such thing.) Bush accepted the endorsement without hesitation.

Similarly, though *The Daily Show* does not normally pounce on politicians from out of the blue, the show's "correspondents" do conduct on-location interviews, in which they investigate local news stories (often those which appear trivial or absurd). The interviewees, some of whom are clearly unaware that they are speaking with a comedian rather than a reporter, are set up for maximum comic effect, often displaying a less-than-flattering side. For instance, during the show's coverage of the Republican National Convention in the lead-up to the 2004 election, correspondents Ed Helms and Samantha Bee interview GOP delegates. The montage of interview responses includes a woman answering a question about whether it would be seen as a conflict of interest to have Fox News sponsor the convention; she states simply and emphatically, "I think Fox News is absolutely awesome."[44] And when a man tells Bee that he is going to be exploring New York for the next few days, she inquires as to whether he has had his picture taken with a black person yet. He indicates that he has not, but would be willing to do so, and cheerily agrees with a deadpan Bee that there aren't many of "them" in his home state of Montana. These interviewees thus unwittingly provided the evidence for existing critiques of the Republican Party as narrow, blindly ideological, and bigoted. In all of its permutations, the pleasure in this popular conceit lies in the fact that real individuals (not caricatures) are drawn into their own satirizing. The victims' responses would not be nearly as entertaining were they fabricated by a scriptwriter.

In addition to the use of real news footage, editorials, and ambush interviews, *The Daily Show, The Colbert Report,* and *The Rick Mercer Report* add one more layer to this blurring of real and fake news. All include lengthy (consensual) interviews often taped in front of their studio audiences. As opposed to the ambush interviews, these interviewees have been booked in advance and are aware of the type of show they are participating in. Guests on *The Daily Show* are sometimes actors promoting a new movie, but are also just as likely to be politicians, pundits, and journalists, like Seymour Hersh, Wolf Blitzer, and Nancy Pelosi. Interviews on *The Colbert Report* are similar though they involve an extra layer of negotiation, as Colbert is quite obviously playing an ironic character. On both programs, the exchanges are conducted in a style somewhere between a straight news interview and a celebrity chat, with both hosts putting their guests at ease by cracking jokes and kibitzing about their personal lives. But, as Baym points out, the informal chat is not the focal point of most of the interviews; rather, it "provides the frame for often-heady conversations about public affairs."[45] Both hosts pose tough questions, particularly when the interviewee appears to be relying on party talking points or is making broad statements without offering proof. Stewart, in particular, is always congenial, but never hides his own opinion, often relishing the opportunity for a debate.

For example, in an interview with author Christopher Hitchens early in the Iraq war, Stewart begins the discussion by asking Hitchens good-naturedly to "help me understand why I am wrong about Iraq." After a back-and-forth in which Stewart presses Hitchens on the urgency for invading Iraq in particular rather than a number of other countries, they move on to American dissent on the war. When Hitchens dismisses "liberals" as believing that terrorism has been created by the United States, Stewart vehemently retorts that such a conflation is disturbing to him, arguing "there is reasonable dissent in this country about the way this war has been conducted," which has nothing to do with a belief that we should "cut and run" or that terrorism is our fault. Hitchens then implies that Stewart has been ridiculing the president precisely for not agreeing to withdraw from Iraq, to which Stewart responds that, to the contrary, he ridicules the president because "he refuses to answer questions from adults as though we were adults and falls back upon platitudes and phrases and talking points that does [*sic*] a disservice to the goals that he himself shares with the very people he needs in his defense." After this exchange, Stewart grabs Hitchens in mock aggression, comically defusing any animosity, then gives a quick plug for his guest's new book and asks the audience to give Hitchens a round of applause.[46] Interviews like this are certainly not fake or fictionalized, nor are they played entirely for laughs. Instead, lighthearted irreverence combines with a serious discussion of the issues of the day, further eroding the dividing lines between news, satire, and political debate. While some of these interview segments are fluffier than others, many offer a more in-depth and transparent discussion of topical issues than can be found on many of the straight news programs.

Rick Mercer's long-form interviews are often less policy-oriented, but are more focused on his unique goal of showing Canada to Canadians, something Tinic points to as a form of maturation from the project of defining the country in opposition to its neighbors, as in the earlier "Talking to Americans" segment. As Mercer put it in an interview, "I think a lot of the problems we have in this country have to do with the fact that the country is so bloody big, there's so few of us and it's so difficult to get around."[47] Because of this belief, his show differs from the others in that he often travels to a different part of the country for an episode, doing stories on particular professions, engaging in local pastimes, or hanging out with Canadian celebrities (often creating comedy out of his own good-natured ineptitude in the new environment). When he interviews politicians, he spends an extended period of time with them on location. In 2006, when he interviewed Bob Rae, then a candidate for the Liberal

3.3. Typical of his interview style, Stewart heatedly discusses policy with Christopher Hitchens, vehemently but congenially disagreeing with his guest's perspective. *Comedy Central, Aug. 25, 2005*

Party leadership, the two spent the day traveling by seaplane to a remote fishing locale. The aired footage included a mixture of jokes and political discussion and ended (controversially) with the two going skinny dipping together in the lake.[48] Again, these interviews are neither wholly like a comedic talk show nor like a straight current affairs program. Instead, the parodic, not-quite-news-host throws himself into the real political world.

The interpenetration of the mimetic and the real within the genre allows for the manipulation of existing footage within the satiric frame with the intention of affecting broader discourse. The theses advanced by these shows based on their investigation and rearrangement of existing footage often do become a part of the political record. For instance, on a *Daily Show* episode focusing on the results of the 9/11 Commission's report, Stewart, as anchor, plays footage of an interview that Vice President Dick Cheney had recently participated in on CNBC, during which he emphatically refutes the interviewer's assertion that he had once said that a meeting between one of the 9/11 hijackers and an Iraqi government official had been "pretty well confirmed." Stewart quickly segues from this footage of Cheney insisting that he absolutely never said those words to the original footage of him saying exactly that, handily exposing the blatant lie.[49] This segment, then, became a form of evidence within the real-world political discussion. In these instances, the program becomes performative, in that it creates that which it names and enacts in the moment. The revelation of this lie did not result in Cheney's firing, nor even in any sort of public reprimand, but it did become a part of the larger debate.

In a similar way, when public figures appear on these programs, their actions sometimes become news events in themselves, later reported by the serious news networks. This may involve favorable or neutral publicity for the politician, as when Pakistani president Pervez Musharraf dropped by *The Daily Show* for an interview, or it may result in increased scrutiny and related repercussions. In 2004, Liberal MP Carolyn Parrish appeared on *22 Minutes* in what was to be a lighthearted skit. The outspoken member of Parliament had come under fire in the past for her blunt criticism of the Bush administration in the United States, having referred to Bush as a "war-like" man and described Americans in general as "bastards." In the *22 Minutes* segment, she was interviewed by cast member Mark Critch, who encouraged her to speak her mind, handing her a Bush doll and goading her into stomping on it for the cameras.[50] When publicity footage was released prior to the actual airing of the show, a national newsmagazine picked the story up, repeatedly playing the doll-stomping segment and attracting a flood of subsequent press attention and speculation. Parrish was also shortly afterward quoted denouncing Paul Martin, then prime minister and leader of the Liberal Party, and the series of events soon led to Martin dismissing her from the Liberal Party caucus. Though perhaps not the sole cause of Parrish's party banishment, the comedic interview she participated in for *22 Minutes* undoubtedly had real-world ramifications. The intertwined nature of satire and serious political debate on these shows means that the newsworthy segments and exchanges that take place within them are by no means safely cloistered in the realm of entertainment but are very much part of the general political discussion.

Both the mimetic and the real are equally important components of this genre. The simultaneity of the two is a characteristic specific to performative parody. In most forms of textual parody, the parodist may

3.4. Liberal MP Carolyn Parrish agrees to stomp on a doll of President Bush on *This Hour Has 22 Minutes* (subsequently attracting censure for the action). *CBC, Nov. 19, 2004*

allude to real people and events, poking fun at real-world policies or personalities; however, his/her texts normally exist outside of and as commentary on the political world. Similarly, even in other performed parodies in which actors might create impersonations of public figures, these performances are typically separable from the day-to-day workings of public and political life, existing in a demarcated space of fictionalized entertainment that seems removed from the world of political fact. The parodic news shows, however, work hard to blur the line between the parodic and serious political discourse, as the comedians physically interact with the real, literally dialoging with the day's news footage or interviewing the newsmakers themselves. Undoubtedly, there is something more potentially dangerous and unpredictable about this interaction than there is in a fictional send-up of a public figure. Tellingly, a viewer of *22 Minutes* expressed her discomfort over this element via a letter to the editor of a local newspaper, beseeching the cast of the show to stop their ambushes, arguing, "you are all brilliant actors so impersonate politicians, by all means, or whomever, as much as you wish. Then those skits can be truly funny and you will have achieved that without debasing the personal dignity of our politicians."[51] Of course, judging by the popularity of these programs, there are many more fans who take pleasure in this potential to seriously impact and interact with the political world. Here, the hybridity of the genre is inseparable from the performative. Viewers tune in to watch the performers comedically interrogate, critique, and transform the real. The pleasure in this transformation is, I believe, created through a melding of two traditions: comedic improvisation combined with what television theorists have pinpointed as the historic allure of television itself—the aura of "liveness."

IMPROVISATION AND DIALOGIC INQUIRY

From its inception, the television industry marketed its product by emphasizing its difference from cinema. Television programs were live and immediate, and, as Lynn Spigel has demonstrated, they represented a means of unifying newly dispersed suburban homes, allowing one a connection to the larger community while remaining in the comfort and safety of one's living room.[52] From the names of programs to their stylistic markers and genre conventions, television has claimed the concept of liveness. As Jane Feuer argues, "[T]elevision's self-referential discourse plays upon the connotative richness of the term 'live,' confounding its simple or technical denotations with a wealth of allusiveness."[53] In fact, she explains, while television actually now involves less of an equivalence between the time of an event and the time of transmission, "the medium seems to insist more and more upon an ideology of the live, the immediate, the direct, the spontaneous, the real."[54]

If there is one type of program in particular that is built on this promise, it is the news show, which one watches with the understanding that one is receiving the most current information on world events as they unfold (regardless of how far in advance some of the pretaped sequences have been filmed), witnessing the revealing of information among a community of viewers tuning in at the same moment. Though this community may be dispersed in space, they are united in time. To reassure the viewer that this is the case, news shows routinely employ markers of their liveness, including references to the date and time, as well as a generalized format of "direct address," which Jérôme Bourdon defines as "the sequence where a person looks straight at the camera (as if at viewers) and addresses the viewers, using the appropriate deixis [proof of 'liveness']. The most evident part of this deixis is of course the personal pronouns 'I' (the host) and 'you' (the viewers at home)."[55] The fake news shows play off these same markers, partially as a means of parody (imitating the tropes of the genre) and partially for similar reasons as the straight programs themselves. These shows are also reporting and reacting to events as they unfold, offering their redaction of the day's or week's stories. Audiences watch not simply for comedy, but for relevance.

Within the genre, this general reliance on topicality also combines with the tradition of comedic improvisation. While related to much earlier folk theater traditions, such as commedia dell'arte, modern stage improvisation became a codified performance tradition in the late 1950s. It is an unscripted form of sketch comedy in which actors create the material in the moment, sometimes based on suggestions from the audience or simply in collaboration with one another, and it is a form from which these shows draw heavily. With the ambush interviews in particular, the skills of the performers must be considerable in order to maintain their personas while adapting to whatever their victims say, playing the straight men to the victims' unwitting comedy. Similarly, in the interview segments, the host improvises both comedically and journalistically in his unscripted exchanges with his guests. Indeed, in an interview with Charlie Rose, Colbert made reference to his background as an improviser and how it aids him in the interview segments, since he never knows "what is going to happen in the interview."[56] As in watching stage improv, the audience takes pleasure in seeing something created on the spot, as the performer comes up with just the right provocations and responses to further the scene. And with the exception of the on-location ambushes, the bulk of the show is filmed in front of a live studio audience, once again drawing on the aura of immediacy and community this creates. The monologues are written beforehand, but the hosts also ad lib in response to audience reaction, making the home audience feel as if they are part of the live performance (though they are not watching it in real time). *The Daily Show* has also made an occasional habit of doing live (real-time) specials concurrent with particularly important events, such as after a presidential debate or on election night itself. These specials serve to further blur the line between satire and reportage, as the cast improvises their responses to the events simultaneously with the ranks of pundits providing their analyses on other channels. In one sense, this combination of improv comedy with the timely incorporation of nonfiction material defines the developing genre I have been calling the parodic news show.

Rather than sending-up one particular program or newscaster, most offer a broader satire of larger ills within the news genre as well as hypocrisies in the day's news stories. Here, the incorporation of nonfiction material serves to add an entirely new level to the unmasking abilities of parody and satire. Linda Hutcheon defines *parody* as a form of "inter-art discourse,"[57] arguing that what distinguishes parody from pastiche (mere similarity) is the use of ironic "transcontextualization" to provide critical distance from the original. Hutcheon is clearly referencing more direct textual parodies within fine art and literature, offering such examples as the transcontextualization of Shakespeare's words in Tom Stoppard's play *Rosencrantz and Guildenstern Are Dead*. However, I would argue that the concept of transcontextualization is also a useful one for the fake news programs. Rather than the transcontextualization of one fictional text or work of art within another, an official's real-world actions or words are transcontextualized within the frame of the show, so that the two texts or performances exist side by side: the original act and the host's interpretation of that act.

The reason that Jon Stewart can get a laugh from simply playing a clip of President Bush at a press conference is not because Bush's statements were considered funny when he first said them or even when they were aired on the evening news, but because they have been transcontextualized into a comedically deconstructive frame. Since the audience of *The Daily Show* is primed to watch the material with a critical eye, the original footage suddenly reveals a wealth of hidden meaning. In a similar manner, when an ambushed politician or representative of a corporation is caught on tape, his/her official statements, which might otherwise be read as authoritative, are transcontextualized into a new frame, rendering them pompous and hollow. Much of the audience's pleasure is derived from watching real, serious news material ironically transcontextualized and stripped down in front of their eyes.

Here, parodic news does what the straight news cannot, which is stage an ongoing dialogue with itself. As Baym points out, while traditional news is monologic, presenting a closed, authoritative version of what the issues of the day are and why they are important, parodic news shows are dialogic, playing multiple voices against each other. While the straight news "claims an epistemological certainty, satire is a discourse of inquiry, a rhetoric of challenge that seeks through the asking of unanswered questions to clarify the underlying morality of a situation."[58] This becomes possible, in large part, because parodic news is not beholden to the same industry standards as the straight news is supposed to be. Traditional news programs are expected to adhere to a type of dispassionate objectivity that frowns on any sort of subjective display on the part of the journalist. As discussed in chapter 2, in the post-9/11 era in particular, this tenet has too often translated into a hesitancy to question the statements made by officials for fear of appearing partisan or "unpatriotic," meaning that a political party's public relations talking points become presented as fact without any interrogation of their veracity. This is a critique now frequently leveled at the mainstream media and one that Jon Stewart explicitly articulates, arguing, "[T]here are—should be—you know, truths, actual truths, and someone should be there to help arbitrate that, and it seems to be that media should be the forum for that."[59] His function as a fake news host, then, is to act as a comedic interrogator. In contrast to the seeming inadequacies of the broadcast news, the comedians in all of these programs are able to draw on a process of dialogical interaction, cross-examining the rhetoric both of public figures and of standard news discourse.

The Daily Show provides a particularly good example of this process, as Stewart so often literally stages a conversation between himself and the news footage he plays for his audience, stopping and starting the clip in question in order to provide his own interjections. For example, the day after the Iraq Study Group issued its assessment of the Iraq war in December 2006, Stewart did a lengthy piece on its reception. After opening with a montage of newscasters offering such grim summations as "a complete overhaul of U.S. policy in the Middle East" and "Bush would have to concede, he got just about all of it wrong," Stewart explains that White House press secretary Tony Snow nevertheless has remained loyal to the president and then segues to footage of him taking questions from reporters. Snow is shown accusing one of the reporters at the press conference of being partisan, to which the reporter responds, "You are suggesting that by quoting the report, I am trying to make a partisan argument?" Stewart then stops the footage to say, "It's the way you quote it. You're quoting with a partisan inflection," adding with a comical voice, "the president's policies are not woooorrking." We are then returned to the footage, in which Snow is still responding to the reporter, explaining, "The question is, can you read this as anything but a repudiation of the president's policy, and the answer is yes, I can." Stewart responds, "You absolutely can. It could be read as a nineteenth-century comedy of manners," at which point he brandishes a copy of the report with a flourish, reading from it "pull out the majority of troops by 2008. Saucy!" Finally, Stewart closes with a short montage of Snow repeatedly answering questions by saying that he needs more time to "parse" the report. Stewart imitates Snow, adding, "I need time to parse, to split hairs. See, right now, you are not getting my top-quality bull-[bleep]. It's not fair to you, the public I lie to."[60]

The parodic news hosts use their own subjective responses to dissect the discourse of public officials and organizations. In so doing, these comedians act as the everyman's stand-in. If a regular newscaster cannot roll an eye or arch a brow at a politician's statement, the comedian can fall off his chair doing so. Thus, he is able to act as the viewer's surrogate, screaming at the newsclip in frustration or summarily labeling someone "full of shit." As opposed to the average citizen, however, these comedians have an audience of millions at their command. For those of us without such a luxury, we can take vicarious pleasure in hearing our own opinions aired on national television. Indeed, this is an important component of the genre's appeal. In one newspaper article on *The Daily Show,* a journalist interviews members of the studio audience and quotes a 78-year-old woman, who explains her love of the program and of Jon Stewart in particular: "'he can really see through things and some of the shams that we're being fed,' she says. 'And I'm tired of the shams. I want a little truth to come out. I want somebody to see some of the things I see and Jon does that for me.'"[61] These performers are still clearly recognized as comedians, but as our stand-ins they have also garnered a unique form of status and respect that is certainly not routinely granted to the average stand-up comic or sitcom actor.

SLIDING INTO PUNDITRY

Due to the hybridity of the genre, and because these programs are so heavily reliant on and critical of contemporary political events and the evolving discourse surrounding them, they have themselves become a fairly substantial presence within that discourse, while some of the more outspoken performers have been elevated to the status of legitimate political pundit. In documenting the wider, growing genre of political entertainment on television, Jeffrey Jones notes that the hosts of the new political television "have increasingly come to be seen as political commentators by fans and others within the television industry."[62] When referring to *22 Minutes,* for instance, particularly in its early years, journalists frequently paint it as possessing a voice to rival those of the individual political parties. In a 1997 article in the *Toronto Star,* Susan Riley describes it as a sort of "Unofficial Opposition."[63] Much of the praise for *22 Minutes* takes on a populist rhetoric, as the show's digs at those in power are depicted as the amplified voice of the people. This is also how members of the show tend to represent their work. In an interview about the program's celebrated ambushes of politicians, for example, senior producer Gerald Lunz explains, "the drama is in the questions—we ask the questions Canadians would ask if they got the chance."[64]

The performers in the cast who have done the most overtly political material, Mary Walsh and Rick Mercer in particular, have developed a large following of admirers, not necessarily for their skills as actors, but for their political critiques. Before leaving the show, Walsh became notorious for her ambush interviews, using the innocence and guilelessness of the characters she developed as an excuse for asking politicians impertinent questions. Mercer, as noted, has become most famous for his political rants, a tradition he has exported into *The Rick Mercer Report.* In this newer show, his one-man, distinctively Canadian, news-magazine format has built him a reputation as the voice of the country. At this point, it is certainly not unheard of for people to cite Mercer's political advice to the nation as they would any established political speaker. In a column about Canada's status as a worldwide peacekeeper (and its sparse military resources), for instance, a writer in the *Hamilton Spectator* cites Mercer's on-air pronouncement on the matter verbatim: "'If we're going to ask people to leave the best place on earth and go to the worst places on earth and keep the peace and do it in the name of Canada, the least we can do is back them up with the Gold Card.'"[65] He goes on to explain that "there is a growing public recognition—à la Rick Mercer—of a moral obligation."[66] Mercer has now become both a ubiquitous Canadian celebrity and a pundit, winning the Arthur Kroeger College's Award for Public Discourse, an honor normally bestowed upon think tanks, magazines, and associations. Notably, he has even been tapped for his expertise south of the border in interviews with the *New York Times* and *Washington Post.* In a 2004 episode of PBS's *NewsHour,* Mercer appeared with a columnist for the *Globe and Mail* and a University of Toronto professor in a roundtable discussion (with Gwen Ifill) on Canadian-American relations, speaking insightfully on popular Canadian perceptions of the Bush administration. He was sought out not for a comedic monologue, but for his knowledge of current affairs.[67]

Jon Stewart and the staff of *The Daily Show* have received even more public attention. When *The Daily Show* began airing with Craig Kilborn as its host, it was less focused on political critique and more often was described as a spoof of *Entertainment Tonight* than of a serious news program. However, when Stewart took over in 1999, the show began to change, garnering a huge amount of attention over its coverage of the 2000 presidential election and winning several awards. Then, the show's coverage of the 2004 presidential campaign catapulted it into the spotlight. Viewers eagerly tuned in for the cast's deconstructions of the party primaries, stump speeches, debates, and poll results, all of which were reported under the title "Indecision 2004." Early in the campaign, John Edwards announced his candidacy for the Democratic ticket while on the show, and during the crucial last months of campaigning, presidential hopeful John Kerry dropped by the program for an interview, while declining offers from numerous other news shows.

Public attention snowballed as the season wore on. Leading up to the election, Stewart landed on the cover of numerous magazines and did interviews on a plethora of news programs. At the same time, he and the other writers for the show released a faux textbook called *America (the Book): A Citizen's Guide to Democracy Inaction* that immediately became a bestseller. In the midst of it all, the show received a Television Critics Association award, not for comedy, but for outstanding achievement in news and information. Suddenly, everyone was asking Stewart's opinion on every nuance of the campaign and the media's coverage of it, while journalists speculated over what his influence would be on the election itself. A reporter for *USA Today,* for example, argued, "Stewart has become not just a TV phenomenon but also a cultural force, if not hero, influencing discourse at the dinner table and in the college dorm and even, some believe, turnout at the polls."[68]

Meanwhile, a few weeks before the election, Stewart was invited on CNN's *Crossfire* to promote his book. Stewart had previously criticized this program on his own show, using it as an example of political debate that has degenerated into a shouting match between caricatured representatives of the left and the right rather than a discussion of facts. During his live appearance on *Crossfire,* though, he surprised everyone by refusing to confine himself to the role of comedic entertainer and instead sincerely begged the hosts to stop "hurting America," accusing them of engaging in "partisan hackery." When one of the hosts, Tucker Carlson, tried to goad him into lightening up, he persisted with his critique, eventually referring to Carlson as a "dick." News of the incident spread immediately, with hundreds of thousands of people downloading the footage and thousands of fans writing emails (primarily in support) to the Comedy Central network.[69] As one reporter put it, "[I]nstant Internet buzz about the extraordinary 13 minutes of television universally hailed Stewart as a refreshing and clear-eyed critic of an increasingly trivial television news media and skyrocketed him to a new rank in his comedic career—from wry commentator to serious provocateur."[70] As Boler and Turpin point out about the episode, though other media critics and commentators may have made similar critiques in the past, "the frustration expressed by Stewart clearly resonated with the sentiments of thousands of viewers who were keenly grateful that Jon Stewart had the status and authority to represent the 'average citizen.'"[71] In that moment, Stewart took on legendary status as a heroic truth-teller, which was only increased by CNN's subsequent decision to drop *Crossfire* from its schedule.

The point here is not simply that Stewart has become an extremely popular comedian, which he certainly has, but that, through his parody, he has achieved legitimacy as a political speaker, which sets him apart from most of his predecessors. While at the helm of "Weekend Update" on *Saturday Night Live,* Chevy Chase was never asked seriously for his analysis of political events. Stewart, on the other hand, is now sought out for his growing reputation as a media watchdog, while his show is gaining a significant voice within political discourse. Thus, when in early 2009, Stewart ended up in an even more well-publicized dust-up with another media figure—CNBC's Jim Cramer—both the press and fans waited with bated breath to view the much-anticipated drubbing. And, indeed, Stewart did not disappoint.

The feud began when another CNBC reporter, Rick Santelli, delivered an on-air rant about President Obama's stimulus plan, yelling that he was uninterested in subsidizing the mortgages of "losers" (those facing foreclosure). *The Daily Show* responded with a withering piece on the business network's track record leading up to the financial crisis, highlighting a number of bad calls its reporters had made and showcasing some of its interviews with corporate CEOs that were far more fawning than probing. Some of the material was from Jim Cramer's program, *Mad Money,* and Cramer took umbrage at the critique, disputing Stewart's logic, particularly the insinuation that he had advised viewers to buy Bear Stearns stock shortly before the company collapsed. Stewart responded by pretending to apologize for the accusation, but then played more clips from earlier episodes of Cramer's show when he did, indeed, tout the stock. Cramer continued to complain about the critique in appearances on a number of other programs, fanning the flames of controversy, until finally he appeared on *The Daily Show* itself several days later. Almost the entirety of the episode that evening was devoted to the interview, and though the two men started by joking about the tension that had built up between them, Stewart then forcefully and in great detail laid out why he thought that CNBC, and Cramer by extension, was doing a poor job of business journalism. While Cramer sheepishly admitted to having made mistakes, Stewart played a number of incriminating clips of Cramer candidly discussing borderline illegal activity he may have engaged in while a hedge fund manager and relentlessly called him to task for the dishonesty of the industry.[72] The exchange was widely reported and was overwhelmingly framed as a slam-dunk trouncing by Stewart. As a reporter from the *Los Angeles Times* put it, the episode "provided one of those memorable television moments that distill the public mood—in this case, angst about the economy's swift decline. Stewart also displayed the tough interviewing skills that belie his insistence that he's merely an entertainer."[73]

Though *The Colbert Report* is a younger program, Stephen Colbert also has quickly garnered widespread fame as a truth-teller and political provocateur. From the beginning, Colbert seemed to have his finger on the cultural zeitgeist, coining in his first episode the term *truthiness,* a word that both perfectly sums up the satiric targets of his show and seems, to many, to accurately describe the state of public discourse. According to Colbert, *truthiness* is truth that comes from the gut rather than hard evidence or logic, "what you want the facts to be as opposed to what the facts are. What feels like the right answer as opposed to what reality will support."[74] The term caught on instantly, making its way into multiple newspaper articles and television discussions about truth and fact (all referencing the show) and leading *Merriam-Webster's Dictionary* to name *truthiness* the word of the year for 2006, further attesting to Colbert's "quotability" and to the timeliness of his parody.[75]

Though Colbert already was attracting notice, as with Stewart, the moment that brought him the most attention as a political bomb thrower was a public appearance on another platform. In April 2006, Colbert gave a scheduled performance at the White House Correspondents' Association dinner in front of an audience of reporters, celebrities, and politicians (including President George W. Bush). He performed a monologue in his character as television host personality, ostensibly praising and offering support for Bush, but actually heavily ironic and critical of the president's policies. He explained, for instance, "I stand by this man. I stand by this man because he stands for things. Not only for things, he stands *on* things. Things like aircraft carriers and rubble and recently flooded city squares. And that sends a strong message: that no matter what happens to America, she will always rebound—with the most powerfully staged photo ops in the world."[76] He also picked on the press corps itself, wondering out loud why there had been a recent surge of critical reports on topics like NSA (National Security Agency) wire tapping and secret prisons in Eastern Europe, opining, "Those things are secret for a very important reason: they're super-depressing. And if that's your goal, well, misery accomplished. Over the last five years you people were so good—over tax cuts, WMD intelligence, the effect of global warming. We Americans didn't want to know, and you had the courtesy not to try to find out. Those were good times, as far as we knew."[77] The performance drew some laughter from the live audience but also appeared to make many (including Bush) visibly uncomfortable.

The next day, press coverage of the dinner largely omitted detailed discussion about Colbert, much of it focusing more on a preceding Bush impersonator who collaborated on some jokes with the president. However, footage of the monologue (which originally aired on C-SPAN) began circulating on the internet and quickly became a viral phenomenon, with millions downloading it and forwarding it to friends. On the internet and in the alternative press, a wave of indignation spread, with many accusing the mainstream press of deliberately choosing to ignore Colbert's biting critique. The ensuing controversy then trickled back into mainstream coverage, with pundits and reporters weighing in on the issue. The two sides of the debate were largely divided along political lines, liberals arguing that Colbert had audaciously spoken truth to power, voicing the critiques of the administration that others in the media had been unable or unwilling to make, and, better yet, doing so in front of the president himself. Some made the argument that Colbert had then been shut out by the overly timid mainstream press. A website was set up called *Thank You Stephen Colbert,* which logged tens of thousands of "thank yous" in the first few days after the dinner. Conservatives, on the other hand, scoffed at the idea of a media conspiracy, arguing that Colbert was just not funny. Neither side was necessarily dissimulating. Rather, it was the type of humor that many on the political right did not find all that amusing, or that was interpreted as plain rudeness, while for many on the left, the skillfulness of the joke delivery was almost beside the point, as Colbert had succeeded in articulating the critiques that they had been longing to hear within mainstream political discourse. Again, a comedian had slid into the role of serious political pundit, as audiences vicariously looked to him to speak their viewpoint within the public realm.

Instead of conceptualizing the actions of these entertainers as mere commentary on the political field from the jokers on the sidelines, it seems clear that their work functions as political speech in and of itself, affecting the direction of public discourse while elevating the parodists to the level of legitimate political experts. It appears that, while the parodic news show certainly takes comedic jabs at the conventions of television news, it also paradoxically borrows some of the authority imbued in those conventions. Performers such as Stewart, Colbert, and Mercer, who appear on television to speak about current events with obvious knowledge and command (and irreverence), absorb some of the authority of real pundits and newscasters while simultaneously mocking those roles. Similarly, while the average comedian would presumably not normally be granted admittance to political functions, *The Daily Show*'s correspondents routinely secure press passes to official events, such as political party conventions, where they then lampoon the authority and purpose of the real-world participants. One correspondent, Rob Riggle, even gained access to the U.S. military, conducting a series of interviews on location in Iraq. And in 2009, Colbert taped an entire week of his program in front of the American troops in Iraq. In an interview with *Bust* magazine, *Daily Show* cast member Samantha Bee marvels over the fact that so many people have told her she could, in the future, get a job as a real newscaster if she wanted to. She says, "I don't want to believe that it's true. But I almost do. Our impression is just good enough that we could be newsreaders. It's pretty sad. . . . It's ridiculous that we get the access we get. Why in the world would I be talking to Madeleine Albright? Why in the world would she stop to talk to me? It's crazy."[78] Far from remaining solely in the world of comedic entertainment—or fake news—the parodic commentary offered by these shows has launched them into the midst of the very real political sphere.

There is some danger inherent in this expanded legitimacy, however. The popularity of *22 Minutes* in Canada has come to mean that many politicians who once would have tried to avoid the show's roving cameras like the plague are now eager to be featured on the widely viewed program. Likewise, since developing his own show, Rick Mercer has made it a habit of securing interviews and whimsical outings with high-profile politicians, including what was presented as an impromptu "sleepover" at Prime Minister Stephen Harper's residence in 2006, which certainly did not do any damage to Harper's image. Similarly, *The Daily Show* has become a hot spot on the interview circuit for politicians, pundits, and authors. For some fans, this begins to raise the question of whether the once dangerously unpredictable satire is becoming domesticated.

In a scathing article on Rick Mercer, a *Toronto Star* reporter blasts the performer for, among other things, appearing in a commercial asking Canadians to help reduce energy use as a means of meeting the Kyoto protocols, advocating policies developed by the Liberal government at the time. He writes:

> Let's acknowledge what's been lost here. When Mercer was young, struggling, and a Newfoundlander—when he was, in other words a natural outsider—he did true satire, blasting not just the government but its supplicants and Canadian culture in general. . . . The contrarian who once said, "It would be very disturbing if I found a government I agreed with" is now a shill for the government, and a comfortable Crown corporation employee whose specialty as a "satirist" is roasting the Leader of the Opposition.[79]

The criticism is somewhat unfair, as Mercer presumably agreed to tape the commercial out of a personal commitment to a particular environmental issue, not allegiance to a particular party, but his increased visibility within Canadian media culture has left him vulnerable to the charge of selling out. Though Stewart has, for the most part, continued to win over fans through his coverage of successive American elections, during the 2004 presidential campaign, there were some rumblings of criticism after John Kerry's appearance on the show, particularly because Stewart did not ask him very tough questions. A writer for the *Boston Globe,* for instance, mused that "the spot raised the unsettling prospect that as *The Daily Show* grows in popularity and significance, that program will lose its wily edge. How can Stewart and his writers continue to make fun of the very people now clamoring to get cozy on his studio couch?"[80] Indeed, in the initial stages of the 2008 campaign, Stewart appeared to struggle to critique Barack Obama (whom the audience seemed unwilling to laugh at) or John McCain (with whom he had developed a relationship over the course of numerous previous interviews). As Baym points out, however, he soon found his critical edge (and anger) after McCain picked Sarah Palin as his running mate, articulating his clearly impassioned belief that McCain had lost his principles.[81]

NOT NOT NEWSCASTING

Beyond the question of the satirists' coziness with their targets, the increased legitimacy of the programs, combined with their slippery combination of the mimetic and the real, has sparked some cultural anxiety, much of which has been focused on *The Daily Show.* As Stewart's profile was rising during the presidential campaign of 2004, a flurry of reports was produced on who was watching the show and for what reasons. The Pew Research Center for the People and the Press released a study in January 2004 that reported that 21 percent of Americans aged 18–29 regularly learned about the campaign and the candidates from comedy shows like *Saturday Night Live* and *The Daily Show.*[82] The survey from which these data were gleaned asked respondents if they "regularly learn *something* from . . ." (my emphasis) and then gave a list of various sources, including "comedy TV shows." As Russell Peterson points out, nothing in the survey posed the sources as either-or options, meaning that the same respondent could potentially report learning something from a wide variety of media outlets.[83] However, in subsequent articles and television discussions, the results became redacted to statements such as: *The Daily Show* was chosen as "the preferred election news source by one-fifth of surveyed Americans ages 18–29."[84] This dubious statistic soon became fodder for much musing on the state of the voting public.

The idea of fans receiving information from the show has provoked hand-wringing from several quarters. In a spontaneous late-night exchange on the floor at the Democratic National Convention in 2004, Ted Koppel whined to Jon Stewart that "a lot of television viewers—more, quite frankly, than I'm comfortable with—get their news from the comedy channel on a program called *The Daily Show.*"[85] While Stewart countered that his fans watch for a comedic *interpretation* of the news, Koppel insisted that they use the show for information. When Stewart appeared on Bill O'Reilly's Fox News program, O'Reilly infamously referred to Stewart's audience as "a bunch of stoned slackers," opining, "You know what's really frightening? You actually have an influence on this presidential election. That is scary, but it's true. You've got stoned slackers watching your dopey show every night and they can vote."[86] Fans of the show were vindicated when, within days of O'Reilly's comment, the National Annenberg Election Survey concluded that viewers of *The Daily Show* were far better-educated and affluent than the national average and were more knowledgeable about the presidential campaign than those who do not watch any late-night television.[87] As a *PR Newswire* writer gloatingly pointed out, viewers of O'Reilly's show were significantly less wealthy and well-educated than those of *The Daily Show.*[88] There was no mention of which audience was more stoned.

Much of the rhetoric about *The Daily Show* functioning as a news source has taken on a familiar tone. Like condemnations of soap operas or tabloids, the anxiety is over a perceived other (in this case, young people), who might be unable to tell the difference between truth and fiction, real life and entertainment. Writing about tabloid television, Kevin Glynn addresses the destabilization caused by the blurring of news and entertainment. He argues, "[T]abloid television disturbs not only the figure of the traditional anchorman . . . but equally the definitions of truth, seriousness, and authority that he embodies,"[89] a disturbance that undoubtedly accounts for at least some of the revulsion it engenders. Jason Mittell also points out that genre mixing, in general, often creates a certain amount of controversy. As he argues, "[A]ny programs which are generically mixed, either through parody or fusion, do face a particularly tumultuous cultural life, easily buffeted by competing contexts of reception."[90] In this case, the mixture of comedy with news and political commentary creates anxiety in some that the show will somehow be read as straight news by others.

What detractors don't understand is that these programs would have little appeal were they simply slightly hipper versions of the straight news. They are not attempting to become another incarnation of the existing real, but to hold the real up for scrutiny, an operation that requires that audience members remain aware of the deliberate use of artifice. In fact, if the hosts and their casts are to maintain legitimacy as *satiric* newscasters, it is important that they continue to appear to be obviously playing a role. Stewart and Mercer in particular must retain the aura of the cheeky journalistic outsider throwing stones rather than seeming like a part of the political establishment they critique. Their unique status stems from their ability to embody the authority of a pundit or newscaster while still being several steps removed from the profession. To borrow the terminology Richard Schechner uses when describing performance, they will maintain this status as long as the audience knows that they are both not newscasters and not not newscasters.[91] It is worth noting that the hosts' physical being is also important to this operation. Returning to an idea mentioned in the introduction, they simultaneously embody the authority of a television expert (due to their ability to perform white, male, middle-class respectability), while remaining somewhat removed from the mainstream by virtue of religion (Stewart makes frequent references to his Jewishness) or region (Rick Mercer and the cast of *22 Minutes* are from Newfoundland), which allows them to play up their outsider's eye for absurdity. Ultimately, it is through their incorporation and engagement with the real, without actually becoming identical to it, that they are able to critique the real.

For many fans, there is something about the hosts' playful manipulations and dissections of the real world of television news and political debate that end up coming closer to reality than the original itself, returning us to the idea developed in chapter 2 of overproduced earnestness seeming suspect, while ironic self-referentiality maintains an aura of sincerity. The parodic news shows happily point to their own fakery, while highlighting the dissimulations of the self-serious. The parodic news hosts present themselves as the everyman surrogate, who can display his disgust and amusement on our behalf and who responds as anyone would to the crazy situations at hand, speaking out loud what we are all thinking, if perhaps in a somewhat wittier manner than we are able. And, within the ironic, not-quite-real universe of the show, they are able to effortlessly shape the real into evidence for the critique their audience has grown to crave.

Given the popularity of this critique, however, these shows have attracted a great deal of suspicion about what message the audience is ultimately taking away from them. Since there is a growing body of fans who revel in reading the news ironically, in parodically poking fun at the straight news media, and in knowingly laughing at the flawed nature of contemporary public discourse, there is concern over whether these fans are becoming disillusioned with the political discussion as a whole. The critique that has plagued this young genre, both in popular and in academic writings, is that the form begets cynicism, that it trivializes the serious, and that it leads viewers to see the political world through detached amusement. While these worries are clearly linked to the ongoing debates that have shadowed the more general modes of satire and parody from the beginning, the fact that this particular genre is so closely intertwined with the real political world lends a new aspect to old concerns. Further, these programs are not as unmistakably activist in intent as the documentaries or activist groups profiled in the coming chapters, meaning that they can appear to be more detached from the issues they seemingly casually critique.

CYNICISM AND ENGAGEMENT

Within academic circles, there has been a great deal of debate and worry about exactly what the audience of *The Daily Show* in particular is taking away from it, much of it stemming from the question of whether or not the program encourages cynicism. At the 2006 meeting of the National Communication Association, for example, one of the most popular panels was a mock heresy trial in which Jon Stewart was accused of engaging "in unbridled political cynicism" (the proceedings of which were later published in *Critical Studies in Media Communication*). Though the audience seemed to be overwhelmingly on the side of the defense, the prosecution, Roderick P. Hart and E. Johanna Hartelius, staunchly maintained that the popularity of Stewart's program signaled a level of dangerous detachment and a too-seductive desire to feel good about feeling bad about politics, though they struggled to persuasively link this charge of detachment to the actual contents of the program.[92] Along similar lines, in 2006 Jody Baumgartner and Jonathan S. Morris published the results of a study they claimed proved that exposure to the program led to increased political cynicism among viewers. One of the major flaws with the study, however, was that they never defined *cynicism,* instead inferring its presence based on their own somewhat hazy criteria. Their method consisted of having undergraduate students watch either a clip from *The Daily Show* or a clip from a CBS evening news broadcast—both explicitly treating the then-upcoming 2004 election and the candidates—and then fill out a questionnaire. Participants were asked to rate their agreement or disagreement to questions such as "I have faith in the U.S. electoral system," "I trust the news media to cover political events fairly and accurately," and "Sometimes politics and government seems so complicated that a person like me can't really understand what's going on."[93] The participants were also asked to indicate how well a range of personality attributes described both President Bush and presidential contender Kerry.

The authors found that those who had viewed *The Daily Show* gave lower evaluations of both presidential candidates and that they were less likely to express faith in the U.S. electoral system or in the mass media's ability to fairly cover political events. These results were intensified for those who were not already regular viewers of the program. Finally, the researchers found that viewers of *The Daily Show* were more likely to express confidence in their ability to understand politics. From these findings, they concluded, "*The Daily Show* generates cynicism toward the media and the electoral process," while simultaneously making "young viewers more confident about their own ability to understand politics,"[94] which was due, they suggested, to comedy's tendency toward simplification. And though they did not ask the participants about their intentions regarding political participation, they speculated that since the program is so popular with young citizens in particular, it could end up "driving down support for political institutions and leaders among those already inclined toward nonparticipation."[95] However, cynicism here seems to lie entirely in the eye of the beholder, as it would seem that a lack of blind faith in the electoral system or particular candidates might just as easily be described as healthy skepticism, as an understanding of nuance and complication, or as engaged frustration with a less-than-perfect political field. Nowhere in the study did they persuasively link distrust in the system or in particular candidates with a belief that these things cannot be changed for the better nor with a lack of desire for that change.

Part of the problem here, as with Hart and Hartelius's paper, is that the authors do not do any textual analysis of the show's contents. On one hand, Baumgartner and Morris explicitly argue that "the effect of *The Daily Show*'s humor on youth is somewhat unique,"[96] distinguishable from that of Jay Leno or David Letterman, whose jokes are shown to have little impact on audience evaluations of particular politicians. However, the authors nevertheless assume that all political comedy can be described uniformly, lumping Stewart back in with Leno, Letterman, and all other political comedians in their assertion that "political comedy is largely focused on personal traits of public figures rather than policy, and the jokes tend to draw on preexisting negative stereotypes people have of these public figures."[97] However, if they had examined *The Daily Show*'s contents, they would have found that its targets and techniques are widely divergent from those on a program like *The Late Show with David Letterman* and that, while some other manifestations of political comedy might be construed as encouraging cynicism, the intent of the parodic news shows seems precisely the opposite.

There certainly is a tendency in some political comedy to focus on personalities rather than on more substantive policy or structural issues. Indeed, as discussed in the introduction, it is this tendency that has led numerous theorists of satire to argue that it ultimately serves a conservative function, sending the message that everyone is equally inept and immoral and that there is not much to be done about it. This could be described as the "equal opportunity offender" school of comedy that, in the vernacular, seeks to demonstrate that "everybody's shit stinks." The parodic news shows are by no means above the targeting of character flaws or other personal foibles, and they would likely garner less respect if they did not take the opportunity to lampoon the bumble of the day without regard for which political partisan made the error. However, there is also a clear desire in these shows to additionally dissect substantive political policies and structures, not, I would argue, out of a sense of smug detachment, but out of concerned engagement. This is evidenced in the very structure and pacing of the segments.

As Baym points out, the programs to which *The Daily Show* is often compared, such as *Saturday Night Live* or *The Late Show with David Letterman,* mimic the delivery of many news programs in their "now this" approach to the jokes. The comedians move from punch line to punch line, quickly flitting from issue to issue, while "no topic is placed in wider context or receives elaboration."[98] Straight television news, he argues (citing Neil Postman), has a tendency to reduce "the importance of political information to a form of 'trivial pursuit'—political information and knowledge become fodder for quiz shows and trivia games, containing little perceivable real-world importance or relevance."[99] When topical comedians mimic this rapid-fire approach, then, they "further reduce any sense of engagement with or connection to the political public sphere."[100] *The Daily Show,* however, has developed a different mode of delivery. During his monologues, Stewart often spends several minutes covering a particular story, far longer than the few seconds it would be granted by someone like Jay Leno. He also makes liberal use of footage from other news programs or from congressional television, employing the clips not just as comedic props but as evidence in an expanded dissection of the issue at hand. These segments might include a potshot or two at a particular politician's missteps, but they most often focus more broadly on policy, frequently providing historical details and other background information to contextualize the current development. Ironically, then, a segment on sectarian violence in Iraq might contain more historical analysis of the roots of the current conflict than most real news programs' coverage of the same story (albeit along with a scatological joke or bad pun).

The Daily Show and *The Colbert Report* both excel at pointing up the cycle of public relations spin and media amplification without interrogation that seems to define contemporary political discussion, which is certainly a more foundational and complex issue than is typically engaged by late-night comedians. While it is not unusual for a comic to imply that the political administration is deceitful, the parodic news show tends to go an important step further in drawing our attention to an administration's particular techniques of mystification, as well as in analyzing how the mass media contribute to the lack of substantive political debate. Peterson fleshes this out further, arguing that there is a clear distinction between a comedian who is simply a truth-teller and one who exposes truthiness and demonstrates how popular truths are used and manipulated. He asserts that it amounts to the "distinction between merely pointing out the fact that the emperor wears no clothes and leading us to understand how we could have been led to ignore his nudity in the first place."[101] The primary appeal of Colbert's humor stems from this exposure of the truthiness impulse in contemporary debate. As the exaggerated parody of a conservative, opinionated, but ill-informed pundit, he calls attention to the flaws of mediated political discourse while pretending to be enthusiastically in favor of those flaws. It is in this guise that he fulminates against facts and against things written in books, both of which his character believes to have an elitist, liberal bias, arguing that whatever he feels in his gut is far more important. In addition to the concept of truthiness, Colbert also coined the term *wikiality,* referencing the user-compiled internet encyclopedia in his ironically enthusiastic endorsement of fact as determined by majority rule: if enough people are led to believe something is true, then it *is* true.

After the Democrats took over as the majority in Congress in January 2007, Colbert explained that, when the Republicans were in power, it was worth ignoring facts for their version of reality, but the Democrats' "version of reality is, unfortunately, based on reality," meaning that he must fight their use of facts with his own "factiness": inflated innuendo and accusations based on information that is somewhat true, or that at least cannot be proven to be untrue. He then proceeds, in illustration, to target Democratic senator and then possible presidential candidate Barack

3.5. Stephen Colbert ironically derides the Democrats' use of facts, arguing that they can be combated by "factiness." *Comedy Central, Jan. 8, 2007*

Obama by emphatically announcing that his middle name is Hussein (a fact), which clearly links him, Colbert argues, to deposed Iraqi dictator Saddam Hussein. He also slyly demonstrates how the factiness tactic is actually used in the mainstream media by playing footage from a CNN broadcast in which a reporter points out the similarity in dress between Obama and Iranian president Mahmoud Ahmadinejad (jacket with no tie) and muses that this is likely not the type of comparison a presidential contender should be inviting.[102] What makes Colbert's invented terminology so funny and incisive is that it does an excellent job of describing the tenor of much contemporary political debate.

Baumgartner and Morris acknowledge this function of critiquing the news media in a second study on *The Daily Show,* this one focusing directly on the program's effect on attitudes toward the media. Once again, as a starting point for the study, they begin with the assumption that the show has a cynical attitude toward the news media, hypothesizing that individuals who themselves suffer from "videomalaise," or a general distrust and dissatisfaction with the media, will be more attracted to the program, but also posing the question of whether young viewers with still-malleable political ideas will be pulled into non-preexisting video malaise by exposure to the program. In another clip-viewing-and-questionnaire experiment, they find that respondents who have watched *The Daily Show* are more likely to agree that the media are motivated by profit rather than the goal of providing legitimate news, and they are less likely to say that they trust the news media to cover political events fairly and accurately. Once again, they interpret these responses as de facto evidence of cynicism about the news media. Though they enumerate the reasons that viewers might be dissatisfied with the press (including growing commercialism and sensationalism), they do not consider that this disapproval could be an engaged form of wishing for something more, but assume it to be a cynical form of disengagement and apathy. Indeed, they ominously conclude that, as Stewart's "criticism of mainstream news gains greater attention, more and more young adults may begin questioning the legitimacy of the mass media. This may, in turn, limit the media's ability to serve as a watchdog of elected officials,"[103] completely ignoring the fact that, if there is one theme in all *Daily Show* episodes, it is precisely a plea for the media to serve as better watchdogs of elected officials.

A number of other commentators have pointed to the fact that *The Daily Show* not only critiques the flaws of contemporary journalism but itself tries to model the form of journalism it repeatedly calls for. As Dannagal Goldthwaite Young argues, the program "rejects the problematic norms of objectivity, drama, personalized and fragmented news, reacts to the game of politicians rather than embraces it, and stands outside the media pack commenting on the spectacle that the symbiotic relationship between media and politics has become."[104] As Baym articulates, the critique *The Daily Show* makes ultimately stems from a committed belief in a deliberative theory of democracy, "the notion that only civil and honest conversation can provide the legitimate foundation for governance."[105] It seeks to point out where the 24-hour news media fall short of this ideal and to model the ideal in its own interview segments.

Importantly, in all of these programs, it seems clear that the comedians believe there can and should be alternatives to the poor leadership, dishonest political debate, and sensationalist news coverage they highlight. Though they do so by making jokes, all of the hosts candidly reach toward solutions. Colbert, as the only one of the hosts who is a fictional character, is the most slippery, but he is so obviously ill-informed, bellicose, and over-the-top that we understand that Colbert the comedian holds exactly the opposite beliefs to those of his alter ego. When ostensibly celebrating a particular situation, he often rattles off a litany of damning statistics that make a tight case for the other side. For example, on the fifth anniversary of the opening of the U.S. prison in Guantanamo Bay in 2007, Colbert announces that the program has clearly been a resounding success, as "out of the 517 detainees, 10 have been charged with crimes, and as many as several know what they are accused of. All that with only about 600 criminal investigations into prisoner abuse."[106] There is no doubt we are to get the message that both the policy and the oversight of the prison have failed. Though Colbert's character cannot tell us what should be done about the prison now (since he supposedly believes it to be working well), he then brings on Kenneth Roth, the head of Human Rights Watch, to make the case for him. The human rights lawyer explains that the majority of the people at the Guantanamo jail were brought there after being accused of having terrorist ties by countrymen lured by the promise of reward money, and they have still not been given a chance to prove their innocence after five years of imprisonment. The only way forward, he explains, is to formally charge everyone in a court of law, allowing the few who might actually be terrorists to be convicted and the rest to finally be released. Colbert, meanwhile, periodically makes fun of his interviewee for wanting to "coddle our enemies," but his own opinions are presented as so wildly absurd that the interviewee is quite obviously the voice of reason in the conversation. The lengthy piece is not, by any stretch of the imagination, a detached series of jokes about inept leaders, but a quite lucid analysis of flawed political policy and an appeal for what should be done next.

Unencumbered by the complications of an ironic alter ego, Stewart and Mercer are able to more explicitly bemoan the problems they see in contemporary politics, almost always from the perspective of "we deserve better." Mercer, for instance, frequently concludes his trademark rants with a direct appeal to a particular politician or political party or with a suggestion on how things could be improved. While often framed in irreverent or comedic language, the advice is clearly sincere, whether it be his summation of a particular party's misguided strategy of the day or a warning to government officials that he, and the rest of the country, can see through their politicking. Though not always as frankly polemical, Stewart's news reports are often laced with clear disappointment and reproach when he believes that events should have developed otherwise.

It is during the interview segments, though, that Stewart makes his most obvious appeals for *solutions* to political woes. His guests include politicians, pundits, reporters, and academics from all points on the political spectrum, many of whom have recently finished a book or are promoting a particular agenda. Indeed, as Joanne Morreale points out, the show is now one of the only television programs on which serious books are still promoted and discussed.[107] In all of these interviews, Stewart attempts to have a genuine conversation about the guest's ideas. Though he gets impatient with interviewees who seem to be repeating platitudes, the attitude he most often takes is of someone searching for solutions, someone interested in what his guests think the answers are and in how political compromises and areas of consensus can be reached. One of his favorite themes is the desire to overcome entrenched political partisanship. In a 2007 interview with then Arkansas governor Mike Huckabee, for example, Stewart points out that Huckabee describes himself as a conservative and an evangelical Christian, attributes that strike fear into the heart of the blue-state foundation, but that many of the ideas presented in his book actually seem quite liberal. This gives Huckabee the opportunity to expound on the fact that he is pro-life, meaning he believes that life begins at conception, but that he does not believe "pro-life" ends at a child's birth; rather, governments have to be concerned with a child's housing, education, health care, and access to clean air and water. His explanation causes the studio audience to burst into applause.[108] In many ways, this interview is typical for the show, as Stewart generally approaches the exchanges, not as a self-satisfied comic, but as a citizen (again, acting as the audience's surrogate) seeking answers to the questions that confound him. One quality that all of these popular hosts seem to share is less a smug detachment than a passionate enthusiasm for the political world and a desire to spread that interest to their audiences.

It would seem, then, that these television shows are anything but cynical, as they actively engage the political issues of the day, provide context and background to contemporary dilemmas, dissect the ways in which both politicians and the press work to cloud political discussion, and encourage the development of solutions. In the process, they certainly find many faults with both the political system as it currently exists (in whichever country the show is operative) and the mainstream news media. However, since the dominant political discussion is itself profoundly cynical, it seems anything but cynical to want to hold it accountable. As Robert Hariman put it in defense of Stewart at the mock heresy trial, "[I]n a public culture where one has to wonder if real news is fake, and where one often wishes that were so, the question 'Are you really serious?' becomes every citizen's question and a good test of public speech."[109] There are undoubtedly many ways of asking "are you really serious?" and we do want to be able to distinguish between those that are constructive and those that are simply mean-spirited, and we should acknowledge there will be some crossover. However, to decide that all forms of satire, irreverence, irony, and humor breed cynicism when mixed with the political is to discount a powerful current of political critique within contemporary culture.

It seems that most of the critics who charge programs like *The Daily Show* with cynicism or who worry about the parody being taken too seriously read its humor as a nihilistic shrug, assuming that the ironic edge that gives the parody its bite must be the disengaged and detached variety, as outlined in chapter 2. However, an examination of these shows' contents reveals instead an engaged irony, one that may revel in absurdity but that believes strongly in alternatives. Writing about another form of televisual satire—the long-running program *The Simpsons*—Jonathan Gray refutes similar accusations of cynicism by referring to the results of his interviews with fans. He explains that his interviewees "were hardly disenfranchised, embittered, and/or alienated individuals removing themselves from society";[110] instead, "[t]he joking around with media and politics that *The Simpsons* and their talk about it involved may even have helped them to face the realms of media and politics again with renewed vigor, optimism, and engagement. Moreover, they spoke of it glowingly, not as a weight around their ankles, dragging them and their optimism downward."[111] Though I have not conducted any extensive audience analyses of the parodic news shows, given the intensely avid (often wonkish) fan activity around these programs and the flurry of gleeful web forwarding that follows a public political outburst by one of the hosts, it seems clear that these viewers similarly gain energy and pleasure from witnessing the critical deconstruction of contemporary public debate, and they clearly use the show as a form of connection with others.

Though I don't have the space to fully explore the issue here, a number of researchers have focused on the uniquely engaged relationship that fans of Stephen Colbert, in particular, have to his show, as they eagerly step up to play the role of the adoring fan for his self-obsessed character, collectively vandalizing Wikipedia pages when requested, creating user-generated video content, and ballot stuffing in online contests. As Jeffrey Jones articulates, fans of the show happily play the dual role Colbert requires of them, celebrating "the playfulness, ingenuity, and creativity of the comedian's performance, while simultaneously ridiculing and vilifying the inanity of his distorted logic,"[112] following his directives, while also enthusiastically applauding his guests' rational retorts to his character's simplistic thinking. Indeed, a 2009 study commissioned by Comedy Central (for the purposes of advertising) found that hosts Colbert and Stewart both engendered not just fans but intensely impassioned fans, many of whom identified themselves as having a deep personal connection to the shows.[113] The overwhelming enthusiasm, engagement, and energy of these fans seem a far cry from the thin pleasure of smug cynicism. If this genre generates anxiety, it is not because it foments cynicism, as accused, but because it troubles boundaries and expectations, functioning as a substantive political forum while appearing to be "only entertainment."

* * *

The fact that parodic news shows are encroaching on the serious world of political debate to such an extent, both supplementing and prodding that debate, does not mean they are overreaching their bounds, but that perhaps the debate itself is underreaching. And the popularity of the genre demonstrates clearly that there is a craving to hear some sort of critique. As Aaron McKain argues about *The Daily Show,* "Stewart's authority almost has to be derived from more than merely the News's aphasia and his ethos; it must also be tied up with the audience's desire that this view be articulated and its belief that this view is ethical, or just, or valid."[114] The shows then become focal points for particular opinions, frustrations, and intuitions, while the high-profile hosts become de facto spokespeople for their viewers.

Interestingly, it is not necessarily an overtly partisan worldview that is advanced. Though the hosts may be fairly open about their own political beliefs (which certainly skew left of center, though not wildly so), their function is to perform a more generalized critique of political dissembling and media excesses. The actual political commentary on the most popular of the parodic news shows is rarely overtly abrasive or self-righteous. The interviews may include heated policy debates and loaded questions, but they generally remain congenial, allowing interviewees a fair chance to articulate their views. Similarly, even the ambush interviews on a show like *22 Minutes* are conducted without overt anger or stridency. The people chosen to perform the ambushes are Marg Delahunty and Gavin, the awkward teenage correspondent, both of whom make controversial comments and ask provocative questions, but do so out of feigned naïveté rather than antagonism. This is in contrast to someone like Michael Moore, who is profiled in the next chapter. He has a lot of ardent fans, but he also attracts an enormous amount of vitriol, often because of his perceived self-righteousness and anger. This is likely because the parodic news shows are, after all, on television, a medium that is rarely explicitly activist in its intent. Additionally, the critiques are often directly opposed to the way in which political discussion can be misshapen by extreme polarization.

Nevertheless, these shows do attempt to further a critique that is opposed to many elements of mainstream political discussion. It is important to recognize these programs as spaces in which elements of the dominant discourse are unpacked and evaluated. And, while these spaces have developed to appeal to a fairly targeted population, after generating enough momentum, the critique then trickles back into broader publics. Though the shows may be rooted in particular taste cultures, their popularity has provided an entrée to wider dialogue. The practice of narrowcasting allowed these programs to develop, but their hosts have moved beyond their niche to heavily hyped interviews on the networks, cover stories in popular magazines, and invitations to high-profile events. Narrowcasting has here provided the gateway to more mainstream encounters, affecting the broader political discussion.

While we might not want to go so far as to include the viewers of *The Daily Show,* for instance, as an actively politicized counterpublic that mobilizes itself as such, Stewart's audience nevertheless is an engaged viewing public, a crucial component of the contemporary public sphere. As John Hartley argues, "[J]ust as the popular press of the nineteenth century was responsible for the creation of the mass reading public, and hence the public, so TV became the place where and the means by which, a century later, most people got to know about most other people and about publicly important events or issues."[115] These particular programs are currently providing a powerful locus for critique, debate, and communion. In fact, their function begins to approach that which many public sphere theorists have classically hoped for in straight news programming, while still standing a parodic step removed so as to provide the knowing critique. In a historical moment when all sides of the political spectrum bemoan the flaws of straight news, these shows' brand of "fake" news has emerged as a trusted filter through which to engage with the debased real. The contemporary blend of political nonfiction and satire happens to provide particularly fertile ground for the dissection of public discourse, providing a welcome outlet for many who are already critical of that discourse. This theme will play an even greater role in the next chapter in the discussion of counterpublic communities formed around politically charged satiric documentaries.

FOUR

Heroes and Villains: Satiric Documentarians Spearhead the Debate

Long an art-house curiosity, the documentary film has muscled its way into the thick of mainstream political debate. As a reporter for the *Chicago Tribune* put it in the election year of 2004, "documentaries, traditionally a speck on the cultural periphery, have moved front-and-center in the national discussion, achieving a relevancy and popularity that would have been inconceivable just two years ago."[1] At the heart of this larger shift has been the blockbuster popularity of a new genre of documentary. The satiric documentary, as I have termed it, combines a playful, satiric style with unabashed polemic, resulting in a product rooted simultaneously in mass culture entertainment and political activism, guerrilla theater and documentary exposé. These elements are brought together through a narrative centered around the filmmaker's own personal quest, tracking his interactions and explorations. Highly self-reflexive, these films can be described as performative in that the documentary takes as its subject the coming into being of itself, based on the filmmaker's interactions with his subjects. As I will demonstrate, the satiric documentarian plays two important roles: on-screen, he performs the classic fool, asking the most revealing of questions out of (feigned) naïveté, while, as the filmmaker, he also gets to be the preacher, providing the context and framing for how these interactions will be interpreted. I will argue that the primary achievement of these filmmakers is that they have successfully nurtured the creation of oppositional political communities, or counterpublics, which are anchored by the films but then sustained by books, websites, interviews, and other media appearances. As objects within popular culture, the films serve as accessible nodes of identification, energizing those who already share similar opinions and functioning to shift some of the terms of debate within the wider public sphere.

The figure most readily identified with this type of film is Michael Moore. Though he is far less photogenic and endearing than a typical celebrity, Moore has become an iconic media personality. He came to public attention with his first film, *Roger & Me* (1989), a cheeky exposition of the disintegration of the town of Flint, Michigan, after General Motors closed its local factories, which is structured around Moore's quest to speak with the head of the company, Roger Smith. Produced on a tiny budget when Moore was an unknown, first-time filmmaker, it became a surprise hit. Since then, he has built on the style he developed in *Roger & Me* in five more full-length documentaries: *The Big One* (1997), also about corporate downsizing and the use of overseas labor; *Bowling for Columbine* (2002), an exploration of gun culture in the United States, which uses the Columbine High School massacre as its narrative focal point; *Fahrenheit 9/11* (2004), an election-season attack on President George W. Bush's record, focusing on his response to the September 11 attacks and the subsequent invasion of Iraq and making the argument that his administration played on the public's fear in order to engineer an unnecessary war; *Sicko* (2007), an exposé of the flaws of the U.S. health care system; and *Capitalism: A Love Story* (2009), an analysis of the pitfalls of letting markets manage themselves without regulation, which was released in the wake of the 2008 economic meltdown.

In addition, Moore produced *Slacker Uprising* (2007), a documentary chronicle of his 2004 speaking tour aimed at galvanizing students into getting out the vote, which he made available for free internet downloading in 2008. He has also developed two television series, *The Awful Truth* and *TV Nation* (both of which employ a similar documentary style), and written three bestselling books. He makes regular appearances on the television talk-show circuit, conducts extensive speaking tours, and hosts a thriving virtual community via email missives. In all of his work, Moore sets his sights on a particular political issue and invites his audience along to dig up the dirt, hounding CEOs for interviews and staging elaborate stunts designed to shame the socially irresponsible. As John Corner explains of *Roger & Me,* "Moore's attempts to be widely popular, critical of corporate policy and also anti-conventional in the form he uses puts *Roger* at an intersection point unique in recent documentary history . . . and it will be surprising if its contribution to popular documentary does not continue to be recognized at the same time as its methods and forms provoke further debate."[2] Michael Moore has now popularized the style of satiric polemic to such an extent that it has had a significant influence on the documentary world. Since Moore is a major originator of this type of filmmaking, I will concentrate heavily on his work in this chapter.

Although Moore has popularized the genre, other directors have followed in his wake; the most prominent is Morgan Spurlock, whose films include a satiric jab at fast-food culture, *Super Size Me* (2004), and *Where in the World Is Osama bin Laden?* (2008). Like Moore, Spurlock was also a previously unknown director who attracted an enormous amount of attention with his first film. The premise of *Super Size Me* is that, after hearing that McDonald's was defending itself from a lawsuit by obese customers by arguing that its food is part of a healthy diet, Spurlock reportedly decides to test the chain's health effects by consuming nothing but McDonald's food, three meals a day for 30 days, while getting as much exercise as a typical American—almost none. Along the way, he explores America's obesity epidemic, school lunch programs, and fast-food marketing. He interviews a host of experts and sutures the whole thing together using quirky music, animation, and commentary. When it was first released, the movie became the third highest-grossing documentary of all time (behind only Moore's *Fahrenheit 9/11* and *Bowling for Columbine*), leading Spurlock to write a similarly themed book titled *Don't Eat This Book*. In 2008, he released *Where in the World Is Osama bin Laden?* built around the premise that he is on a one-man mission to hunt down the world's most wanted terrorist, ostensibly because he is about to become a father and wants to make the world safe for his child. Along his journey through a number of different countries, he stops to talk to people about their perceptions of the United States and its foreign policy. As I will explore, however, this film was not nearly as popular or critically well-received as his first. Finally, Spurlock was also the producer and sometimes star of his own television series, *30 Days,* which ran for three seasons on the FX network, and was the producer of the movie *What Would Jesus Buy?* (discussed in chapter 5).

Other documentaries that have followed in Moore's and Spurlock's footsteps include *Expelled: No Intelligence Allowed,* a 2008 film starring

Ben Stein that proceeds from a conservative Christian perspective to expose the perceived scientific and educational conspiracy blocking the teaching of intelligent design as a plausible theory of the beginning of life. That same year saw the opening of another film similar in style but polar opposite in slant. *Religulous,* starring Bill Maher, skewers organized religion and the perceived credulity (and dangerousness) of its followers. I will touch on both as part of this larger genre, though my emphasis is on Moore and Spurlock due to the relative impact of their work.

It should be noted that both Moore and Spurlock (and Maher) hail from the political left (and are regularly accused of being from the far, far left by those who wish to dismiss them). Both attempt to popularize critiques that are relatively marginal within the mainstream political discussion. And since their work frequently has undisguised political intent, it is both loved and despised, often eliciting strong reactions from fans and detractors alike.

Like a parodic news show, a satiric documentary incorporates a hybrid mix of genres, forms, and styles, which creates a number of competing demands on how it should be read. And, again, I believe that a lot of the anxiety and dislike it engenders on both ends of the political spectrum can be attributed to these competing contexts of reception. In this case, the use of the word *documentary* to describe these films seems to be one of the things that makes detractors most incensed, as it is a word that, for many people, is associated with qualities like objectivity, neutrality, and transparency. As I will explore, documentary film has never fully been able to live up to these ideals, nor has it always been expected to. Many contemporary documentary theorists take it as a given that documentary, as Stella Bruzzi puts it, is not about transparently relaying the real, but is rather "a negotiation between reality on the one hand and image, interpretation and bias on the other."[3] As she argues, many contemporary "performative" documentaries (this is Bruzzi's term, and she points to Moore's work as one example) now explicitly foreground this dynamic, placing the focus on the dialectical relationship between reality and filmmaker. Bruzzi seems to assume that this understanding of documentary is now self-evident, meaning that "the spectator is not in need of signposts and inverted commas"[4] in order to keep it in mind. However, while I certainly agree with her characterization of the relationship between documentary and reality, and while I concur that most contemporary media consumers have some understanding that all media messages are constructed, it would seem that many people are not convinced of their neighbor's ability to understand this.

The critics of Moore's and Spurlock's films on the political right, in particular, complain loudly about the movies being polemical and biased, often explicitly arguing that they are propaganda and thus do not deserve to be called documentaries. As one man puts it in a fairly typical letter to the editor, "*Fahrenheit 9/11* is incorrectly labeled a documentary, which for me confirms its gushing reviewers' lack of appreciation of the genre. It is a political propaganda film, and it can be rightly judged within that category."[5] Another man, who was offering a buyback program for copies of *Fahrenheit 9/11* DVDs, explained in a press release that the initiative was "designed to protect Americans from harm, especially young children who might accidentally slip this dangerous propaganda into the living-room DVD player."[6] The implication is frequently that gullible audience members might be duped into believing that, say, Moore is offering an objective picture of Bush's record and the war in Iraq in *Fahrenheit 9/11* or that Spurlock is producing an even-handed account of fast food in America in *Super Size Me,* precisely because these films are billed as documentaries.

Similar to the anxiety about young people not understanding that "fake" news is not real, the fear is that unsavvy viewers will take the texts too literally. But while the high-profile performers discussed in the last chapter—Jon Stewart, Stephen Colbert, Rick Mercer—may not be universally adored, they do not draw anywhere near the intense loathing from detractors that Michael Moore does. Though some do grumble about the news hosts being biased, they have not attracted websites devoted entirely to keeping an eye on (and refuting) every one of their statements, as Moore and Spurlock have (www.spurlockwatch.typepad .com and www.moorewatch.com, among others). Critics of these filmmakers see them as potentially dangerous due to the combination of unabashedly polemical work, the ability to attract large audiences, and the cultural legitimacy that the word *documentary* is perceived to confer. The fact that these films are described using the same moniker that is applied to a sober, seemingly objective, historical piece narrated by Ken Burns is simply unconscionable to many, particularly to those whose views are opposed to the filmmakers' own.

On the political left, there are some critics who explain that they agree with many of the premises in these films, but they are nevertheless unhappy with the resulting products. Here, the anxiety is not over the fact that the films offer an explicitly political analysis (and whether or not this disqualifies them from documentary-hood), but over the quality and consistency of the analyses and what the films hope to accomplish. The criticism, in this case, is not necessarily about the films living up to expectations about objectivity and fairness in documentary, but about standards of well-reasoned, rigorous political criticism or tests of efficacy in political activism. As I will touch on later in the chapter, some of these critiques seem to demand the impossible, expecting one film to be able to single-handedly spark momentous political change, while others train a spotlight on more easily correctable flaws. Most of these critics seem to want to treat the films more as definitive political analyses than as highly personal, opinionated, satiric explorations of particular issues. Again, the question is: To what standards should we hold this new genre?

One of the most damning sins that these films have all been accused of, however, that would seem to transcend differences in genre expectations, is that they contain lies and half-truths. Though my focus throughout this chapter will not be on evaluating every individual statement made in each film, the general charge of deceit is weighty enough to merit some exploration. The film that has garnered the most media attention and hence the most scrutiny around this issue is *Fahrenheit 9/11*. Knowing that it would be picked over so thoroughly, Moore reportedly had a team of lawyers vetting each cut of the movie as he went along. After it was released, however, critics (particularly those on the political right) immediately wrote reports attacking numerous individual points made in the movie, giving commentators reason to dismiss the whole thing as misleading and false. Many of the claims and counterclaims have centered on the first half of the film and the exact details of the flights the Saudi royals took out of the country in the days after the September 11 attacks, the level of Saudi involvement with the Bush family, and their precise amount of investment in the U.S. economy. Much of this continues to be contentious, as no single investigator or journalist has access to *all* of the relevant information. Ken Nolley, one of the contributors to a special *Fahrenheit 9/11* edition of *Film and History,* spent some time assessing the claims made by each side, and though he does not come down unreservedly in defense of Moore's conclusions, he has this to say about the charges that Moore deliberately lies:

> [I]t is utterly clear that Moore *has* sources for most of his claims and that for the most part he follows them closely. And that is to say that even if the claims he makes are inaccurate, they cannot necessarily be described accurately as lies. In any case, they are certainly not simply Moore's lies, and to insist on calling them such is to engage in precisely the same sort of inflammatory and misleading rhetoric that Moore's critics profess to decry in the film.[7]

When one examines the substance of many of the complaints lodged about other moments in the film, the argument, though ostensibly about facts, is usually about the broader conclusions that Moore comes to. Robert Toplin, who published a book devoted exclusively to the movie in 2006, puts it this way: "The major disagreements between admirers and detractors of *Fahrenheit 9/11* are primarily over the *interpretation* of facts, not whether the facts themselves are true. Moore's principal evidence is not inherently incorrect, but what one makes of it can excite animated disagreement."[8] For instance, though most would agree that, in fact, there turned out to be no weapons of mass destruction in Iraq, many have taken umbrage with Moore's description of Iraq as a "nation that had never attacked the United States, a nation that had never threatened to attack the United States, a nation that had never murdered a single American citizen," arguing that Saddam Hussein's regime had, in fact, posed a sizable threat to the United States and its allies. In all of the assaults on Moore's logic and conclusions, however, the vast majority of critics have focused almost exclusively on the accuracy of secondary textual details in the film (often with their own dubiously factual assertions), without addressing the movie's central theme—as Toplin puts it, "that the Bush administration had exploited the public's fear after 9/11 and driven the country toward an unnecessary and counterproductive war with Iraq and occupation of the country,"[9] or, I would add, that wars are inevitably controlled by the powerful but actually fought by the most powerless in society. While the repeated use of words like "lies," "deceit," and "fiction" by Moore's critics have shrouded the film in a cloud of suspicion, the charges frequently boil down to existing left-right political schisms in assumptions about foreign policy, civil liberties, and political cronyism, while rarely striking at the heart of Moore's critique.

This is not to say that Moore's methods, either in *Fahrenheit 9/11* or in his other films, are beyond reproach. On the contrary, for someone who knows that his work will be heavily scrutinized, he is often sloppy about the way he builds his arguments. In the first half of *Fahrenheit 9/11,* for instance, Moore clearly wants to reveal all of the information he has unearthed about the Bush family, their connections to the Saudi royals, and their mutual business interests. However, since he takes on far more than he can possibly follow up on in a two-hour film, the result is a jumble of innuendo. Though much of the information does deserve to be aired and debated in a public forum, Moore's rapid-fire series of leading questions without definitive answers leaves him open to charges that he is a conspiracy theorist, while, as Nolley points out, the loose argument relies on "the weak suggestion that association equals influence and collaboration."[10] And, ultimately, this serves to detract from some of the stronger assertions and revealing footage in the second half of the film. Likewise, in *Sicko,* Moore's over-the-top romanticization of the Cuban health care system allows critics to easily dismiss the film as pure propaganda without their having to grapple with some of the truly shocking material, for instance, interviews with American health insurance industry employees explaining how they are instructed to actively deny care whenever possible.

In his earlier movies as well, Moore has been accused of haphazardly arranging events in order to create the best narrative arc for his story without giving the viewer a clear sense of chronology or context, again displaying a sloppy heavy-handedness with the way supporting material is sutured together. Additionally, he can occasionally take cheap shots at relatively innocent bystanders, making the narratively unimportant Miss Michigan look quite silly in *Roger & Me,* for instance, by surprising her with a question about unemployed auto workers as she floats by in a parade. Finally, and importantly, although Moore often attempts to expose racism in his movies (for instance, the disenfranchisement of numerous black voters in Florida in the 2000 election), he nevertheless often replicates racist assumptions through his choices of supporting images. In an article in *Counterpunch,* Robert Jensen points to the subtle racism that creeps into *Fahrenheit 9/11* due to its reliance on ethnic and national stereotypes, as well as Moore's convenient focus on exclusively white victims of civil liberties infringements, without so much as a mention of the systematic profiling of Muslim Americans after 9/11. And, ultimately, the fact that Moore's presentation of someone in a keffiyeh or turban is supposed to be evidence in itself of nefarious intentions is not an excusable flaw. This is an area in which Moore's reliance on overly breezy logic is seriously detrimental.

Though there is less of a canon of criticism about Spurlock's techniques (since his has not yet been anywhere near as lengthy a career), both filmmakers are vulnerable to the accusation that their filmmaking style effectively stacks the deck; they selectively seek out material that best supports their arguments (or garners the biggest laughs). Spurlock, for instance, was criticized after the release of *Super Size Me* for designing his experiment to dramatically increase his fat intake while reducing his exercise, virtually guaranteeing, critics say, that he would suffer negative consequences. Notably, however, he received almost no vitriolic critique for his second film from the politically motivated, likely because, as I will explore, that film did not have as clear a political message or intent. Both filmmakers do unabashedly come to conclusions or advance theses based on their own particular worldviews, though I am not convinced that this is necessarily problematic. In *Bowling for Columbine,* Moore makes the suggestion that there is a telling connection in the fact that missiles that wreak violent death around the world on behalf of the United States are manufactured in the same community as the Columbine High School massacre. Is this something that can be definitively proven or disproven through documentary evidence? Absolutely not. But that should not preclude Moore from leading his audience to consider the possible parallels.

Ultimately, if we look to the satiric documentary to uphold standards of objectivity, neutrality, and fairness, or to produce a nuanced, even-handed political analysis, it is going to fall short. This is not where the genre excels, nor even what it strives for. Rather, it is opinionated, satiric, and intimate and, as such, has its own resonance, strengths, and appeal. The individual and embodied presence of the filmmaker is key to the genre's draw, as he (and thus far it seems to always be "he") takes the audience vicariously along for the ride on his own individual quest. Much like an op-ed, it offers a personal, animated, and engaged treatise on a particular social issue, though unlike a written piece, it builds its case partially on evidence gleaned through particularly revealing interviews and recorded real-world encounters that can resonate on both intellectual and emotional levels.

The strength of these filmmakers is in articulating a point of view or particular critique that may already be shared by many, but that is not normally heard within the dominant public sphere, and in doing so in an entertaining and engaging manner. Their films serve as accessible nodes of identification, attracting counterpublic communities around them, energizing those communities, and affecting the direction of wider public debate. As Toplin argues about *Fahrenheit 9/11* in particular, in the lead-up to the 2004 election, "no single work of speechmaking, writing, filmmaking, or television producing sparked as much debate about the direction of U.S. domestic politics and foreign policy as *Fahrenheit 9/11* did."[11] And as Jeffrey Jones points out, the huge popularity of the film suggests that it also "served the important communal function of expressing, reifying, and confirming the frustrations of many citizens on the political left who were opposed to the Iraq war and Republican leadership."[12] Because Moore and Spurlock have had so much success in attracting notice and energizing viewers, they are now widely credited with spearheading this newly powerful genre, while commentators have noted that documentaries in general, a form that has long struggled for cultural relevance, have recaptured the public imagination, "thanks in large part to the attention-grabbing techniques of Michael Moore in *Fahrenheit 9/11* and *Bowling for Columbine,* and Morgan Spurlock in *Super Size Me.*"[13] The particular form of the satiric documentary has clearly had a profound impact on the contemporary political discussion.

THE DOCUMENTARY TRADITION AND GUERRILLA THEATER COLLIDE

Though I speak of the satiric documentary as being a relatively new and innovative genre, the innovation resides primarily in the way in which elements of past forms are pieced together in newly dynamic ways. This should not be seen as a teleological line of development culminating in these particular documentaries; rather, as Bill Nichols argues, a different mode comes into being in a given time and place in response to particular historical circumstances: "once established, though, modes overlap and intermingle. Individual films can be characterized by the mode that seems most influential to their organization, but individual films can also 'mix and match' modes as the occasion demands."[14] The films of Moore and Spurlock are rooted in a contemporary hybridized and self-referential aesthetic, while also harking back to the polemics of the early documentary form pioneered by John Grierson. Their uniqueness hinges on the combination of political didacticism with pop culture aesthetics and lighthearted comedy. I will argue that these elements are brought together through the incorporation of guerrilla theater stunts.

While much of the press coverage of these films fixates on the fact that they are obviously polemical, the articles rarely acknowledge that, from its inception as a concept, documentary film has been firmly linked to the art of rhetorical persuasion. Though elements of the documentary form can be located in the early films of Dziga Vertov, European and North American newsreels, and early travelogues, John Grierson coined the modern usage of the term *documentary,* and he was consequently able to set the standards for how it would be conceptualized. While studying at the University of Chicago in the 1920s, Grierson was preoccupied with combating the alienation between citizens, especially new immigrants, and government. As Jack Ellis explains, Grierson "postulated that what was needed was to involve citizens in their government with the kind of engaging excitement generated by the popular press, which simplified and dramatized public affairs."[15] His friend Walter Lippmann suggested using film rather than print as the means by which to educate citizens about the factors to be considered in making democratic decisions. Grierson went on to work for Britain's Empire Marketing Board and, later, the general post office, where he became the head of a fast-growing documentary film movement.[16] He then moved in 1939 to Canada, where he helped to create the National Film Board, spearheading the country's prolific documentary production throughout World War II.

The brand of documentary he developed was rooted in social realism and was unabashedly didactic and propagandistic, much of it centering on the idea of communal strength and the dignity of the worker. John Corner explains that Grierson's now ubiquitous definition of documentary as "the creative treatment of actuality"[17] refers to a practice that is "grounded in a considerable degree of discursive skill and creative 'vision' (revelatory, 'deep-seeing'), it is not simply a result of any 'capturing' performed by the camera."[18] While Grierson and those who worked with him sought out images plucked from reality, it was assumed that these images would then be molded into a carefully constructed social and political narrative. Though critics of Moore and Spurlock invariably argue that their films do not deserve to be called documentaries as they are polemical, biased, or, according to some, even fictional, they are much closer to the initial aims for the form than the more journalistic television documentaries with which contemporary audiences are familiar. In addition, Grierson's desire to draw from popular culture in order to engage a wide audience is similar to the self-professed goals of Moore and Spurlock, who have explained that they aim to make accessible, popular work. However, the style of these contemporary films is vastly different from those of Grierson's era, as Moore and Spurlock are part of a long legacy of filmmakers who have rebelled against the formal properties of the Griersonian tradition.

The first large-scale rebellion against the Griersonian mode within the North American and European tradition began in the 1960s with the popularity of observational filmmaking. The invention of lighter and more portable camera equipment allowed filmmakers to shoot more intimately and spontaneously, meaning that subjects could be shown reacting to one another in the same manner as in fiction film. Almost simultaneously, writes Barry Keith Grant, observational cinema began to develop in France, Canada, and the United States, the two major schools becoming "cinema verité" and its American counterpart, "direct cinema." One of the hallmarks of this type of documentary is a distrust of the heavy-handed documentary voice. While the films of Grierson's era had relied on authoritative voice-overs or title cards to guide the viewer, there was now a demand to show instead of tell and a rejection of any sort of narration, music, re-creation, or theatrical lighting. Proponents of the new form argued that the "filmmaker should in no way indicate that any action is preferred by him over any other. The filmmaker acts as an observer, attempting not to alter the situations he witnesses any more than he must simply by being there."[19] Some of the techniques and stylistic markers of observational filmmaking have remained popular to this day, especially on television. As Corner points out, though it does use elements such as voice-over, much of "reality TV" relies on a "neo-verité" style, billed as "fly-on-the-wall" coverage, regardless of the fact that the situations are heavily manipulated. In fact, many of the commentators who have remarked on the recent surge of interest in film documentaries partially attribute the renewed interest to the popularity of reality television.

In film criticism, however, cinema verité and direct cinema have been heavily critiqued, not necessarily because of the films they engender, but due to the overblown rhetoric of their more zealous proponents, who give the impression that the form allows access to an unaltered, objective "real." The enthusiasts fail to acknowledge the creative and editorial choices a documentarian invariably makes, nor do they entertain the possibility that the filmic events might have transpired precisely because there was a camera present. However, the more naïve belief in total objectivity is not shared by all of the observational filmmakers themselves, nor is it always evidenced in their films. In particular, the documentaries of Frederick Wiseman, one of the most prolific and well-respected of the observational cinema auteurs, illustrate a skilled melding of observational footage into films with a clear message, a style that has had a continued influence on other documentarians. Wiseman has centered many of his films around social institutions, such as a school, a police station, a mental hospital, often creating a subtle form of exposé, revealing, as Grant explains, "the ironic quality of the gaps between an institution's stated goals and its practices."[20] While Wiseman certainly does not "tell" his audience how to react to his subject matter, he allows his camera to focus on elements of a scene that are especially revealing, such as the wiggling finger of the sexist gynecologist addressing a group of boys in *High School* (1968). Though this technique is far more restrained than that of Moore or Spurlock, they too rely heavily on the spontaneous reactions of their subjects as "evidence" in order to create their narratives—also like an exposé. As Corner points out, in *Roger & Me,* Moore uses a technique of "investigative verité," insofar as the "pro-filmic events are the activities of enquiry themselves, shot as ongoing action."[21] The power of the ambush interviews and the narrative of the filmmaker's personal quest in the satiric documentary would not be possible without an established understanding of the verité style.

Besides the false claims to transparency, another of the shortcomings of many of the observational films was, as Nichols articulates, that they "seldom offered the sense of history, context, or perspective that viewers seek."[22] Writing in 1988, he explains that, for this reason, "in the past decade we have seen a third style that incorporates direct address (characters or narrator speaking directly to the viewer), usually in the form of the interview."[23] Many of these films have sought to question the official record of events. Connie Field's 1980 film, *The Life and Times of Rosie the Riveter,* for example, is made up of interviews with several women who worked in the shipyards during World War II, all of whom challenge the received opinion that these women provided an emergency service only and were more than happy to return to the home after the war had ended.

Documentarian Emile de Antonio uses a somewhat different style, scavenging from existing interviews and historical footage, then making a collage of the clips to create a sharply polemical critique of various official narratives of U.S. history. He relies heavily on a technique of ironic juxtaposition, often to humorous effect. As Bruzzi explains, "de Antonio is a strong advocate of bias and of the foregrounding of opinion, thereby undermining the notion that documentary is principally concerned with transparency and non-intervention."[24] The critically acclaimed film *Atomic Cafe,* released in 1982, is also built around this collage style, similarly skewering American cold war policy by turning the state-produced propaganda films in on themselves, editing them in such a way as to highlight the delusional quality of the cold war rhetoric. This technique is one that Michael Moore draws heavily from, mining the archives for film clips and music that can be used ironically. The opening sequence of *Roger & Me,* for instance, is primarily a collage of old promotional movies made by General Motors back when Flint was a thriving company town. One could argue that the earlier collage and interview films inaugurated the beginning of the spate of documentaries that Linda Williams refers to as "anti-verité," meaning those characterized by "an attempt to overturn this commitment to realistically record 'life as it is' in favor of a deeper investigation of how it became as it is."[25] Doing so has involved attempts to play with, structure, and comment on the filmed material.

Beginning in the late '80s and early '90s, documentary criticism became preoccupied by the sudden glut of films that were borrowing expressive techniques that had previously been associated with fiction film and with those that were incorporating a self-reflexive focus on the filmmaking process itself. Singling out Michael Moore's *Roger & Me,* along with Ross McElwee's *Sherman's March* (1986), Tony Buba's *Lightning over Braddock* (1988), Nick Broomfield's *Driving Me Crazy* (1988), and

Errol Morris's *The Thin Blue Line* (1988), Paul Arthur writes that these documentaries share

> a perhaps unprecedented degree of hybridization. Materials, techniques, and modes of address are borrowed not only from earlier documentary styles but from the American avant-garde and from Hollywood as well. Voice-over narration, found footage, interviews, reenactments, and printed texts mingle in a pastiche that implicitly rejects the boundary distinctions of prior filmic modes. However, unlike related media and literary practices, the new documentary's most salient quality is an explicit centering of the filmmaking process and a heavily ironized inscription of the filmmaker as (unstable) subject, an anti-hero for our times.[26]

In Nichols's opinion, documentary seemed to be moving toward making its assumptions more visible, drawing attention to itself as a form of representation. Arthur is less enthusiastic about the evolving characteristics, taking pains to point out that these new conventions are no more guarantees of an authentic relationship to the real than the cinema verité techniques were.

Most would not claim that these films were entirely different than anything that had come before, as both the self-reflexive and the expressive, poetic techniques had made appearances in earlier works. However, it was more immediately remarkable that a highly hybridized amalgam of these traits had become a norm in itself. By now, this formal eclecticism and the "postmodern" centralization of the filmmaking process have become more taken for granted. For this reason, it is no longer as interesting to speak about the films of Michael Moore and of Errol Morris in one breath, as they are, in many respects, very different. I am particularly interested in the satiric documentary, as I believe it has been undertheorized in relation to other postmodern documentaries. While the films of Morris and McElwee begin with personalities and then open up to allow politics to seep in, the genre developed by Moore begins with more of an overt agenda (harking back to the Griersonian era and to the more recent collage films). Moore's style also involves a conscious drive to attract audiences through the use of comedy, an unusual trait within documentary. Both elements are incorporated through the use of guerrilla theater stunts.

The guerrilla theater approach, used in combination with a first-person narrative, allows both Moore and Spurlock to construct a David versus Goliath story. The audience watches as one man (and film crew) takes on a multinational corporation or powerful public figure. Within this frame, the narrative becomes unmistakably polemical, while the surprise encounters and developments can be quite humorous. Moore first developed his guerrilla theater tactics in *Roger & Me,* during which he stalks Roger Smith, the CEO of General Motors, staking out his office, his yacht club, his country club, and a stockholders meeting, attempting to find and convince him to talk to the workers he has recently laid off and to visit the devastation wrought by the local plant closures. He then continues to barge into offices and to create public spectacles in his two television series and subsequent films, though he tones down the technique somewhat in his later films, *Fahrenheit 9/11, Sicko,* and *Capitalism: A Love Story.* In all of them, he targets the powerful, whether corporations or politicians, attempting to hold them publicly accountable for their actions, using the neo-verité film style to frame the way in which these encounters unfold. Many of the stunts are elaborate, such as staging a mock funeral for a man outside of his insurance company's headquarters after he has been denied coverage for a crucial operation (*The Awful Truth*). Importantly, these tactics are strikingly similar to those pioneered by performance activists.

Politically motivated theater has a history as old as theater itself. However, as far as modern Western political theater is concerned, Bertolt Brecht is one of the most influential figures of all time. Beginning in the 1930s, Brecht devised theatrical forms that were to be in direct opposition to the established, bourgeois theater. He argued that the emphasis on illusion in traditional theater tricks the spectators into believing that the stage has really been transformed into another world, while the stress on empathy creates the feeling that "everyone behaves like the character concerned,"[27] serving to render the play's events inevitable and to naturalize the status quo. Through his own productions and theoretical writings, Brecht sought to create an "epic theater" that does not try to represent the "eternally human" but that represents "what men of specific social strata (as against other strata) do in our period (as against any other)."[28] One of his central concepts is the "V-effect," or the use of alienation, a technique that instructs the actor not to strive to "be" his character, but to be a step removed, so that the actor looks at and judges the character's actions from the outside. The goal is to induce the audience to think critically about the action, rather than simply identifying empathically with the character. Brecht sought to entertain but also instruct, historicizing all the events depicted onstage. As opposed to presenting plots determined by fate, epic theater highlights the fact that characters make particular choices, when they could make others, and, by extension, demonstrates what could be changed. This desire to historicize or denaturalize taken-for-granted realities and assumptions continues to be one of the central thrusts of much political art.

In order to create his often large-scale productions, Brecht was content to remain inside traditional theater buildings with a separated stage and audience seating. In the 1960s, however, the next generation of politicized theater artists, who were seeking to disrupt assumptions, moved outside the proscenium stage. Peter Handke, for instance, argues that the traditional theater was about play and that "seriousness of purpose in places meant for play is deceitful and nauseously false."[29] The committed theater, he explains, is now in lecture halls, streets, churches, and department stores. Peaking in the '60s and '70s, there was a widespread move to begin catching people unaware in everyday spaces like parks and supermarkets, to personally confront figures of power, and to produce shows in public for spectators who might not otherwise come to a theater. Depending on which particular performance or troupe one is focused on, this newer style of theater has been given several different names: "guerrilla theater," "radical theater," "street theater," "people's theater." All are mobile forms of performance designed to confront audiences and to reframe debate. As Jan Cohen-Cruz explains, "radical street performance" "draws people who comprise a contested reality into what its creators hope will be a changing script."[30] Much as in Brecht's theater, the intention is to spur spectators into thinking about their world in a new way, except that this type of theater does not wait for spectators to come to it.

Another helpful concept is provided by Richard Schechner, who uses the somewhat broader term "public direct theatre"[31] to refer to all street performances, including political demonstrations and Mardi Gras parades. He further divides the category, though, into events that are officially sanctioned and those that are not, arguing that the scenography and choreography vary greatly. In official events, street displays are well scripted; they follow a predetermined path and normally have a previously scheduled beginning and end. Conversely, rebellious events do not have a fixed conclusion; they randomly take over public space and are often interpreted by the authorities as being out of control. These events typically involve elements of the carnivalesque "in that the struggle—at certain key moments—is an exposure of what is wrong with the way things are and an acting out of the desired hoped-for new social relations."[32] Michael Moore's method, in particular, involves utilizing the strategies of rebellious direct theater. He consistently takes over public (and private) spaces and attempts to make as big a spectacle as possible. He never phones ahead to book an interview but instead shows up unexpectedly with a tenacious determination to stay.

In one early episode of *The Awful Truth,* for example, he sets out to satirize the impeachment of Bill Clinton during the Monica Lewinsky scandal by showing independent counsel Ken Starr how to conduct a cheaper witch hunt. His camera follows a group of actors dressed as Puritans, who invade Capitol Hill. The women run after several politicians yelling "Sinner!" and falling down in swoons at the mere sight of Newt Gingrich's office, while a man dressed as Thomas Jefferson interrupts Starr's speech to Congress and confesses to the affairs he had while in office. At a particularly poignant moment, Moore is met with baffled silence as he questions Republican Bob Barr, one of Clinton's harshest critics, about reports that he was seen licking whipped cream from an entertainer's nipples. Later, in editing, Moore adds commentary to the episode, referring to the $40 million spent by Ken Starr on the impeachment proceedings, compared to the measly $560 Moore spent on his witch hunt. Though many of the real politicians giggle at the unexpected scene, there is an atmosphere of nervousness surrounding the event due to its unpredictability. In other such stunts, there is much less tolerance from officials.

When Spurlock's debut film, *Super Size Me,* was released, it was almost impossible to find a review of it that did not explicitly compare it to Moore's work, as critics consistently pointed to traits like Spurlock's use of the "regular-guy populist style of documentary rabble-rousing pioneered by Michael Moore."[33] In the movie, Spurlock takes aim at America's fast-food industry and the country's obesity epidemic, mixing statistics set to quirky music and cartoons with health expert interviews and an exploration of school lunch programs. The narrative centerpiece of the film, however, is Spurlock's personal medical experiment, using himself as the guinea pig in order to test the health effects of a 30-day McDonald's diet. The results end up being worse than anyone predicted. The team of doctors monitoring his progress start begging him to stop the experiment halfway through, as he gains copious amounts of weight, suffers massive mood swings, develops a cholesterol nightmare, and turns his liver into "pâté," according to one of the doctors, all of which is meticulously chronicled by his cameras.

The contents of Spurlock's stunts are actually quite different than Moore's. He is much less confrontational. The central stunt of *Super Size Me* only immediately victimizes himself (though it clearly indicts the McDonald's corporation as a whole). And though he does interview several food industry public relations people, allowing them to entangle themselves in phony corporate-speak, one *New York Times* reviewer writes, "rather than barge into McDonald's headquarters with tissue samples from his Quarter Pounder–bedeviled liver, for instance, he is content to document the frustration of trying to reach a corporate official on the telephone."[34] It is this element that ends up winning him nods from several critics who admit to finding Moore abrasive. However, the comparison between the two filmmakers is inevitably drawn because of their similar emphasis on the "first-person guerrilla style,"[35] or one quirky individual's absurd trysts with an entity much more powerful than himself.

Moore's and Spurlock's stunts vary from guerrilla theater in one crucial way: they are the ones with the camera. Though any sort of street theater can attract a large live audience, in most cases, the goal is to reach a much larger group through mass media attention. Schechner writes that "the direct theatre is itself a reflexive first theatre, or raw material, for a near-universally displayed second theatre, the television newscast which includes (often improvised) responses to the first theatre."[36] Schechner explains that street performers ultimately have little control over how their actions will be portrayed on the news that night or on talk shows the next day. Editing and commentary (not to mention the choice of whether or not to cover something in the first place) play an enormous role in determining what sort of message is disseminated electronically. Because both Moore and Spurlock use their stunts as raw material, editing, framing, and packaging them into a finished art form, they are in control of the way the narrative unfolds. Since they are the main actors in their own stunts as well as the films' directors, they have the advantage of playing two different roles. I will argue that, as on-screen presences, they perform the classic role of the fool, while as editors and narrators they are also able to play the role of the preacher, an option not normally available to the fool and one that is ultimately not under the control of guerrilla theater artists who are reliant on media coverage.

FOOL AND PREACHER: DUAL PERSONAS IN THE SATIRIC DOCUMENTARY

In an analysis of *Roger & Me* written shortly after its release, Miles Orvell observes, "Moore turns the tables on traditional documentary: he himself becomes the 'powerless' subject."[37] That film deliberately foregrounds his status as a nobody filmmaker (which he was at the time) pitted against the army of security guards and PR people surrounding his rich and powerful subject. It is a formula he has continued to rely on (though some would now call it a contrivance), as the premise of most of his work is the attempt to make the powerful accountable to the public, or to expose them as unaccountable, by asking them the questions a journalist might not and filming every snub along the way. To get anywhere on this mission, though, requires more than just a thick skin. It also necessitates that the on-camera Moore seem to have the innocence to truly believe, for instance, that the guards at Guantanamo Bay will allow Moore and his boatload of sick Americans to receive access to the free medical care offered to the prisoners there (in *Sicko*).

Although this is a strategy that may be new to the world of documentary filmmaking, it has, of course, long been a tool of satire. Hans Speier describes the archetypal fool as the "Undeceiver General."[38] He is a person who defies social standards in some way. Traditionally, he often has noticeable physical deformities (which speaks to Moore's penchant for playing up his scruffy, overweight image), but more important, he flaunts behavioral norms, either as a simpleton or as an eccentric. Seen as harmlessly childlike, he is granted enough immunity that he may slyly go about unmasking the pretensions of those around him. As Mikhail Bakhtin explains, the fool uses the technique of "not grasping"[39] in order to dissect the conventions of his society. He appropriates the "right to act life as a comedy, and to treat others as actors, the right to rip off masks, the right to rage at others with a primeval (almost cultic) rage—and finally, the right to betray [to] the public a personal life, down to its most private and prurient little secrets."[40] Early in his career, as the wide-eyed guy from Flint with a camera and a conscience, Moore was able to capture remarkably revealing, shocking, and absurd footage with ease, likely because no one seriously believed that this inexperienced nobody would be able to actually do anything with it. (This has, of course, become more challenging as his fame has grown.)

The narrative premise of *Roger & Me,* for instance—that he will try to bring Roger Smith back to Flint for a discussion about policy—is a recognizably naïve one. Moore, with apparent innocence and wearing jeans and a baseball cap, attempts to walk into Smith's office to have a frank chat with him, and the camera captures the contempt with which he is greeted. Feigning obliviousness to this contempt, he offers his Chuck E. Cheese member card as identification when a guard implies he has no credentials. Of course, the film is about much more than Smith himself, since one could easily pillory him without going to all this trouble. Rather, it is about systemic ills. Smith's conspicuous absence from the movie points up the fact that, within the corporate system, he really does not have any obligation to address the suffering of the people of Flint. Moore wants us to ask ourselves, "Why not?" This point can be made because he depicts himself as having the innocence to assume that human empathy would triumph over profit motives if he were given the chance to reason with Smith. I would argue that these repeated, now almost clichéd moments in Moore's work of him naïvely trooping into some corporation's headquarters are constructed to expose the failures of the modern public sphere, echoing many of the criticisms made by Jürgen Habermas. Corporate America is powerful enough to speak only in PR sound-bites and has no interest in rational debate with the person on the street.

This technique is also an effective means of cornering his opponents. Moore's performance of the fool would have little impact were he the only actor involved. Thus, as opposed to more traditional forms of satire that critique real but absent officials, or documentary exposés that build their cases from afar, Moore brings his script to his targets (whether they be single individuals, large institutions, or representatives of a particular position), forcing them to play *themselves* within his frame, providing the

4.1. Playing the fool, Michael Moore attempts to offer a GM official his Chuck E. Cheese frequent visitor card as identification in *Roger & Me* (1989).

damning confirmation for the thesis he has already set up. Much as in the parodic news shows, the material then serves to function as a form of evidence within the larger political discussion. His targets have the choice of either attempting to dodge participation or trying to represent themselves in a positive light. In most cases, however, they don't come off well, as they have already been set up to produce a parody of themselves, mouthing the lines we expect of them. This is inevitably the case when the target is a corporation's abuse of power, since what is easily explained away in official press-release rhetoric never appears genuine in real human interactions. But the strategy works equally well in other scenarios, too. In an episode of *TV Nation,* Moore brings a film crew to the house of an anti-abortion activist notorious for harassing abortion doctors in their homes. Moore hypothesizes that this man will understand their approach since it is the one he prefers. The man responds by telling the group that they are a bunch of fanatics and yelling at them to get out of his yard, providing the precise note of irony Moore had been seeking.

In a similar way, Spurlock also plays the fool. Though he spends less time trying to trick individuals into revealing too much via loaded questions, in *Super Size Me* he uses a "foolish" conceit as an excuse to expose the dirty secrets of an industry. As many of his less enthusiastic critics have testily pointed out, Spurlock clearly must have known that a McDonald's diet combined with little exercise would be bad for him, but he undertakes it with the naïve attitude of "how bad can it be?" In the process, of course, he is then able to shock his audience with the details of how bad it really *can* be. From the outset, he sets himself some arbitrary rules, such as one stipulating that he will have to "super size" his meal if he is incited to do so by the cashier. He ends up having a super-sized lunch on the second day of the diet, and he has himself filmed ordering and then eating the giant meal in the front seat of his car. After we watch him marvel over the size of his French fries and happily commence chewing, a title screen pops up periodically to tell us how much time has elapsed, while he speaks about his growing stomach pains. In the last shot (at the 22-minute mark), the camera captures him force-feeding himself the remaining bites, and then it careens over to film him vomiting out the car window. In this scene, as in the movie as a whole, Spurlock is foolish enough to make himself physically sick in order to faithfully bring us the results of his experiment, literally making himself the guinea pig for our amusement, disgust, and edification. Beyond providing the setup from which to prove his point, it also gives him a comedic, human-interest hook with which to draw audiences.

Upon being questioned on whether the message of the film gets lost in the gimmicky-ness of the conceit, Spurlock argues, "[M]y doing this diet has really given the film accessibility. You know, now we've created a movie that has a story line that is interesting, that is intriguing, that people want to see,"[41] adding that the audience gets to laugh at his expense. In a sense, he combines the gross-out stunts of popular culture blockbusters, like the movie and television series *Jackass,* with a more political crusade.

Replicating this formula proved a bit trickier in his second movie, however. At the start of *Where in the World,* we learn that Spurlock is planning to embark on another absurdly foolish quest: to personally hunt down Osama bin Laden in order to make the world a safer place for his unborn child. After a peppy introductory animated sequence about all the

4.2. Morgan Spurlock is about to vomit after force-feeding himself his first super-sized meal in *Super Size Me* (2004).

potential dangers lurking in wait for his baby, he wryly tells the audience that if he has learned nothing else from big-budget Hollywood action movies, it is that the biggest problems are best solved by one lone guy on a mission. The beginning of the film is actually quite inspired, including an animated video-game sequence featuring a Spurlock avatar facing off against a bin Laden avatar, each of whom have funny secret weapons like Spurlock's "mustache attack" and bin Laden's "reign of terror." After some self-defense training and preparation, Spurlock then makes stops in Egypt, Saudi Arabia, Pakistan, and Afghanistan, interviewing a variety of average locals on the street as well as journalists, activists, imams, and others. Many of these exchanges are interesting, often providing a window on how, for instance, U.S. foreign policy affects lives in Egypt and the dim prospects for children growing up in the impoverished neighborhoods of Morocco.

The problem, however, is that Spurlock sets himself up to be too foolish about a complex topic. Though he likely had a fairly clear idea of the types of encounters he would have, he nevertheless has to play the American everyman abroad, entirely surprised at hearing less-than-rapturous evaluations of U.S. foreign policy. Likewise, his repeated questionings of men and women in markets and shopping malls about whether they know where bin Laden is are amusing the first couple of times and then seem

4.3. One of the opening sequences of *Where in the World Is Osama bin Laden?* (2008) introduces a playfully self-referential element by depicting Spurlock and bin Laden as video-game avatars engaged in combat.

contrived. And, of course, Spurlock the filmmaker can't possibly believe that he is actually going to find bin Laden, meaning that he is stuck coming up with a suitable conclusion for the film. After reaching the border of a tribal area in Pakistan that a number of people have told him is where bin Laden is most likely to be hiding, Spurlock stares at the sign warning that foreigners are not permitted beyond that point and decides that it is ultimately not worth it, supposedly finally coming to the conclusion that, even if he were to find bin Laden, it would make little difference, since the factors compelling him and his followers will remain. He explains that he now understands that his trip was ultimately about going out and talking to people whom Americans are taught to fear. In the last scene, after he has witnessed the birth of his son, Spurlock concludes that there are millions of people out there just like "us" rather than "him" (bin Laden) and that we are ultimately all looking for the same things, including a safe space to raise our kids. It is a fair sentiment, but not a particularly profound or novel revelation.

One could argue that, in *Super Size Me,* as in many of Moore's films, the foolish conceit or quest that sets the movie rolling is always somewhat contrived, but the difference in this film is that there is less of a clear political analysis underlining it all. Though Spurlock undoubtedly wishes to expand Americans' understanding of the Middle East and the concerns of the people in the region, and though he does insert a couple of animated informational sequences about past U.S. involvement in propping up unsavory dictator types, he has no message to impart about what should be done (or not be done) in the wars in Iraq and Afghanistan or in the campaign against global terrorism more broadly. In the end, he seems to have lost whatever political edge might have been motivating him, and the conclusion seems facile and obvious, unworthy of an entire filmic journey. Spurlock's on-screen fool ends up looking a little too foolish when not balanced by a strong directorial voice. What is missing is the role of the preacher.

When all is said and done, the fool is fairly powerless on his own; after we all have a good chuckle, he is vulnerable to being dismissed as just eccentric or crazy. But in the majority of their work, Moore and Spurlock ensure that, as directors, they are also able to play the preacher. Normally working from within a self-consciously situated political position, they structure their footage accordingly. No matter how innocently confused Moore's on-screen persona may be, his true opinions on the subjects he tackles are always clear, as are the aims of his pranks. The simplest and most effective technique he has available to him is, of course, merciless editing. In contrast to a journalist faithfully reporting official statements and ignoring flubs, Moore deliberately emphasizes moments in which his targets make potentially incriminating comments. He also relies heavily on ironic juxtaposition as a means of deconstructing seemingly innocuous statements or to draw attention to revealing parallels.

A good example is the marine recruiter scene from *Fahrenheit 9/11.* Moore himself does not appear in the scene, nor does he seem to even be present. Instead, a silent camera crew films two marine recruiters as they troll a shopping mall in Flint, Michigan, in search of potential recruits. In the preceding scenes, the narrative has followed the escalation of the insurgency in Iraq, with Moore as narrator wondering where they are going to find the additional soldiers needed. He answers his own question by stating that they would be found in economically destroyed cities around the country like his hometown of Flint. We are then taken on a tour through the town's run-down buildings and unemployment lines, scenes which are intercut with a conversation Moore has with a group of local teenagers who explain that they all have relatives or friends in the army and that there is someone recruiting at their high school nearly every other week. We are then segued to the marine recruiters preparing for a trip to the mall while smooth disco music plays in the background, as if we are about to witness an attempted seduction. Moore's narration explains that they are not going to the more affluent mall in Flint's suburbs, but to the *other* mall. Once there, the two recruiters approach numerous youngish-looking men to talk about enlisting. The footage is edited to show them repeatedly alerting each other to potential targets with "we got two over here" or "green hat, right behind you," as if they are stalking prey. Like used-car salesmen, they tell each potential recruit what he wants to hear, sleazily explaining to one teenager who wants to go into the music industry that he is going to need to learn discipline to manage all the money he is going to be making and that the marines can help. An edited mini-montage then draws attention to their repeated suggestions for potential appointments with the young man until he finally agrees to a meeting the next day. The point of the scene is not to embarrass these two individual recruiters in particular but to advance Moore's implicit argument that, while the rich and powerful are the ones engineering and profiting from the war, the country's poor are its manipulated victims.

In addition to featuring montages of the most incriminating footage, Moore's films are also structured around a pointed voice-over and held together through the use of stock footage, music, and titles. The playful, parodic style allows him to incorporate many pop culture references and pastiches of other movies and television shows, creating comedy but also a clear thesis—for instance, the memorable *Fahrenheit 9/11* sequence in which the Bush administration's architects of the invasion of Afghanistan are superimposed onto the title sequence of an old Hollywood western, depicting them as sound-stage cowboys playing at war. Likewise, one of the most remarkable segments of *Capitalism: A Love Story* consists of borrowed footage from a film about Jesus' life, redubbed so that scenes of healing the sick and feeding the hungry are edited to include free-market platitudes about self-sufficiency and not giving anyone a free ride. The segment handily drives home Moore's point that capitalism as it is currently practiced is at odds with Christian teachings on morality. Similarly, in *Super Size Me,* Spurlock intercuts the ongoing drama of his eating adventures with interviews with nutrition experts, doctors, and marketing watchdogs who provide the damning background facts. He then structures it all with animated maps, charts, and other visual aids

4.4. In *Fahrenheit 9/11* (2004), Moore uses stock footage and music to drive home his point that members of the Bush administration acted like Hollywood cowboys in their handling of the invasion of Afghanistan.

set to peppy music, also creating a clear position piece. In one notable scene, for example, he follows the progress of a man who has developed diabetes due to his poor eating habits and has opted to have a gastric bypass to solve his problems. Spurlock creates an amusing sequence of disgustingly graphic footage of the operation set to dramatic classical music, as if documenting a ballet, which highlights the incredible lengths that many now go to in order to counteract the effects of a destructive lifestyle. Some of the stronger sequences in *Where in the World* similarly distill the more pointed informational segments into cheeky cartoon interludes. Both filmmakers use techniques borrowed from fiction film as means of making their didacticism entertaining, clearly preaching to their audience while also keeping them amused.

This is, of course, a delicate balance to keep in play, and both directors have had a great deal of success with it due to their skill as storytellers. Some of the other films that have emulated the genre have (like *Where in the World*) not quite got it right. The films *Religulous* and *Expelled: No Intelligence Allowed,* for example, which were both released in 2008, were regularly compared to Moore's films, but they had mixed success in achieving similar goals. Not incidentally, though both are structured around the first-person protagonist on an investigative mission, neither Bill Maher of *Religulous* nor Ben Stein of *Expelled* were the directors of the films, so the sense that one is viewing a personal, unified, authorial vision is somewhat diluted. Both films make similar use of old black-and-white footage as a form of ironic commentary and for pop culture appeal, but they are heavy-handed. The scales tip too heavily toward the preacher function. In the case of *Religulous,* the clips are more often than not used to undercut and make fun of the interviewees (for the most part, religious believers), belying the idea that Maher is actually interested in how the religious make sense of their belief systems. In *Expelled,* much of the stock footage is of Nazi Germany and of the Berlin wall, which is used to drive home the narrative through lines that Darwinism led to the horrors of the Nazi death camps and that academics have erected a sort of Berlin wall between science and religion. Neither topic is funny, though the film is clearly aiming for comedy. The movie was also pounded for its dishonesty in not including any mention of the history of discrimination against Jews in Europe or the position of Germany after World War I, giving the impression that it was Darwinism itself that led to the Holocaust.

Though both Maher and Stein attempt to play the role of the naïve inquisitor seeking answers, neither is convincing. Maher, in particular, hardly gives his subjects the chance to finish their sentences, impatiently refuting what they have to say, while the director often then cuts away to Maher laughing about their statements back in the car. Rather than playing the low-status fool, Maher smugly comes across as believing he is the only one of intelligence for a good distance around him. This is enjoyable when the target is, for instance, a nattily dressed, self-satisfied preacher who has clearly enriched himself on the backs of his congregation, but it feels more mean-spirited when directed at average citizens. Of course, many similarly complain that Moore is smug, and he can certainly go after particular high-level targets with barely disguised venom, but he also allows most of his subjects to have their say, preferring to let his targets hang themselves with the rope they are given (with the exception of, say, the ill-conceived ambush of Charlton Heston in *Bowling for Columbine*). And a good many of his interviewees are not actually on-screen to be vilified; rather, Moore is often happy for others to make his case for him, playing dumb to let their intelligence or personality shine. In other words, he is careful to balance the directorial preacher with the on-screen fool.

FILMMAKERS AS PUBLIC FIGURES

As far as Moore and Spurlock are concerned, the two roles, fool and preacher, importantly also bleed into their public appearances outside of the films and into the way they are characterized within the media. The fact that they are featured so prominently in their documentaries makes them immediately recognizable—already celebrity figures—which both men (though Moore especially) certainly fuel by cultivating a high public profile, doing a multitude of interviews and speaking tours. Perhaps not surprisingly, then, because these filmmakers put their own bodies in front of the camera as the vehicle for making political points, they themselves become highly contested signs in the media battles surrounding the films.

With Moore in particular, a great deal of the distaste his films engender in opposing political camps manifests in direct attacks on his person. Moore's physical appearance is particularly striking, as he is unusually homely for someone who is now a celebrity. He has not adjusted his dress much since *Roger & Me,* appearing most frequently in jeans and a baseball cap. He is also noticeably overweight and often unshaven. The frequent sneers made about his physicality tend to take two tacks. On one hand, he is routinely mocked in cartoons, on late-night talk shows, and in print for being a fat pig, the implication being that this is indicative of character flaws such as greed or stupidity. On the other hand, he is incessantly accused of being a phony, since he is now a millionaire but still looks like someone from the working class. When pressed by Barbara Walters about his choice to always wear a baseball cap, Moore questioned why the fact that he has been successful would mean that he should have to change who he is.[42] His position and those of his critics are, of course, both strategic. It aids the repeated narrative in his films of one man on an investigative crusade for justice if he continues to look like an average Joe rather than a media personality. As Larissa MacFarquhar of the *New Yorker* observes, "Michael Moore, the fat man, is the big guy in his baseball cap, the way Charlie Chaplin was the little tramp in his bowler."[43] For his critics, on the other hand, demonstrating that he is enacting a persona allows them to imply that he is interested only in cynically manipulating people in order to sell more books and movies.

To a certain extent, critics of Spurlock's first film also tried to take aim at his person as a way of discrediting the movie, arguing that he deliberately gorged himself (secretly sneaking extra desserts and snacks) in order to disfigure his body and disgust viewers, meaning that nothing else in the film can be taken seriously. And, like Moore, Spurlock soon inspired an anti-fan website set up to discredit the film. However, in comparison to Moore, there were fewer vocal critics (who weren't industry-backed) seeking to attack Spurlock on a personal level when the film came out. This is partially due to the fact that he was a relative unknown, which Moore is no longer. Though Moore was more easily depicted as a working-class hero speaking truth to power after the release of *Roger & Me,* journalists wishing to attack his credibility now routinely make sneering reference to his New York penthouse. As A. O. Scott points out in a *New York Times* review of *Super Size Me,* not being a celebrity allows Spurlock "to inhabit the ordinary-guy-with-a-camera persona a bit more persuasively than Mr. Moore can."[44] This seems not to have changed all that much even after he exported much of the *Super Size Me* formula to a successful television series called *30 Days* in which other social experiments are conducted for a month, involving, for instance, Spurlock and his girlfriend attempting to live on minimum wage, or sending a devout Christian to live with a Muslim family. Spurlock narrates and appears periodically in front of the camera in each episode. The program drew a variety of reviews and some interest; however, it did not garner the same level of attention as a mainstream film, while Spurlock's second documentary was far less successful and high profile than the first and also had a mushier political agenda, presenting less of a target. For now, the *Spurlock Watch* website is not being maintained, though Spurlock could easily become a somewhat polarizing figure again, depending on future endeavors.

The fact that Moore and Spurlock put themselves into their films, structuring their narratives around real interactions, not only makes them objects of scrutiny, it also serves to complicate the literary-based theories of satire. As indicated in the introduction, one of the prevailing assumptions held by theorists of satire and political humor who argue that these modes ultimately have little political effect is that the key to satire lies in its detachment from the real political world. Much like the parodic news show hosts, however, filmmakers like Moore and Spurlock are not simply making quips from afar, but are physically engaged in their critiques. Viewers watch not as they do imitations or make jokes about topical issues, but as they interact with real individuals and stage real-world stunts. The first-person narrative allows for material that is performative, engaged, and improvisatory. None of these filmmakers (including Maher and Stein) has been accused of being detached from the issues they cover. Instead, they are regularly attacked for being overtly partisan or for making films that should not be considered documentaries since they are so obviously structured around one individual's crusade.

Satire theorist Leonard Feinberg argues that all satirists ultimately reinforce social norms, since they usually fail to "attack the basic problems of their societies. They tend to criticize hypocrisy, dullness, snobbishness, and folly and to avoid such issues as the political and economic structure of their specific society."[45] As a result, Feinberg argues, particular public figures may be harmed by satire, but the larger system is never called into question. However, what the particular form of the satiric documentary allows for, far more so than even the parodic news show, is a detailed exploration of one particular issue, providing hours of time in which to flesh out a layered and complex analysis. In *Bowling for Columbine,* for instance, Moore crafts a quite complicated critique of the culture of fear in the United States and its relationship to social hierarchy and control. And while *Fahrenheit 9/11* does skewer Bush (perhaps focusing to too great an extent on one individual's psychology), it also raises larger questions about social class and war. Spurlock's *Super Size Me,* though often construed as a film about McDonald's, offers a broader meditation on the fast-food industry and corporate responsibility. Here, we return to the role of the preacher, both within the confines of the films and beyond them, as the directors often continue preaching to audiences about their issue outside of the movie theater—in television interviews, speaking engagements, and online.

In Feinberg's characterization of satire, audience enjoyment is possible because everyone knows it is only entertainment, not a call to action, while "the satirist is motivated by the aesthetic desire for self-expression far more than by the ethical desire for reform."[46] Charles Schutz goes one step further, arguing that satire relieves the audience of any need for action that it might previously have had. He states that the satirist translates anger or resentment into a satiric attack in place of a literal one and that, in every instance, the "audience has participated vicariously in the satirist's sublimated aggression. They too have been purged of the need for more direct action in expression of their aggression."[47] These theories come up short, however, when we consider the mixture of entertainment and activism that makes up the satiric documentary. Even more so than the parodic news hosts, both Moore and Spurlock routinely remind their audiences that there are alternatives to the problems portrayed in their films, often specifically entreating their viewers to take action. Beyond the film or television text itself, they have also mined appearances across a variety of media for their potential in presenting alternative worldviews and encouraging the feeling of community in opposition. Both have worked to build a politicized counterpublic around their work.

NURTURING COUNTERPUBLICS

Moore and Spurlock have each attempted to fuel and sustain a counterpublic through the networking of multiple media, using their recognizable persona as both figurehead and primary commodity. Since Moore, in particular, is so prolific, he has been able to parlay his successful films into discussions of similar issues in several bestselling books, television programs, and speaking tours, all of which also encourage fans to visit his website, www.MichaelMoore.com. The site contains updates on the issues covered in his work, links to newspaper articles, humorous rants about current events, and lots of activist information. In addition, having amassed an enormous email list he refers to as "Mike's Militia," Moore frequently sends out letters about what he is working on, often presenting requests to the group that they consider particular issues or airing his own open letters to officials about upcoming political decisions. On the web, the role of the fool is gone. Moore certainly still writes with humor but as a polemicist or, perhaps more accurately, as a community organizer. On his website and in his emails, he writes to the presumed converted, urging everyone in the group to take action. Leading up to the 2004 presidential election, for example, he sent out numerous impassioned letters urging everyone to volunteer their time, to speak to nonvoters, and to contribute money to some of the tight congressional races. He also booked live speaking engagements at universities in swing states, referring to the engagements as the Slacker Uprising Tour.

In a similar manner (though perhaps on a smaller scale), Spurlock has attempted to sustain interest and attention in the issues raised in *Super*

Size Me far beyond its disappearance from the theaters. He, too, came out with a book, which provides more information on fast food, the American diet, and nutrition, including resources for parents and educators. His website contains chat rooms and discussion forums designed to sustain dialogue, and he has continued to appear both in high schools and in public venues to speak about health and nutrition. Both filmmakers have managed to prolong a continued circulation of discourse around their pet issues.

As discussed in the introductory chapter, Fraser argues that a singular public sphere can never adequately represent all factions within a stratified society, meaning that it has always been essential for subaltern groups (those that are economically or socially marginalized) to form their own counterpublic spheres. She stresses that these smaller publics are not inevitably about separatism; rather, they function as "bases and training grounds for agitational activities directed toward wider publics."[48] The obvious objection to using the language of counterpublics to discuss the fan communities of quite mainstream movies would be that members of these audiences are not necessarily "subaltern" in most respects. However, I am relying on Michael Warner's more expanded definition of counterpublics as those publics constituted through a conflictual relation to the dominant. Assuming that all publics are simply spaces of discursive circulation, counterpublics are specifically structured by different dispositions and assumptions than those found elsewhere in the culture, meaning that they are somehow subordinate to the prevailing culture, but they do not, he argues, have to be made up of otherwise marginalized individuals. He points to Christian fundamentalism and artistic bohemianism as examples of counterpublics whose members may not be otherwise socially disadvantaged. Importantly, though, "dominant publics are by definition those that can take their discourse pragmatics and their lifeworlds for granted, misrecognizing the indefinite scope of their expansive address as universality or normalcy."[49] Thus, counterpublics must fight an uphill battle in order to be heard within the larger culture. But, like Fraser, Warner implies that counterpublics are not separatist realms; rather, they "are spaces of circulation in which it is hoped that the poesis of scene making will be transformative, not replicative merely."[50] Along these lines, I would argue that Moore and Spurlock have attempted to nurture and sustain publics interested in challenging some of the narratives that are more typically circulated within the mainstream media.

It is no coincidence that, in all of his public appearances, Moore consciously tries to act as the spokesperson for a community. He continually references the popularity of his books and movies as *proof* of the popularity of his political views. Upon hearing that *Fahrenheit 9/11* had been nominated for a People's Choice Award a month after the 2004 election, for instance, Moore characteristically proclaimed that "the election has not altered or made irrelevant, unfortunately, a single one of these issues. That they (and the film that dealt with these issues) are still at the forefront of the majority of the public's minds should give serious pause to Mr. Bush as he brags about a nonexistent 'mandate' and begins to spend his 'political capital.'"[51] It should be noted that it is not merely self-aggrandizement for Moore to speak as if he were the leader of or figurehead for those opposed to Bush's policies or to the actions of particular corporations. The media also, particularly surrounding the release of *Fahrenheit 9/11,* were eager to depict him as representative of the entire political left. Moore regularly made the rounds of talk shows and news programs as a pundit, was selected as a devil's advocate columnist by *USA Today* during the Republican convention of 2004, became the favorite whipping boy of Fox News, and inspired a multitude of anti-Moore websites, books, and retaliatory documentaries. And in 2008, director David Zucker released a slapstick comedy film called *An American Carol,* which follows the overweight, slovenly, "anti-American" filmmaker Michael Malone as he is taught to see the error of his ways by several spirits from the past (à la *A Christmas Carol*). Though the movie ended up being quite unsuccessful (both in terms of critical reception and audience numbers), conservative figures like Bill O'Reilly and Rush Limbaugh urged their supporters to go see it as a means of registering a vote within the culture war. Other conservative critics and commentators critiqued the movie's quality and lamented that Zucker was granting Moore too much importance. But the widespread use of Moore himself as a signifier for a particular brand of political critique (by both supporters and detractors) attests to his success at popularly spearheading a number of political crusades.

It is important to note, as Warner makes clear, that neither publics nor counterpublics are groups that somehow preexist the circulation of particular texts. This is *not* to say that those watching *Capitalism: A Love*

Story, for example, were previously a blank slate but were suddenly radicalized by the film. Obviously, there were people predating Moore who held similar political views. However, his work does offer a temporary focal point for those views, allowing people, regardless of how politically active they are, to identify through the consumption of and interaction with particular popular culture texts, while providing an easily shared reference. Moore has consistently worked to draw attention to issues and opinions that have been relatively ignored by the national media, pushing them into the larger political dialogue. Though he portrays himself as speaking for the majority of Americans, he works to get issues and perspectives that are peripheral to the dominant into the wider public sphere. Those already interested in taking up such a debate often invoke his books and movies in order to do so, as they have become part of a shared lexicon.

Importantly, not everyone on the left appreciates Moore's ubiquity nor agrees with the logic of his arguments, but his success in driving the discussion of numerous issues in popular culture has, nevertheless, made him a signifier for a whole system of beliefs and made one's relationship to his media a means of performing those beliefs. Even within Congress, Representative Maxine Waters dedicated her objection to the ratification of Ohio's 2004 electoral votes to Michael Moore, thanking him for "educating the world on the threats to our democracy and the proceedings of this house on the acceptance of the electoral college votes for the 2000 presidential election,"[52] referring to the fact that *Fahrenheit 9/11* had included the first mainstream airing of footage of African-American congressional representatives attempting to challenge the 2000 election results based on charges of systematic disenfranchisement. Barbara Walters, who profiled Moore as part of her "Most Fascinating People of 2004" special, introduced him with the quip, "Suddenly you can tell a whole lot about a person by the way they react to a single name—Michael Moore."[53] The point here is not that one man has made himself the center of attention, but that his films and books have made particular political issues a part of popular culture, while becoming a conduit for counterpublic discourse. And for so doing, like the news hosts, he has garnered a lot of fans who look to him to speak their opinions.

Morgan Spurlock is not nearly as polarizing a figure (nor as widely recognizable), but with his first film he did become popularly identified with the issues surrounding the American obesity epidemic, fast-food culture, and corporate accountability. While Eric Schlosser's popular book *Fast Food Nation* (2001) had certainly already attracted some attention to the issues, the success of films like Moore's had, to a large extent, primed the pump, meaning that distributors, audiences, and journalists were familiar with the idea of a mainstream satiric documentary. *Super Size Me* did exceedingly well at the box office, while Spurlock racked up an impressive number of interviews and spotlight profiles, launching him on a talking-head career. As with Moore, Spurlock's interviewers focused heavily on the political import of what he was doing. Depending on his/her own leanings, journalists gleefully reported that McDonald's had eliminated its super-size options shortly after the film debuted at the Sundance Festival, or they grilled him on the fairness of his experiment. With the popularity of the film, Spurlock succeeded in creating an object of identification for, among others, the health conscious, those suspicious of megacorporations' power, and those opposed to the practice of aggressive marketing to children. Like Moore, he managed to push these issues out from the margins into the wider public sphere, providing the impetus, for instance, for several television specials on fast food and health concurrent with his movie's release.

While Spurlock has managed to sustain a counterpublic of sorts around *Super Size Me* and subsequent media encounters, since that one film remains his most successful work, his influence is more narrowly defined around the one issue in comparison to Moore's. It is also a somewhat less divisively controversial issue than those that Moore has tackled over the years, as it is less obviously aligned with a particular political ideology. This has certainly worked in Spurlock's favor as far as his popularity is concerned. As a reviewer from the *National Post* (Canada's more conservative national newspaper) puts it, "While *Super Size Me* is at its essence a propaganda film, it's propaganda for living healthier. . . . I can get behind that."[54] The central issue of the film also seems to have a good deal of resonance for the average person. Several critics, such as David Edelstein of National Public Radio and Roger Ebert, began their reviews of the movie with personal tales of dieting woes and fast-food indulgence, while others remarked on the timeliness of the movie, arguing that it was just what the ever-fatter country needed. Thus, while Spurlock has sparked some circulation of discourse surrounding the fast-food industry, popularizing an otherwise more marginal critique, for the time being he is not publicly associated with a particular worldview beyond that one issue (though his television show and second film have garnered him a reputation among a much smaller fan base for a somewhat diffuse desire to increase tolerance and dialogue between diverse social groups). Moore, on the other hand, has long been inextricably linked to a particular political outlook in the public's imagination.

Surrounding *Fahrenheit 9/11,* in particular, the extent to which Moore became popularly identified as the head of a political counterpublic likely exceeded even his own expectations, as at least one journalist covering the sentiments of the divided electorate referred to the opposing camps as the "Bushies and Michael Moore-ites,"[55] treating Moore as the more logical ideological opponent to President Bush than even the Democratic candidate, John Kerry. As *Entertainment Weekly* proclaimed: "John Kerry you can relax—the Republicans have a new Public Enemy No. 1."[56] This figurehead slippage did not always work in favor of Moore's goals, however (nor, presumably, for Kerry's), as Moore did become an easily targeted straw man for the other side. For instance, in a *Chicago Tribune* editorial, Kathleen Parker dismisses criticism of the Republican administration's move to raise the terror alert level shortly after the Democratic National Convention of 2004 by arguing that the critique was coming only from deluded "Michael Moore disciples."[57] Though Moore himself had made no public statement on the issue, Parker uses a rant against Moore's movie as proof that any questioning of the Bush administration's motives stems from dangerous paranoia. Similarly, in the less formal venue of internet chat rooms, calling Moore stupid, deceitful, or fat was regularly interpreted as a blow against Kerry, regardless of the fact that neither Moore nor Kerry had actively embraced the other.

After the election, *Time* magazine published an article titled "Winners and Losers" in which it profiled Moore as one of the most prominent losers of the election,[58] implicitly linking Moore's own fortunes to those of the Democratic Party (though he has continued to be a vocal critic of the Democrats). The anti-Moore websites were also crackling with glee, as one chat room participant announced Moore's demise: "Michael Moore's mentality, his movement, his message, and his movie have all been soundly, embarrassingly, decisively defeated. Remember this day folks: He lost, *and he lost real bad.*"[59] In post after post, participants appeared much happier about Michael Moore's "loss" than John Kerry's, as he seems to incite a more visceral loathing in his foes than Kerry ever did. This is likely because it has been more difficult to tell what Kerry stands for and who he is, while it has always been very clear who Michael Moore is and what his aims are—which is also a major part of why the reception for *Fahrenheit 9/11* was so polarized.

In his book on *Fahrenheit 9/11,* Robert Toplin argues that operatives on the political right worked hard to discredit the documentary from the beginning, surrounding it with words like "distortion," "manipulation," and "lies," making many suspicious of the film and cultivating the feeling that one would be actively supporting something sinister by attending a screening; many who might otherwise have considered viewing the movie decided that they should not. This was undoubtedly the case, but Toplin also intimates that had the film been released in a more neutral environment, more Republicans likely would have been swayed by its message (something that was apparently predicted by an initial Republican Party audience study). However, I do not think a neutral environment was ever possible. This was not exclusively the doing of Republican strategists, but equally of Moore himself. Since his physical body and explicit political opinions have been primary components of his art, we probably should not be surprised when these factors become the most publicly salient. It is now impossible to separate his persona from the issues in his films. And his persona incites both admiration and rage.

Consequently, from the moment the film began being publicized right up until the day of the election, the majority of the media coverage focused on the horse-race quality: whether Moore and his movie would succeed in persuading a significant number of undecided voters, effectively deciding the election. After Bush's win, some conservatives argued that Moore had succeeded only in galvanizing his opposition, sending more Republicans to the polls. Moore and his fans, however, pointed to the record turnout in the youth vote and the unprecedented number of impassioned election volunteers. Despite the pronouncements from both sides, however, it is impossible to know how many votes Moore single-handedly succeeded in attracting or repelling. In fact, looking at the issue in those terms seems almost absurd, as it implies that one cultural text could or should be expected to single-handedly cause quantifiable political change.

However, this is precisely the standard of judgment implicitly relied on by many of Moore's critics, particularly those on the political left. For example, in an article entitled "The Perils of Michael Moore" published in *Dissent* magazine shortly after the release of *Bowling for Columbine,* Kevin Mattson argues that, though Moore has commendably succeeded in making a leftist worldview popular, he does so often at the expense of substance and real politics, entertaining rather than accomplishing anything. Mattson's central critique seems to be that Moore's attempts at cornering CEOs and politicians generally fail. These powerful figures rarely change their policies as a result of Moore's stunts, meaning that the subsequent spectacle demonstrates only "that confrontation—especially when laced with humor—is too easy to sweep aside."[60] What really rankles him is that people consider Moore subversive. As he explains, it "could all be chalked up to a joke, except that Moore thinks of what he's doing as political. Here he inherits the New Left's conflation of 'guerrilla theater' with politics."[61]

Certainly, there are often significant weaknesses in Moore's work, as I have discussed, and it is important to note these flaws. However, I think Mattson's particular criticism is wrongheaded and misleading. His argument rests on the assumption that there is a clear distinction between art or culture, on one hand, and real political debate and struggle, on the other. According to this logic, for a play, book, or movie to be genuinely "political," there must be a one-to-one relationship between consumption and political action. This is a remarkably common conception of political efficacy and is likely why most theorists of satire, even the most optimistic, are loath to claim that satire can actually contribute to political change, as no one wants to be caught arguing that a particular cultural text can do something so concrete. Edward and Lillian Bloom, for example, argue passionately that the best examples of literary satire strive to remind us of our failings and to correct moral wrongs, practically gushing about the satirist's sense of hope and his quest for the quality they label "humanitas."[62] However, they too hedge on the question of political effect, feeling the need to explain that satire "alerts us to moral lessons and yet stops short of initiating remedial action or organized benevolence,"[63] assuming that efficacy is analogous only to material returns.

The problem with defining political effect so narrowly is that it risks reducing all democratic politics to what one does at the polls, ignoring the political groundwork that precedes any type of change. It negates the much lengthier process of altering structures of feeling, or what Carol Burbank refers to as "reiterative resignifying,"[64] and it elides the importance of building political communities. Ultimately, this sort of critique discounts the important component of *deliberation* within a democracy. Later in his article, Mattson critiques Moore for not being movement-based, but seems to assume that cohesive oppositional movements spring from the head of Zeus fully formed. As Stuart Hall reminds us, a group "does not become a class or a unified social force until it begins to have forms of intelligibility which explain a shared collective situation."[65] While I think it is highly unlikely that Moore himself expects that he will be able to single-handedly transform every CEO with whom he comes into contact, he joins the efforts of other counterpublic agents to "transform notions of the common good and to reprioritize items on public and official agendas."[66] Thus, as with the parodic news shows, it is more useful to examine the impact of these films in terms of their ability to galvanize and their influence on political discourse.

Moore's most noticeable achievement is in creating work with which people identify, both through the consumption of his popular culture texts and in opposition to the targets of those texts, and thus creating the sense of a larger community of dissent. In reviews and articles on *Fahrenheit 9/11,* it was widely noted that, in many theaters around the country, particularly amid the charged atmosphere of the first weeks after its opening, audiences were spontaneously bursting into applause at the end of the film. It seemed that Moore had succeeded in articulating a point of view that many shared and were longing to hear confirmed. As Toplin puts it, "[I]t was clear that Moore had done more than preach to the converted. He had energized them and given them hope."[67] Cheering him on was a way of identifying with and becoming a part of a larger movement or community in opposition, one that suddenly seemed tangible and that was unexpectedly making inroads into the national debate. Likewise, as reviewers in the *American Journal of Bioethics* point out in their discussion of *Sicko,* though the film would not likely sway committed conservatives, the movie's promise is rather "its apparent capacity to mobilize supporters to demand change."[68] And, indeed, Moore seems to point this out himself at the end of *Capitalism: A Love Story,* as he tells the audience that he is tired and clearly can't solve the problems of the system himself.

He implores viewers to take up the charge and join him on the crusade. Numerous reviewers of the movie pointed out that, after stoking anger at the excesses of contemporary capitalism and the management of the economic crisis, he urges change but gives little indication of what the solutions might be. This is certainly a valid critique (producing definitive academic analysis is not Moore's strong suit), though providing a new economic manifesto was likely not his intention. Instead, he proffers new case studies of abuses of wealth and power and, in so doing, encourages fans to identify in like-minded outrage, leaving them to fill in the blanks of how that outrage could be channeled.

In his films, books, television programs, and interviews, Moore holds much of dominant discourse up for interrogation, allowing for the process of what José Muñoz terms "disidentification." As Muñoz explains, disidentification stems from a desire to rework and resignify the norms and values imposed on one. Thus, "identities-in-difference emerge from a failed interpellation within the dominant public sphere. Their emergence is predicated on their ability to disidentify with the mass public and instead, through this disidentification, contribute to the function of a counterpublic sphere."[69] He stresses that disidentification is neither complete identification nor rejection, but rather a "strategy that works on and against dominant ideology."[70] He explains that "the process of disidentification scrambles and reconstructs the encoded message of a cultural text in a fashion that both exposes the encoded message's universalizing and exclusionary machinations and recircuits its workings to account for, include, and empower minority identities and identifications."[71] Most important, disidentification, like Brechtian alienation, holds received truths up for examination in order to demonstrate that things could be otherwise. This process seems a crucial one for political movements, and the satiric documentary excels at it. Moore, for instance, relies on narratives of patriotism and of the American dream, but works hard to reinvest these tropes with new meaning. Rather than distance himself from these ideas, he critiques the hypocrisy of particular people and institutions that have invoked them in the past.

As Todd Gitlin argues, "[O]ne core task of opposition movements is to contest the prevailing definitions of things, the dominant frames. They must 'rectify names,' they must change the way people construe the world, they must penetrate and unmask what they see as the mystification sustained by the powers that be."[72] Part of what makes these films political is that they implicitly challenge the dominant assumptions of what is appropriate fodder for the public sphere, in other words, what is considered "private" information and what is of "public" concern. Moore storms the barricades erected around private industry. He drags corporate policies into the spotlight and then calls for a vigorous debate, publicly airing profit statistics and labor practices. Spurlock links the private issues of individual weight gain and health with the public practices of the fast-food industry. Both directors imply that the individual, private concerns of market capitalism are of crucial importance to the larger social community and that they can and should be subject to public debate. As Erik Doxtader argues about counterpublics in general, they are often "opposed less to what the public *is* than to what it *is not,*"[73] as they push for expansions in the scope of public debate.

In her book *No Logo,* Naomi Klein points out that, in our age of hyper-branding, the most effective weapon that activists have is the ability to bring the abstract, disembodied qualities of the brand back into collision with the materiality of the product and the messy conditions that produce and sustain it.[74] In other words, the corporation's painstakingly cultivated public image can be easily tarnished by placing it next to the privately guarded details of the industry. This is a tactic both Moore and Spurlock take full advantage of. Probably one of the most effective moments in Moore's *Bowling for Columbine,* for instance, is the scene in which Moore brings two of the surviving Columbine shooting victims to Kmart's headquarters to return the bullets still lodged in their bodies (all of which were reportedly purchased at a Kmart store). Moore uses the pathos and black comedy of the stunt to hold Kmart accountable for the products it sells. The thesis he sets up is that bullets are not just another commodity, that they have a life after they leave the store, and that it is a violent one. Sizing up the threat Moore poses, Kmart gives in to his demands before he makes them, offering to stop carrying ammunition in all of the company's stores, likely realizing that the family-oriented public image it has worked hard to create could be badly damaged if juxtaposed with the private information of how much profit they have made on bullet-ridden children.

In their attempts to bring private trade secrets under collective public scrutiny, Moore and Spurlock join the larger tradition of muckraking

4.5. In *Bowling for Columbine* (2002), a Kmart official announces that the company will stop selling ammunition at its stores after Moore tries to return the bullets lodged in the bodies of the Columbine shooting victims.

journalism and its filmic equivalent, the documentary exposé. What makes their work unique, though, is their ability to narrativize the revelation of information in a captivating manner through the use of satire, improvised pranks, and humor. The satirical frame is key to the political efficacy of these films and their surrounding media. Like the parodic news hosts, Moore and Spurlock rely on humor as a tool of alienation. They hold their opponents up for irreverent interrogation, highlighting ironies and flaws. When Moore wants to draw attention to social inequalities in *Roger & Me,* for example, he juxtaposes the story of a laid-off auto worker who has had a mental breakdown from the stress with a "Great Gatsby" party that members of the elite are throwing, complete with footage of the costumed guests proffering advice to the workers such as "get up in the morning and go do something." As evidenced by the power of the fool in such interactions, the comedic frame also allows the filmmakers more leeway in transgressing social norms and asking questions that others would not.

In a response to anxieties that an emphasis on comedy can lead only to a "postmodernizing" of documentary over sustained inquiry, Corner references Moore's television program *TV Nation,* in particular, as an example of humor used to critical effect. He argues, "[T]he linking of documentary purposes to comic and sometimes farcical devices can generate an affective power which the more committedly 'sober' tradition of programme-making . . . is hard put to achieve."[75] I would add that the presence of the filmmaker as personable, quirky protagonist and guide is a crucial component both of the comedy and of this affective power. In interviews, both Moore and Spurlock stress that they are interested in attracting as large an audience as possible. As Moore explains about the impetus behind *Roger & Me,* "I made a conscious decision that I wanted to make a documentary that people who don't go to documentaries would watch."[76] He goes on to argue that, by using a comedic frame, he is able "to reach more people with a political message, and in fact, the message is even more pointed. It's a direct, frontal assault."[77] Spurlock argues that the humor of his stunt in *Super Size Me* "got 'em in the tent,"[78] though he arguably mistook this element of entertaining audiences for a need to dumb down the material in his second film, assuming too little about his audience's intelligence or willingness to follow him through a more pointed analysis. Many of the flaws of oversimplification in Moore's films also likely stem from a similar instinct. For both, though, the satiric slant has largely paid off, as many of their films have attracted record audiences, become widely viewed popular culture texts, and insinuated their subject matter into broader political debates. Though, clearly, no film has the power to instantly undo dominant narratives, the satiric documentary, as a genre, works to insert alternative formulations into popular culture, to introduce an oppositional viewpoint into wider dialogue, and to provide an object of identification for those who already share a film's viewpoint.

For these reasons, this newly evolving genre points up oversights in much of the existing public sphere literature. As discussed in the introduction, many public sphere theorists implicitly accede to Habermas's assumption that political dialogue is advanced only through "rational" discourse. Fraser points out that what is popularly recognizable as appropriate fodder for public dialogue, as well as the norms and manners structuring that dialogue, are themselves ideologically produced, but she, nevertheless, does not explore alternative *forms* of discourse. It seems particularly important to consider counterpublics created within the realm of art and entertainment, as well as the differing rhetorical forms they might entail. As John Downing points out, a survey of the alternative media during the age of Habermas's coffeehouses shows clearly that "through their use of irony, satire, caricature, cartoon, slander, innuendo, salacious public gossip, and pornography, that somber, clearly argued debate was no more victorious then, or the dominant mode of discourse, than we see it to be today."[79] When discussing public spheres, then, particularly in reference to the mass media, which allow for the transmission of much more than text, it seems imperative to consider the work accomplished by images, bodies, and modes of being, as well as the work of parody, satire, and irony.

Both of the satiric documentary filmmakers profiled here draw from a variety of popular forms as means of melding entertainment and activism; their films become pop culture phenomena while insinuating more "radical" counterpublic viewpoints into the wider political dialogue. It would be a mistake to see any of their films as merely descriptive, or as simply comments on the existing political scene. Rather, these films, and all of the media encounters they engender, actively contribute to the constitution of our political landscape, its terminology, players, and issues. In attracting such large audiences and generating so much press, these filmmakers have become significant figures in the battle for hegemony between competing discourses. Though these filmmakers offend many, they also inspire many others, attracting strong affective communities around them. They are far from universally respected, and their films are not without flaws, but their talent, it seems, is in continuing to be imperfect, opinionated spokespersons for change who are willing to play all the roles we demand of them in the process—from hero to villain.

FIVE

Irony in Activism

While the television programs profiled in chapter 3 have the advantage of a culturally powerful, stable medium at their disposal, and the films discussed in chapter 4 have a temporary but potentially far-reaching platform, the activist groups examined here have few of the same advantages nor the widespread fame. Instead, their aim is to borrow, beg, and steal the media spotlight if only for a fleeting moment as a means of forwarding their aims. As the realities of mass media communication have evolved, so too have the tactics employed by political activists. More and more groups are now building their actions around a playfully ironic sensibility, creating attention-getting stunts, graphics, and slogans along with prepackaged media sound-bites. Whether parodically assuming the identity of their opponents, or exuberantly creating a temporary incarnation of the world they wish existed, many activists now adeptly create their own cultural texts. Just as the entertainers of chapters 3 and 4 have become more like political pundits and spokespeople, these political agitators have become more like professional entertainers. And though the use of irony may appear trivial to some, it is in the service of deadly serious aims. Irony is used not only to attract attention to the cause, but to actively call upon audiences' shared assumptions and predilections in an attempt to make members of existing discursive communities present to one another and, ideally, to turn those communities into actively politicized ones.

As I have touched on with the other examples, it is remarkably easy to dismiss political critique aimed at those who may already appreciate the critique as merely preaching to the converted, particularly when the intent is so clearly to persuade and move to action, as in the case of political activism. The common assumption is that activists are wasting their time if they are speaking primarily to people who already share many of their convictions. However, it is important to remember that the so-called converted may still be apathetic, or unconnected to a larger movement, or simply in need of some validation. Passively holding a particular opinion or assumption is not analogous to acting on it or even to privileging it as particularly pressing. As Jonathan Gray argues, there is a reason that most (religious) preachers actually do preach to the converted every week; they clearly believe that reminders and reinforcement are important. Each one of us, he explains, "has thousands of opinions, beliefs, convictions, and ideas swimming around in our heads, but they cannot all be at the surface; hence, preaching to the converted involves grabbing hold of such ideas and making them loom larger in our minds by bringing them closer to the surface."[1] Additionally, it is my contention that affirmation and reinforcement fulfill an integral community-building function, which is a crucial component of nurturing a political movement.[2] While the efficacy achieved by ironic activists (as opposed to more traditional activists) is often less measurable in terms of concrete legislative goals, it is instead located in the strengthening of the visceral experience of community and in the attempt to slowly shift debate by turning laughter over a shared joke into anger and engagement.

Once again, in analyzing the poetics of these activist pranks, happenings, and performances, the modes of satire, parody, and irony bleed into one another, thwarting efforts to neatly separate them. Examples of all three are abundant. The group known as Billionaires for Bush, for instance, created exaggerated parodies of Bush's wealthiest supporters, while the Yes Men appear at conferences and on television as officials of companies they do not actually represent in order to satirize real-world economic policy. However, throughout this chapter, I most often use the broader term *ironic* for this type of activism, relying on Linda Hutcheon's description of irony as defined by the simultaneity of both a said and an unsaid meaning, "each of which takes on meaning only in relation to the other,"[3] as I think it best captures the knowing wink these groups offer to those who already share their views. Hutcheon describes irony as "the making or inferring of *meaning* in addition to and different from what is stated, together with an *attitude* toward both the said and the unsaid."[4] More specifically, I will focus on a practice I term *identity nabbing,* in which participants pretend to be people they are not, appear in public as exaggerated caricatures of their opponents, or ambiguously co-opt some of their power. Members draw on irony to rhetorically head opponents off at the pass, performing their own version of the other side. All are examples of embodied irony, a form that involves the communication of a said and an unsaid, or performed and unperformed, meaning but that is created largely in the moment by live bodies interacting with one another, and thus is reliant on improvisation and exchange. The examples profiled here are of activists and artists who create embodied irony through the dissonance between their performed identities in the moment, their actual statements, and the implied meaning behind them.

The obvious question surrounding this practice is: Why would activist groups in particular, which normally depend on making political demands in as clear a voice as possible, want to use such a convoluted mode of discourse? The answer is at least partially to be found in the coparticipatory workings of irony that Hutcheon lays out. As she explains, the presence of irony requires not only the intention of the ironist but also the intention of the receiver (or audience) to read it as such. In other words, irony is a meaning-making process that must involve both encoding and decoding to be complete. As much as the ironist, the interpreter also performs an act by attributing "both meanings and motives—and does so in a particular situation and context, for a particular purpose, and with particular means."[5] For irony to happen, ironist and interpreter must share certain assumptions, including mutually understood cues (quotation marks, tone of voice, etc.) that mark the utterance and conceptions of what sort of statement is appropriate in a given situation. While many theorists argue that irony creates in-groups (implicitly separating those who "get it" from those who do not), Hutcheon turns the formulation around to argue that "irony happens because what could be called 'discursive communities' already exist and provide the context for both the deployment and attribution of irony."[6] Our membership in existing discursive communities, then, is what makes irony possible.

Notably, her conception of "discursive communities" can be roughly translated as what others might call "publics." Specifically, if we draw on Michael Warner's definition of *publics* as being built on the circulation of discourse, requiring participation (not just demographics) for membership, members of discursive communities *become* publics in choosing to interpret an ironist's statements ironically. It is my contention that the activist groups profiled here rely on existing discursive communities to understand the irony of what they are doing, but that they also attempt to further turn these discursive communities into actively politicized communities, or what I have been referring to as counterpublics. Appealing to shared assumptions about the world, as well as, perhaps, a shared sense of humor, they challenge their audiences to not only get the joke but to actively take up the issues at hand as their own. This co-participatory element is perhaps most pronounced in the case of embodied irony, as it involves the bodily engagement of the ironist with the addressees, demanding somewhat more of its interpreters. While Hutcheon stresses that irony cannot actively create communities, that they must exist prior to the enunciation, she undertheorizes the potential of making members of existing discursive communities present to one another and of strengthening the visceral experience of community.

Finally, another piece of the puzzle about why activists would choose to speak ironically has to do with their positioning vis-à-vis the mass media and their potential audience. These groups are attempting to capture attention that has not already been granted them, often the attention of both passersby and the news media. Thus, for all of the groups, entertainment value is key to the success of their actions as, at the very least, it assures they will be noticed. For this reason, the potential pleasure that particular stunts may afford their viewers is a key concern in their design, a pleasure often conceptualized in opposition to the potential displeasure of the straightforwardly didactic. This courting of entertainment value manifests itself in humorous applications of irony or as spectacular media hoaxes designed to publicly embarrass powerful people or institutions. Likewise, it should be noted, these stunts seem to give the activists themselves a great deal of pleasure, sustaining and energizing those who are often also engaging in other types of difficult activist work.

In what follows, I will draw on some representative samples of the many collectives currently blending irony and activism in order to exemplify different elements of this technique. After tracing a brief outline of some of the earlier groups that have influenced those of today, I will discuss the contemporary activist landscape, focusing heavily on the broad concept of *culture jamming* (the practice of using forms of mass culture against itself through tactics like parody and irony). The concept of culture jamming is an important one for this study as it is a popular phrase among younger activists and is frequently used as a sort of catchall term for much of what I am referring to as ironic activism. I will then turn to several specific case studies, beginning with Billionaires for Bush. The Billionaires attended public events and staged protests as larger-than-life caricatures of the ultra-rich, ostensibly in support of President Bush and the Republican Party, literally becoming their perceived opponents in an attempt to reframe the terms of debate. The Yes Men have further expanded this strategy. They attend conferences and do television interviews as representatives of companies for which they do not actually work, as means of drawing scrutiny to the organizations' policies and practices. They combine the identity nab with invisible theater (as developed by Augusto Boal), rendering the faux identity they have assumed much more difficult to immediately recognize as fake, working to engage and perhaps enrage their audiences, and, ideally, spurring viewers to question their believable but morally suspect replications of corporate, neo-liberal philosophy. Finally, I will turn to performance artist/activist Bill Talen and his character Reverend Billy, a televangelist preacher who presides over the Church of Life after Shopping and who stages a variety of public stunts, including targeted retail incursions at large chains. The interplay between ironist and addressees becomes particularly visible in his work, which relies on a "congregation" of participants providing the "Amens" punctuating his sentences and actively working to produce the semi-fictional reality together.

All of the case studies involve a creative, easily replicable, mediagenic style designed to capture attention. Of course, the ironic forms of play surveyed here are not, by any stretch of the imagination, the only type of activism operating today, nor the only type necessary to effect social change. However, they have taken on a much more significant and privileged role within activism in the twenty-first century. This shift is certainly linked to a more general upsurge of a focus on culture within activist communities, meaning that it is no longer an area considered peripheral to the work of organizing, letter writing, and marching. Addressing this larger phenomenon, Stephen Duncombe explains that culture, both as entertainment and as information, is one of the leading sectors of the economy, so that "the idea of a performed cultural world seems second nature to us. Add into this mix the internet, the virtual world of signs and symbols where an increasing amount of our everyday life takes place, and it's no surprise that activism has embraced culture. Activists have become cultural guerrillas because this is the terrain of the battles they fight."[7] Today's activists are often savvy cultural producers as well as consumers. And it is within this larger context that irony has come to the fore as a type of countercultural dominant.

The irony, humor, and playfulness employed by contemporary activist groups did not materialize as political strategies out of thin air, nor did the emphasis on creatively performing opposition for a mass audience. Around the world, political protest groups have been developing public displays designed to catch mass attention for as long as forms of mass communication have existed. Leslie Goddard details how U.S. suffragists, for instance, carefully crafted public spectacles to garner support for their cause at the turn of the twentieth century, producing amateur pageants and plays as well as public marches. The suffragists were demonized by much of the rest of society, depicted as manly, unattractive, and deviant, while the suffrage debate was delineated as a choice between normality and the disintegration of sex roles. The suffragists had to find a way of countering these conceptions without having direct access to the newspapers or the political arena. Their pageants were designed to invert the stereotypes, drawing a picture of themselves as unopposed to marriage, adept at housework, and great at providing intelligent conversation for their husbands, while getting in a few digs at anti-suffragist women as vain and frivolous. As Goddard argues, "[T]heater served as a primary arena in which suffragists could link themselves with popularly understood signs of ideal womanhood, naturalize their own beliefs about women's proper role in society, and legitimize their own cause by moving their beliefs into the realm of the commonsensical and universal."[8] Most spectacular were the parades, which were considered shocking due to the simple fact of women marching through public streets. These events had a quite dramatic effect on public opinion since the materiality of the bodies on display served to showcase the wide range of movement participants, demonstrating that they really could be one's daughter, sister, wife, or next-door neighbor.

I could point to a number of examples throughout the early twentieth century of performative protest designed to shift cultural perceptions through creative public action, but I would argue that the scale and tenor of the specific tactics changed dramatically in the 1960s as young activists, the first generation to have grown up with television, grappled with the ubiquity of the medium and attempted to harness its power. It is worthwhile to briefly trace this history, exploring the background from which the contemporary tactics have emerged.

MASS-MEDIATED ACTIVISM

Several groups achieved near-celebrity status during the 1960s, most notably the Yippies in the United States and the Situationists in Europe, both of which were recognizable for their shocking, nose-thumbing irreverence and their mediagenic style. Guy Debord remains the most famous Situationist, founding the Letterists and then the Situationist International in 1957. Disappointed at the way that the work of the Dadaists and surrealists had become easily co-opted and commodified, the Situationists sought to radically redefine the role of art in the twentieth century and to revolutionize life. Debord wrote of the "society of the spectacle," a society based on the fetishism of commodities in which direct experience and action are replaced by passive reception. The spectacle, according to Debord, "says nothing more than 'that which appears is good, that which is good appears.' The attitude which it demands in principle is this passive acceptance, which in fact it has already obtained by its manner of appearing without reply, by its monopoly of appearance."[9] In the Situationists' manifestos, art was no longer to remain separate from the everyday, a commodity produced by professionals, but would rather be a way of life. Their mission was to seize control of modern culture and use it for their own purpose. To this end, they developed the technique of *détournement* (which literally means "misappropriation"), the repurposing and rearranging of existing textual fragments, a "re-use, that 'adapts' the original element to a new context. It is also a way of transcending the bourgeois cult of originality and the private ownership of thought."[10] And, I would add, it is a method of using irony, parody, and nonsense for political ends. Members experimented with painting over existing works bought at flea markets, creating books of collages, and, in Debord's case, making films that were heavily reliant on existing footage sutured together with an original voice-over. All were developed as radical statements.

Though they did not actively seek to recruit new members (and, indeed, regularly purged existing members), the Situationists were talented at advertising their ideas. As Jappe argues, their strength was their trademark style, including

> the systematic use of insult; the reliance on "low" cultural forms such as comic strips, graffiti, and satirical songs; the ostentatious lack of respect for authorities and conventions (a respect that was traditionally stronger in France than elsewhere); the refusal to care whether adversaries saw one as "reasonable" or "acceptable"; the mockery of things that other people felt were already very daring or innovative.[11]

By 1968, their ideas had exploded in popularity, so that they became major players in France's May uprisings, and their slogans were graffitied on walls across the country during the strikes. As Hulton Getty puts it, "Daniel Cohn-Bendit, the activist formerly known as Dany The Red, may have been the public face of *les evenements* of May '68, but—despite being the smallest and least well-organised of the various factions—the Situationists proved the most influential in terms of defining the moment. They uttered the Big No."[12] The Situationists officially disintegrated not long after the uprisings, but Debord has remained a cult figure, and the concept of *détournement* has taken on new resonance for those who now refer to themselves as culture jammers, many of whom see themselves as direct descendants of the Situationists.

During roughly the same period in the United States, at the height of the Vietnam War protests and general cultural upheaval, a new protest group began to make itself known to the media. The Yippies (the name was derived from the Youth International Party), most charismatically represented by Abbie Hoffman and Jerry Rubin, became a countercultural sensation due, in large part, to their spectacular stunts, many of which drew heavily on an irreverent, ironic sense of humor and playfulness. They helped to organize rallies and events, made inflammatory statements to the press, and generally did all they could to attract attention. One of their most famous actions involved throwing money off the balcony of the stock exchange, causing the traders to nearly trample each other in a mad scramble for the bills and temporarily shutting down the market. They also convened a massive gathering of people in an attempt to levitate the Pentagon and advanced a pig ("Pigasus") for president in 1968. The pranks often conveyed their own critical commentary, the ironic unsaid meaning of the traders' greedy scramble for money, for instance, being a demonstration of what they already did for a living every day. However, the Yippies rarely offered detailed explanations for these actions, preferring the irony to stand on its own and allowing the buzz to build around them as observers speculated over specifics.

As Hoffman describes it, they saw themselves as "cultural revolutionaries,"[13] inspiring others to get involved and start making their own "revolution for the hell of it."[14] Like the Situationists, they were enormously talented at advertising themselves, seizing on the potential of the mass media, and staging their actions for reporters. No doubt influenced by the concurrent surge in guerrilla theater, Hoffman conceptualized what they were doing in explicitly theatrical terms: "We are theater in the streets: total and committed. We aim to involve people and use (unlike other movements locked in ideology) any weapon (prop) we can find. The aim is not to earn the respect, admiration, and love of everybody—it's to get people to do, to participate, whether positively or negatively. All is relevant, only 'the play's the thing.'"[15] Relatively unconcerned by exactly *how* they were portrayed in the press, they saw any exposure as an unmitigated good. As Hoffman exhorted: "The media is the message. Use it! No fundraising, no full-page ads in the *New York Times,* no press releases. Just do your thing; the press eats it up. MAKE NEWS."[16] The Yippies considered every mention on television an unpaid commercial for the revolution that helped in the creation of the myth surrounding them. Since their rhetoric and style were so different from everything else on the news, they saw themselves as expertly jamming the system, implicitly offering an alternative to the "puritanical, sterile culture of the Establishment."[17] Jerry Rubin scoffed at those activists who discounted the importance of the mass media, writing, "You can't be a revolutionary today without a television set—it's as important as a gun! Every guerrilla must know how to use the terrain of the culture that he is trying to destroy!"[18] But he likely underestimated media culture's ability to absorb and recontextualize much of what crosses its path, particularly its penchant for trivializing fringe movements.

It seemed that few activists could match the telegenic style and sheer entertainment value of the Yippies until the creation of ACT UP in the 1980s and '90s. In contrast to both the Yippies and the Situationists, however, who had aimed for total revolution, significantly impacting their respective cultures but certainly falling short of their ultimate goals, ACT

UP was created around a specific issue and aimed for tangible, targeted goals. Founded in New York in 1987 in response to government inaction over the ballooning AIDS crisis, ACT UP participants sought expanded medical research, access to drugs, and nondiscriminatory discussion about the disease. Unlike the Yippies, its members did not see all media coverage as inherently good regardless of the angle; rather, they understood themselves as fighting a semiotic war in which they had to battle against powerful social biases already in place, which is why they became savvy cultural producers. As ACT UP member Eric Sawyer explains:

> We realized early in our ACT UP experience the importance of street theater, witty chants, slick graphics, and sound bites. Often the coverage we received was limited to fifteen seconds on the television news. Reporters seldom covered our issues accurately. We learned that witty chants and slick graphics were a better way to make sure that the media reported the facts correctly.[19]

Though dealing with the morbid, emotionally taxing issues of disease and death, ACT UP pioneered a polished, often ironic, humor-filled campaign. As Benjamin Shepard notes, "[T]he group recognized the subversive effectiveness of a joke."[20] The jokes were used not simply to lift their own spirits, but also to catch media attention, encapsulating their message in one carefully thought-out sound-bite, slogan, or visual representation. What ACT UP did was preframe each action for the media, so that any coverage of its events almost had to include its own witty formulation of the issue at hand.

Depending on the particular battle to be waged, the group combined demonstrations with flyers, sit-ins, kiss-ins, die-ins, letter-writing campaigns, parodic advertisements, pranks, and invasions of public space, including buying hundreds of seats at a baseball game to unfurl banners, creating fake copies of the *New York Times* detailing the newspaper's neglect of the AIDS crisis, delivering the ashes of AIDS victims to companies and officials they believed should be held responsible, and placing stickers on products by pharmaceutical companies they accused of price gouging. As T. V. Reed explains, "ACT UP's basic strategy might be called the politics of shaming. . . . [t]he group sought to draw attention to shameful government sluggishness, shameful corporate profiteering, and shameful media bias."[21] Their methods for doing so were enormously creative and media savvy, and they produced quantifiable results. In his book on culture and activism, *The Art of Protest,* Reed argues that "those of us who now see culture everywhere, even in the movements from earlier centuries, owe a great debt to groups like ACT UP, which have brilliantly highlighted the impossibility of fully separating cultural from political dimensions of movement activity."[22] Indeed, in most contemporary accounts of political activism, commentators explicitly cite ACT UP as pioneering a new type of protest, so that all subsequent groups must be understood as post–ACT UP, benefiting from the tools developed by their predecessors. As Claudia Orenstein puts it, while '60s era groups, like the San Francisco Mime Troupe, invested in developing grassroots culture and kept to noncommercial media and messages, "the generation of activists since ACT UP, however, are media savvy and use the press to advance their own cause, working for short-term, immediate solutions to problems rather than holding out for outright revolution."[23] Designing protest events to capitalize on their media appeal is no longer a novel strategy; it seems to be the only option.

THE CONTEMPORARY BACKGROUND

If we are to define contemporary activists by their media savvyness, this cannot be conceptualized as a static state. In the relatively short period since ACT UP first made a name for itself, the media universe has continued to evolve at a rapid rate, particularly with respect to the internet and other digital technologies. The ease and speed with which people can connect with one another has had an enormous impact on protest culture around the world, as like-minded strangers can easily form global networks and word of an event can spread almost instantaneously. Among other changes, these shifts have led to a new emphasis on creative, do-it-yourself (DIY) activism, or what Andrew Boyd refers to as "viral"[24] protest models combined with broad coalition organizing. These newly developing forces made an important appearance at the 1997 Asia Pacific Economic Cooperation (APEC) conference in Vancouver, when a variety of groups worked to disrupt the conference through street protests, tent cities, mock war-crimes trials, and puppet theater. In addition, one group printed and distributed thousands of copies of a fake version of a local paper, which contained parody news items critical of APEC members and policy, including an article about Nike CEO Phil Knight recruiting a dictators dream team (made up of leaders of the countries in which Nike had sweatshops) to endorse his shoes.[25]

These forces were made spectacularly apparent to the world on November 30, 1999, during the World Trade Organization convention in Seattle. In what has come to be known as the Battle of Seattle, tens of thousands of protesters took to the streets of that city to block delegates from entering the convention center, forcing the conference to shut down for a day and temporarily occupying the city's downtown core. Simultaneously, a virtual sit-in was taking place on the WTO website, meaning that "hactivists" were coordinating thousands of hits on the website, causing the server to be virtually blockaded by the increased traffic while, at the same time, alternative media networks relayed footage of the street protests around the world as they unfolded. The event's success surprised almost everyone, suddenly making apparent the sheer numbers of people opposed to the neo-liberal policies of global organizations like the WTO. As Benjamin Shepard and Ronald Hayduk put it, "[W]hile ACT UP's work embodied the ethos of the new social movements, 'the Battle of Seattle' marked the culmination of that decade's activism."[26] It has also set the stage for subsequent actions.

The event was remarkable not simply for its scale, but also for its breadth. Widely encapsulated in descriptions of the "teamsters and turtles," referring to the presence of both union labor and environmental activists dressed as sea turtles, the protests were attended by an enormous array of smaller, diverse activist and interest groups, many of which had little in common except the shared goal to shut down the WTO. As Reed explains, "[I]t proved a pivotal moment both in the terms of strengthening connections among the component groups of the actions, and in the protesters' use of new media to spread the word about what had occurred in the Emerald City. For U.S. activists it also proved a key step in moving beyond so-called identity politics."[27] From this perspective, Seattle demonstrated the potential power of strategic coalitions, bringing highly diverse interests together without allowing a particular group's dogma to dominate, thus presenting a loosely unified front as a broad global justice movement. On the flip-side, this same element has also led to widespread critiques of the movement's lack of clarity, as no easily quotable message emerged from the media's coverage of the protest. Indeed, as Andrew Boyd points out, "the mainstream media characterized the new movement as chaotic, superficial, self-indulgent, and faddish. As seen through the media our demands were a jumbled laundry list; we were against everything without knowing what we were for."[28] This PR problem has since been met with varied responses and proposed solutions from within. Naomi Klein (who has achieved near-legendary status as an anti-globalization pundit), however, defends the patchwork quality of the new activism, making the argument that it has developed in the image of the internet itself:

> Thanks to the Net, mobilizations are able to unfold with sparse bureaucracy and minimal hierarchy; forced consensus and labored manifestos are fading into the background, replaced instead by a culture of constant, loosely structured, and sometimes compulsive information-swapping. What emerged on the streets of Seattle and Washington was an activist model that mirrors the organic, decentralized interlinked pathways of the Internet—the Internet come to life.[29]

The question of how to move forward from the high point of Seattle's show of people power, while coming to terms with the strengths and weaknesses of the new forms of communication and organization, remain ongoing issues for twenty-first-century activists.

What seems clear is that these looser structures have allowed for a type of activism that is characterized by both accessibility and creativity. Indeed, the ethos of many contemporary groups, including those of our case studies, is explicitly do-it-yourself, organized around openly participatory methods and a belief that "new movements don't need charismatic leaders; any small group of people can create change themselves."[30] For many, it also involves a carnivalesque sense of pleasure amid transgression, an element that is crucial for the ironic activists. Here, the popular Reclaim the Streets (RTS) groups offer a good illustration. The first RTS group came together in England in the mid-'90s in response to the city of London's seizure of a particular street (Claremont Road) and eviction of the residents to make way for a highway. Protesters barricaded and occupied the street, setting up living rooms and cafes in the road, creating art installations and billboards, partying to rave music, and erecting tunnels and bunkers in the abandoned houses, significantly delaying the demolition and attracting a great deal of attention to the issue.

After the eventual removal of each protester, the group re-formed around the idea of temporarily reclaiming London streets from the car-based culture and adapting them for their own use. Group members pioneered a model that spread to cities around the world in which a large mass of people suddenly descends on a particular street, often initially blocking traffic by erecting a tall tripod with a person on top (who would be seriously injured if the structure were knocked down), followed by the quick setup of a portable sound system and the creation of a dance party in the middle of the road. Individual permutations have involved any number of spectacular additions, such as giant puppets, stilt walkers, temporary kiddie pools and beaches, and snacks passed out to the drivers now stuck in the ensuing traffic jam. The DIY model is relatively easy to replicate, and coordinated RTS actions were soon happening in a multitude of countries simultaneously. Writing specifically about RTS, John Jordan argues: "[I]nspired by and following in the footsteps of the protest movements and countercultures of the '60s, '70s and '80s, the DIY protest movement is finally breaking down the barriers between art and protest."[31] The more individual and quirky presences that are contributed to the event, the better.

As Boyd points out, "[B]y the time of the WTO meeting in Seattle, RTS-style protest had taken hold of the activist imagination."[32] The event drew on a similar street-carnival model in which individuals could bring their own creative interventions to the party while still working toward a common political goal. As Reed describes it, "[T]he streets were filled not only with the ubiquitous sea turtles but dancing Santas, jugglers, stilt-walkers, fire-eaters, clowns, drag queens and kings, wood nymphs, Statues of Liberty with 'Stop the WTO' pins, thirty-foot-tall puppets, and self-described 'radikal cheerleaders' chanting jingles like 'Ho, Ho, Ho, the WTO's got to GO!'"[33]

It is against this larger background, both pre- and post-Seattle, that the activist groups profiled in this chapter have developed, drawing on a spectacularly creative, self-organized, easily imitatable, playful form and, as I will argue, more often than not relying on irony and satire as the attention-getting hook. As Boyd puts it: "Before Seattle, irony had the better of us; now we had the better of it. We were neither nostalgic nor snide. We had achieved a new attitude—sly and mischievous, yet full of hope for the future."[34]

CULTURE JAMMING

When discussing the use of irony in contemporary activism and oppositional culture, the first concept one must grapple with is the idea of culture jamming, which has become a sort of countercultural buzzword. Very similar to the Situationists' practice of *détournement* (which is often specifically referenced as inspiration or as part of the wider jamming legacy in the seminal texts and manifestos), *culture jamming* roughly refers to the repurposing, deconstructing, or hijacking of mass culture, using the media as a means to critique the media. The term was first coined by the band Negativland, which has become known since the late 1980s for cutting up songs and subverting their original meanings, for instance, using snippets of advertising jingles for Pepsi to disparage the product in an album titled *Dispepsi.* Cultural critic Mark Dery popularized the concept by theorizing its workings in a pamphlet titled "Culture Jamming," originally published in 1993. Dery argues that the purpose of culture jamming is to wage war against commodity culture and its colonization of the mass media—the tyranny of the "empire of signs."[35] Culture jamming, he believes, is a form of fighting back via semiological warfare. As he explains, culture jammers "introduce noise into the signal as it passes from transmitter to receiver, encouraging idiosyncratic, unintended interpretations. Intruding on the intruders, they invest ads, newscasts, and other media artifacts with subversive meanings; simultaneously, they decrypt them, rendering their seductions impotent."[36] As examples, he lists tactics like billboard banditry, subvertising, media hoaxing, and audio agit-prop.

It is the billboard work that has become synonymous with the concept of culture jamming, with organized groups, several of which existed prior to the introduction of the term *culture jamming,* making a name for themselves around the world. Examples include the BLF (Billboard Liberation Front) in San Francisco, BUGA UP (Billboard-Utilizing Graffitists against Unhealthy Promotions) in Australia, and ABBA (Anti-Billboard Brainwashing Action) in England. Members target large billboard advertisements in public spaces, altering them to convey different meanings than the originals. For instance, the BLF went after the Apple computer campaign that used pictures of historically important figures next to the slogan "Think Different," altering a billboard with the Dalai

Lama on it to read "Think Disillusioned." And, in 2002, in the midst of several corporate accounting scandals, they seized billboards reading "Business Intelligence. Now more than ever," changing the text to "Business Intelligence. No more than ever" and affixing the logos of Enron, Arthur Anderson, and Worldcom. The tone of these attacks varies widely among groups, from the outrightly polemical to the absurd, while aesthetic styles range from graffiti scrawls to slick computer-generated duplicates indistinguishable from the originals. Likewise, the ideology behind the tactics seems just as diverse. But, as Klein points out, most appear to be united in the belief "that free speech is meaningless if the commercial cacophony has risen to the point that no one can hear you."[37] Indeed, as the BLF ironically proclaims in its manifesto, its ultimate goal is a personal billboard for each citizen, but "until that glorious day for global communications when every man, woman and child can scream at or sing to the world in 100pt. type from their very own rooftop; until that day we will continue to do all in our power to encourage the masses to use any means possible to commandeer the existing media and to alter it to their own design."[38] The intent, then, is to speak back to the ads themselves.

A similar philosophy lies behind what Dery refers to as *subvertising,* the creation of parody ads or ads antithetical to consumer culture. Here, the magazine *Adbusters* (www.adbusters.org) has become the best-known practitioner. Rather than vandalize existing advertisements, it creates its own, using a visual language that mimics the products of any marketing agency. Looking like many other glossy magazines, the print version of *Adbusters* contains articles, essays, and activist information, as well as the slick ad parodies that have made it famous. For example, one ad mirrors the style of a popular Obsession perfume campaign, featuring a black-and-white photograph of a young, attractive man in his underwear, though in this version, the model is staring into his underpants. The logo "Obsession" and the words "for men" are emblazoned over his image. The Adbusters Media Foundation also created Buy Nothing Day, to be observed the day after Thanksgiving in the United States (the heaviest shopping day of the year), and it has created several commercials for the holiday that are regularly turned down by television stations.

There is nothing particularly new or cutting-edge about advertisement parody nor about viewing popular culture texts ironically; however, there is something about the concept of culture jamming that seems to have struck a resonant chord with younger generations. As Klein puts it, writing in the year 2000, "though culture jamming is an undercurrent that never dries up entirely, there is no doubt that for the last five years it has been in the midst of a revival, and one focused more on politics than on pranksterism."[39] Since we all exist within a media-saturated environment, one in which commercial jingles and slogans are primary facets of our shared culture, it is unsurprising that this same language is what many gravitate toward when crafting critiques of that culture. As Claudia Orenstein argues, precisely because the average individual is a highly sophisticated and skeptical viewer, "today's activists tend to favor the indirect means of ironic statement to the direct means of didacticism as a way of conveying their messages. Activists now need to master the use of technologies and advertising skills in order to compete with the mainstream media for the public's attention."[40] But this is also precisely where the potential weakness of culture jamming lies.

One of the critiques consistently leveled at subvertisers and billboard alterists is that they flirt so closely with corporate culture that they are either indistinguishable from that culture or are too easily co-opted by it. There are numerous examples of corporations producing their own pre-jammed advertisements. Trading on the hip edginess of culture jamming, they have created billboards that appear to have been already graffitied, or television commercials built around ironic anti-advertising slogans. Indeed, when one does a media search for the term *culture jamming,* many of the first instances of its usage in the mainstream press are in advertising and public relations industry publications. For instance, shortly after Kalle Lasn, founder of *Adbusters,* came out with his book *Culture Jam,* the magazine *Adweek* ran a piece on it in which the author assures her readers that "anti-consumers aren't the enemies of consumerism; they're its cutting edge."[41] She then goes on to list the qualities for which this particular demographic longs, including authenticity, individuality, and freedom of expression, concluding that Lasn has "tapped into the yearnings from which brand identities of the future—including Lasn's own—will be made."[42] That is not to say that advertisers have been entirely successful at swallowing and repackaging culture jamming, nor that they can so easily defang activists' rage over rampant consumerism and the branding of public space, but it is telling that the industry views the culture-jamming aesthetic as potentially another wing of its own house.

This happens to be particularly ironic in Lasn's case, as he is decidedly preachy about the revolutionary power of the culture-jamming movement: "[O]ur aim is to topple existing power structures and forge major adjustments to the way we will live in the twenty-first century."[43] He depicts culture jammers as media activists locked in battle against "The Corporate Cool Machine,"[44] arguing, "it is not inconceivable that the culture-jamming movement will be remembered by our grandchildren for having been one of the catalysts of the great planetary transformation that shook the world in the early years of the new millennium."[45] It is hyperbolic language such as this, of course, which can make culture jamming easy to dismiss. Lasn, in particular, foments against cultural homogenization, corporate wrongdoing, consumerism, and ecological destruction, among other issues, without clearly explaining how culture jamming can help to solve these problems. His targets appear diffuse or grandiose, while the proposed actions seem small. In Christine Harold's analysis of anti-corporate activism, she critiques *Adbusters* for being stuck in negative reaction, which encourages simply "saying no" to the seductions of consumer culture without affirming possible alternatives. The result, as she puts it, is that "the nay-sayer is, in essence, yoked in a dialectic tug-of-war with the rhetoric it negates,"[46] without offering a new locus for the desires the market currently seems to satisfy.

However, there are numerous other culture-jamming practices that draw from a similar spirit of playful, media-savvy, humorous critique, many of which reach beyond *Adbusters'* "asceticism."[47] The long-time group the Guerrilla Girls offers an interesting example. Cited by Dery in his examples of active culture jammers, the Guerrilla Girls also draw heavily on the lexicon of advertising, producing ironically playful texts in support of serious political aims. Founded in 1985, the group began by anonymously producing posters, stickers, and buttons designed to highlight discrimination in the art world, and they appeared in public only when disguised by gorilla masks. Famously, they created an ad featuring a female nude with a gorilla's head, which was placed on the side of city buses; the text read, "Do women have to be naked to get into the Met Museum?" and in smaller type, "Less than 5% of artists in the Modern Art sections, but 85% of the nudes are female."[48] Another poster listed the advantages of being a woman artist, including "working without the pressure of success," "seeing your ideas live on in the work of others," and "being included in revised versions of art history."[49] They have hung similar posters and stickers in the bathrooms of major museums, orchestrated humorous letter-writing campaigns, and sent ignominious awards to art critics, dealers, and gallery owners whom they believed deserved criticism. They have since branched out into other fields, going after Hollywood around the time of the 2003 Academy Awards, for instance, by buying billboard space in Los Angeles for a poster proclaiming, "Even the U.S. Senate is more progressive than Hollywood. Female Senators 14% Female Film Directors 4%," accompanied by an image of the Oscar statue's body with Senator Trent Lott's head.[50] Over the years, the group has generated an enormous amount of press, no doubt due to the entertaining quality of a group of gorillas with an irreverent sense of humor. Their ironic, tongue-in-cheek slogans are both catchy and easily understandable.

The Guerrilla Girls are a relatively early example, but there is now a burgeoning number of groups practicing a form of culture jamming organized around ironic political critique. Many tap directly into a spirit of carnivalesque pleasure amid transgression, much like Reclaim the Streets. Other examples include the proliferation of groups organizing pie-ings of morally suspect public figures, the current popularity of radical marching bands, and the antics of organizations like the Clandestine Insurgent Rebel Clown Army. All are gesturing toward the progressive versions of spectacle called for by Stephen Duncombe, displaying a politics that understands desire, fantasy, and pleasure.[51] It is within this growing movement of affect-based activism with a sense of humor that we find the specific tactic of identity nabbing.

For the Guerrilla Girls, anonymity is a strategy. Members wear gorilla masks for all public appearances and assume the names of dead female artists for interviews. Not only does the technique provide a humorously memorable group identity, it also serves to keep the focus on the group's issues rather than on particular personalities or biographies. Other contemporary activist groups, though, have taken this strategy a step further, not simply letting go of their own personal identities, but actively taking on the identities of their enemies. It is a tactic which draws on irony as a means of reframing (or rebranding) political opponents, while it actively connects to those who already share many of the group's values, entertaining and engaging those potential allies. Identity nabbing can be seen as part of the larger culture-jamming project, but it is an incarnation that is aimed specifically at co-participatory communication between ironist and audience.

THE IDENTITY NAB

Billionaires for Bush provide a good illustration of the identity nab. Originally titled "Billionaires for Bush (or Gore)," the concept was developed in the lead-up to the U.S. presidential election of 2000 in order to draw attention to the influence of big money on politics. After Bush won the presidency, the Billionaires focused on the policies of his administration that they believed were good for the wealthy but bad for everyone else and actively worked against his reelection in 2004. Their formula was fairly straightforward; members dressed up in tuxedos and top hats, fake furs and evening gowns, and assumed ironic fake names such as Meg A. Bucks, Tex Shelter, or Ava Rice. In their original incarnation, they created candidate product comparison charts and campaign contribution return-on-your-investment analyses and appeared at events with signs reading "We're Paying for America's Free Elections So You Don't Have To" and "Free the Forbes 400."[52] Later slogans included "Leave No Billionaire Behind," "Make Social Security Neither," and "Tax Work Not Wealth."[53] Typically, members of the group appeared at Republican campaign rallies or Bush policy speeches, showing up to ostensibly thank him for not pandering to the special interests of everyday Americans, or at anti-Bush events as feigned counterdemonstrators. They also organized their own functions, such as greeting citizens at post offices around the country on April 15 to thank them for paying the Billionaires' taxes and celebrating "Cheney Is Innocent!" day to support him for overseeing "Enron-style accounting" while managing the Halliburton company.[54] Local chapters of the Billionaires organized the Million Billionaire March, an auction of the Liberty Bell, and vigils for corporate welfare, as well as stunts like listing Social Security for sale on the internet auction site eBay.

Part of their strategy was what Carol Burbank refers to as "othering the opposition,"[55] marking one's enemies with essentialist, larger-than-life accusations. Billionaires for Bush tried to actively link images of corporate greed and vast wealth disparities with particular politicians. The aim was to reframe the terms of political debate. If campaign financing,

5.1. Billionaires for Bush during a tax day event. *Photo courtesy Fred Askew*

ties to particular corporations, or budget deficits were not primary topics within mainstream reportage (or were being inadequately framed), the Billionaires attempted to reinsert them into public dialogue via media coverage of the group's appearances. They worked hard to emphasize the communication of concrete facts within the formula they developed: for instance, the precise amount of money donated to the Bush campaign from Enron's Ken Lay. The Billionaires' "Do-It-Yourself Manual" instructs potential Billionaires to "use irony as a Trojan horse"[56] to win attention, but to feel free to then step out of character to explain the message in plain terms, as clear communication of the issues is the ultimate goal.

The gimmick of the Billionaires' identity-nabbing technique was expressly developed with maximum media amplification of the issues in mind. Andrew Boyd, one of the original founders of the group, also known as Phil T. Rich, explains his thinking in terms of "viruses" and what he refers to as "meme warfare," arguing that "memes are media viruses that spread throughout the population. Think of urban legends, fleeting fashions, and idiotic ad slogans that work their way into everyday conversations; these are memes. But memes can also be used as a culture of resistance."[57] With this in mind, the intention behind the Billionaires for Bush model was "to create a humorous, ironic media campaign that would spread like a virus via grassroots activists and the mainstream media."[58] The formula was deliberately easy to follow. Anyone wishing to start up their own Billionaires chapter was encouraged to do so; the website provided downloadable templates for signs and suggestions for slogans, costuming, and major talking points. The idea was to create an easy, do-it-yourself model that could accommodate local inventiveness while still ensuring that everyone would remain relatively on-message.

The concept has proven to be remarkably resilient and appealing, even after the end of the Bush presidency, and the model has been adapted to attack other targets, as in the case of the Billionaires for Tar Sands group protesting the environmental impacts of processing oil in the Alberta, Canada, tar sands. In late 2009, amid the vocal town-hall discussions of the Obama administration's health care proposal, groups referring to themselves as Billionaires against Health and later as Billionaires for Wealthcare began showing up at the protests, ostensibly in support of the anti-reform element, relying on the same formula for costuming, stage names, and ironic messaging. Much like many of ACT UP's stunts, the group's concept creates a much more interesting angle for reporters than simply relaying the number of protesters present at a particular event, and, as Boyd argues in reference to some of their initial outings, "content and humor were tightly meshed. Not only did the humor help carry the content (in the way that laughter makes it easier to bear the truth), but if the media wanted the humor (and they did), they had to take the content too."[59] While the media can report on the Billionaires' presence at an event with factual neutrality or detached amusement, the critique is still implicit.

The ironic identity-nabbing technique sets up a unique relationship between activists and audiences, so that, for people to find the joke amusing and worth repeating, or worthy of reportage, they must participate in the meaning-making process, sharing in many of the group's assumptions. In other words, they must take part in the co-participatory construction of the event. As Duncombe writes about his experience dressing up as part of the Loan Sharks (at International Monetary Fund events), Billionaires for Bush, and Students for an Undemocratic Society, irony served as a tool for participation and interaction, but "irony only works

5.2. Billionaires for Bush adapted their formula to intervene in the health care debate, becoming Billionaires for Wealthcare. *Photo courtesy Ruth Robertson*

in so far as people 'get it,' actively constructing a counter message and idea in their own mind. In other words, we were creating a symbol of the world that we wanted to create, but one that only appeared if other people entered into our joke."[60] Part of the attraction for onlookers is the feeling that they are in on the joke when they understand the unsaid meaning.

As Baz Kershaw explains about radical performance (referring specifically to 1960s and '70s groups in Britain), the indirect attack of "satiric irony" allows for the liberating energies of carnivalesque humor to meet the didacticism of agit-prop theater.[61] Likewise, the Billionaires' irony offers the pleasures of masquerade, mockery, and hierarchy inversions combined with a pointed political critique. However, I do not think the Billionaires have succeeded in winning over many Republicans, nor should they have necessarily. Rather, as with the filmmakers profiled in the last chapter, they attempt to reframe the public debate, pushing issues that may be peripheral to the dominant into the public sphere and politicizing those who may already share many of their assumptions. As Orenstein writes about groups like Billionaires for Bush, "[F]or most people, the lesson is not so much news as a reminder or an affirmation of what they already suspect. For this reason the name alone elicits laughter and, with the precision of any media campaign, succinctly sums up the whole concept and the political critique embedded in it."[62] For those familiar with the criticism that the Bush administration was in the pocket of big-money interests (or that the current health care system works primarily to the benefit of the wealthy), it was (and is) easy to discern the intended, unsaid meaning of the Billionaires' ironic posturing. The political point is clearly targeted, while the clever humor provides a satisfying wink to the audience. Much as with the parodic news shows and satiric documentaries, the aim is to communicate with existing discursive communities that get the joke and appreciate the critique, while amplifying that critique via the mass media.

This idea gets more complicated, however, when the irony employed is so subtle or the identity nab so convincing that the audience becomes entirely taken in. Here, the group known as the Yes Men provide a particularly interesting example in that they deliberately court confusion, attempting to truly "pass" in their assumed identities. The group developed out of ®™ark (or RTMark), a "brokerage" firm that trades in corporate subversion, linking to prank ideas on its website and encouraging those with funds to support the stunts to meet up with others who have the ability to carry them out. The Yes Men project began with parody websites: www.GWBush.com, which mirrored George W. Bush's official site (www.GeorgeWBush.com) while he was ramping up his first campaign for president, and www.GATT.org, which mimicked the World Trade Organization's home page and was developed in the lead-up to the Seattle meeting (the former site is no longer active, but the latter is). Both were sophisticated parodies that almost identically copied the originals. Rather than presenting themselves as obvious or over-the-top spoofs, these sites employed language that, for the most part, could plausibly be found on the legitimate webpages. However, the content was dryly satiric, so that the shadow Bush site, for instance, highlighted such benchmarks from his tenure as governor of Texas as the state's decline to the most polluted in the nation,[63] while the WTO site contained a similarly critical account of the organization's philosophy. To the surprise of the sites' creators, they were contacted by officials from other organizations who had not noticed that the WTO site was a fake, and they were invited (as WTO employees) to speak at several international conferences.

Mike Bonanno and Andy Bichlbaum (both pseudonyms) then began publicly speaking on behalf of the WTO, making presentations that they felt more honestly represented the organization, many of which are chronicled in a documentary and book, both titled *The Yes Men*. Later stunts are relayed in a second documentary, *The Yes Men Fix the World*, which was released in 2009. At their first conference on international trade, for example, Bichlbaum lectured on trade regulation relaxation, explaining why the European Union was endangering competition by striving to keep "violent bananas" grown in oppressive conditions out of their market and later concluding with an endorsement for a system called a "vote auction," in which voters may voluntarily auction their votes to the highest bidder.[64] Shortly thereafter, they seized on an opportunity to represent the WTO in a televised debate on CNBC in the lead-up to the 2001 G-8 summit in Genoa. In the interview, Bichlbaum (as the fictional Granwyth Hulatberi) ostensibly defends global trade practices in light of the widely anticipated protests surrounding the summit. When questioned on the protesters' argument that international trade policies have led to increasing global inequality, he replies that the protesters "are simply too focused on reality, and on facts and figures. There's an enormous number of experts at all the greatest universities in the world, who have read all these books, who have read Adam Smith and everything since it to Milton Friedman, and these people have [a] solid theoretical basis for knowing that things will lead to betterment."[65]

While groups like Billionaires for Bush do take on false personas, perhaps encouraging some initial confusion over who they are, the over-the-top slogans and blunt language the group employs are intended to be read wholly ironically. The Yes Men, on the other hand, are more slippery, deliberately courting confusion and even flirting with fraud. They call their technique "identity correction," which they explain is what happens when "honest people impersonate big time criminals in order to publicly humiliate them."[66] Their belief is that they are merely taking their adversaries' positions to their logical extreme, pushing the neo-liberal market philosophy of the WTO, for example, only slightly further than the organization itself. In an interview, Frank Guerrero (the RTMark pseudonym for the person also known as Mike Bonanno) explains:

> The Yes Men use affirmation to make their point. It is an unusual rhetorical strategy, almost a reverse-psychology approach. Instead of debating their opponents, they assume their opponents' identities and enthusiastically affirm their adversaries' beliefs. It's an unorthodox approach, but hardly new

> or original. In fact, I think something like Swift's "Modest Proposal" also falls into this category, in a sense.[67]

Though there is clearly a link between the Yes Men's practices and Swift's satiric proposals, the difference is that the Yes Men appear in public in their assumed identities (more like Stephen Colbert), directly confronting their audiences with what they believe to be wildly offensive ideas. The intent is both to confuse and to enrage. In interview after interview, they explain that they hope to make people question the rhetoric used by real officials with real power and to take a closer look at the philosophy underlying official actions.

To their surprise, however, it ends up being much harder to shake people up than they expected. They report crafting their presentations to be patently ridiculous, expecting their audience to be enraged by their suggestions, only no one seemed to find anything wrong with them. In response, they raised the absurdity level, even creating a presentation for a textiles conference in Finland that involved the debut of a gold lamé "management leisure suit," complete with an inflatable phallus with a television screen at the end of it with which to monitor workers. When this still failed to rankle fellow conference-goers, they began following stunts with press releases, receiving significant media attention after the fact (publicity also later surrounded the release of the documentaries chronicling these pranks). They also adjusted their tactics somewhat. For instance, in 2004, on the twentieth anniversary of the Union Carbide explosion in Bhopal, India, they appeared in an on-camera interview with the BBC as representatives of Dow Chemical (after media inquiries to another fake website). Instead of actively making Dow look reprehensible, they took the opportunity to announce that, after 20 years of denying responsibility, Dow would liquidate Union Carbide and spend the money to clean up the site and compensate the victims. Of course, Dow was doing no such thing, but the company took two hours to retract the story, attracting a flurry of media reports, which brought the almost forgotten issue back under scrutiny.

Much of the British press, in particular, castigated the group for falsely raising the hopes of the Bhopal victims, arguing that, while the stunt may have been funny on paper, it was "not so funny for those Indians who, for several hours, believed that 20 years of mistreatment and

5.3. One of the Yes Men falsely speaking on behalf of Dow Chemical and officially taking responsibility for the Bhopal plant disaster. The Yes Men Fix the World *(2009)*

suffering were coming to an end."[68] The Yes Men argued, however, that their aim was to push the Bhopal disaster and the ongoing environmental contamination back into the news, explaining, "In getting the news to these folks, we succeeded wonderfully: hundreds of articles about the event made it into the U.S. press, whereas on most anniversaries of the accident, it hasn't even found its way into *one* mainstream source."[69] For the Yes Men, public discussion (or at least acknowledgment) of the issue is what matters most, and while the statements they made toward that end were false, they argued that the denials of culpability and the public relations screen Dow had used for 20 years were more pernicious. Much like the parodic news shows and satiric documentaries, stunts such as the Yes Men's seem to deliberately straddle the line between satire and political dialogue, art and activism, creatively attempting to influence the direction of public discourse, even if that involves a level of fraud. And while I have argued that the performers of the last chapters are becoming more like political pundits, these activists are edging closer toward the territory of professional entertainers, albeit in the service of serious aims.

Hutcheon warns of the potential dangers inherent in the use of irony, in that it can easily backfire. She explains, "[T]hose whom you oppose might attribute no irony and simply take you at your word; or they might make irony happen and thus accuse you of being self-negating, if not self-contradicting. Those with whom you agree (and who know your position) might also attribute no irony and mistake you for advocating what you are in fact criticizing."[70] The Yes Men, it seems, found themselves falling prey to these traps, but have hit upon a method of using the pitfalls to their advantage, allowing audiences to read them seriously and then exposing them for being complicit with the offensive ideas put forward. In hindsight, the irony is much more obvious, meaning either that those present at the live event appear morally unscrupulous or that the media is spurred to engage in reflection about why they were taken in. More important, the revealed hoaxes speak to a growing number of fans who take delight in witnessing organizations and corporations of which they are already critical be publicly pranked, again providing affirmation for existing discursive communities.

INVISIBLE THEATER AND POLITICAL SIMULACRA

The performances of the Yes Men at conferences or in television interviews function as what Jean Baudrillard would call "simulacra": copies of copies with no original. The pair do not impersonate real officials nor attempt to caricature specific mannerisms. Instead, they simply mimic a generalized performance of power and authority, "substituting signs of the real for the real itself."[71] No one challenges their authenticity or hardly ever questions their ridiculous presentations because they have reproduced the signs of officialdom: a clean business suit, a conservative haircut, an air of gravitas and knowledge, and a practiced power-point presentation. It is important to note that, much like for the parodic news hosts, this performance is possible for them because they are both recognizably white, male, and middle class, and therefore not out of context at international conferences or as television spokespeople. One cannot underestimate the power their social positioning already affords them, but they also work to funnel that advantage into the production of the signs of knowledge and authority (many of the same signs that real WTO or Dow Chemical officials would employ), deliberately engaging with the hyper-real.

Interestingly, while Baudrillard characterizes the rise of simulacra as profoundly anti-political, working to conceal and naturalize the lack of a real, the Yes Men create simulacra in the pursuit of distinctly political aims, precisely to reveal that lack. Baudrillard points to attractions like Disneyland, in particular, as functioning to hide the ubiquity of simulacra, arguing, "Disneyland is there to conceal the fact that it is the 'real' country, all of 'real' America, which *is* Disneyland. . . . Disneyland is presented as imaginary in order to make us believe that the rest is real, when in fact all of Los Angeles and the America surrounding it are no longer real, but of the order of the hyperreal and of simulation."[72] Conversely, the Yes Men attempt to draw attention to the fact that legitimacy is routinely granted to men with business suits and fancy titles, whether their ideas are sound or not, so that their status is predicated solely on these signs of power. The Yes Men's aim, then, is to draw scrutiny to the system. The end goal, however, is not to prove the nihilist's version of Baudrillard's theories, to demonstrate that no one is believable or that nothing is more or less true than anything else; rather, it is to encourage evaluation. They argue, "[M]any, many people, regardless of education, are easy prey for the ideas of the corporate decision-makers. Present them with a decision, they will accept it! This is why it is important for citizens to decide what sorts of corporate decisions are and are not acceptable. It is never possible to count on the highly educated to filter the okay from the rotten."[73] Having discovered that it was nearly impossible to offend their immediate audiences with what they believed to be examples of free-market fanaticism taken to grotesque extremes, their method now involves shaming those present and drawing attention to their issues through public reveals of the hoax, sending out their own press releases to drum up publicity. While they deliberately court confusion (not normally the most productive way to make a political point), they rely on the breach of expectations and protocol to generate its own explanations and narrative, ensuring the story's longevity through mediatized controversy. And it is through the subsequent media coverage that they are able to reach their most important audience, not the bored conference participants, but those out there who already share some of the Yes Men's assumptions and basic moral outlook.

In her discussion of pranking, Harold argues that the strategy is more successful than that of an organization like *Adbusters,* which seeks primarily to negate, because pranks instead work through amplification and appropriation. Further, she argues, pranks don't depend on the "aha" moment when the audience becomes conscious of a new reality. Though some pranks are followed by explanations, in her opinion, they have nothing to do with the prank itself, and they may even "dilute the rhetorical power of pranks to confuse and provoke. In other words, attaching an explicit argument or making a prank make sense may undermine what is unique about pranking's asignifying rhetoric in the first place."[74] While I agree that the cleverness of a prank can obviate the need for direct didacticism, I would argue that if it is to have any political or rhetorical effect, a prank must imply some moderately clear critique and must indeed flatter its potentially sympathetic audience with the pleasure of getting it, whether we characterize that as an "aha" moment or not. Taking the position that pranks don't necessarily have to be easily understandable leads one back to the presumption that irony and satire are ultimately a smirking step outside of the political and thus encourage cynicism. Rather, if it is a self-consciously oppositional action (which the pranks of a group like the Yes Men always are), it is implicitly attempting to speak to others within particular discursive communities who will appreciate the critique and who will want to continue circulating its discourse, thereby becoming part of an active counterpublic. While the nuance of what exactly the ironic statement is can certainly depend somewhat on individual readings, the prank must have some fairly clear critical content built into it or risk being nothing more than an exercise in art-student narcissism.

Baudrillard has argued that true "resistance" to the dominant order is nearly impossible, particularly through the mass media, which offer only a one-way flow of speech, meaning "transgression and subversion never get 'on the air' without being subtly negated as they are: transformed into models, neutralized into signs, they are eviscerated of their meaning."[75] However, he does point to graffiti as having an effect, as it interrupts the exchange between transmitter and receiver. Within these terms, we can conceptualize the Yes Men's brand of culture jamming as a type of graffiti in that they scrawl their own messages over those already existing in public space, not waiting for attention but instead crafting their own hijack. And it is precisely through the creation of simulacra that this is accomplished, as corporate public relations rhetoric is shaped into corporate condemnation. Similarly, the billboard alterists profiled earlier create simulacra of the simulacra produced by the advertising industry in an attempt to deconstruct that industry. While Baudrillard sees the proliferation of these copies with no original as self-obfuscating, here the self-conscious creation of simulacra functions as a form of critique. And, perhaps, in a world of simulacra, it is the only form of critique that is palatable. Rather than unhip moralizing, culture jamming of all types speaks the slick language of popular culture while ironically bending it to critical use. It is crucial, however, that this critique be legible if it is to reach a wider audience and to provoke discussion.

To that end, in producing staged scenes that are not immediately visible as staged, the Yes Men can also be seen as drawing on the technique of invisible theater developed by Augusto Boal, including his aim of sparking public debate. Beginning his work as a theater practitioner during a period of military rule in Brazil, Boal inherited from Brecht a concern for demonstrating that things could be different from the way they are, but he was equally interested in engaging spectators in the theatrical action. Rather than presenting the audience with a plot that had already been determined while allowing them to remain passive onlookers, he sought ways to engage the audience in developing solutions to the problems portrayed, empowering them to not only imagine change but to actually practice that change—to literally rehearse the revolution.[76] The concept of invisible theater is one of many techniques he developed, this one involving spectators who do not know they are witnessing a staged event. An example he gave is of a scene in a restaurant involving several planted customers, one of whom orders and eats an expensive steak. When it comes time to settle his bill, however, he announces that he is broke and can pay only with his labor, prompting an exchange about the high cost of the meal in comparison to the salaries of the restaurant employees. Other planted actors offer information about how much the person who takes out the garbage, for instance, makes and that the customer would have to work for 10 hours to buy the meal. The loud, public conversation encourages the others in the restaurant (who do not know that they are watching actors) to join in, coming to the support of the diner or of the restaurant or just whispering comments to their dinner companions, but somehow becoming engaged in considering the issue.

A successful invisible theater performance involves bringing together people who might not otherwise have had any interaction, but are suddenly united by an issue, which transforms them into a momentarily politicized collective. In a similar manner, the Yes Men orchestrate scenes in which only they know that they are following a script, inciting their audiences to recognize themselves in the issue and become involved, and attempting to evoke a critical collective response. As chronicled in their second documentary, for instance, the pair managed to get themselves a speaking engagement at a Gulf Coast reconstruction conference in New Orleans as representatives of the U.S. Department of Housing and Urban Development. To draw attention to the fact that HUD had been collaborating with private developers in tearing down public housing projects that had actually suffered no storm damage, they made the announcement (as Mayor Ray Nagin looked on in surprise) that they would be reversing course. The new plan, they reported, would be to immediately allow former residents to return to the units, while also providing increased money for health clinics and local schools to help the communities thrive. Though the hoax was soon discovered, the intent was to momentarily raise expectations as a way of attracting attention to HUD's real-world policies and to get people collectively questioning the philosophy underlying them. The difference from Boal becomes one of scale when the Yes Men manage to achieve mass media engagement, ideally sparking discussion on a national or international level, reminding individuals that they share opinions, beliefs, and even senses of humor with many others.

It is this goal of fostering discussion and engagement that links these groups and to which the identity-nabbing tactic is aimed. However, the technique need not be used exclusively to other the opposition or lampoon their position. The performance artist/activist known as Reverend Billy, for instance, has a more complex relationship to the character he assumes, borrowing some of that figure's genuine allure while still assuming an ironic distance. Bill Talen has created the persona of Reverend Billy, complete with bouffant hairdo, booming voice, and Jimmy Swaggart bravado, who presides over what was originally the Church of Stop Shopping, now the Church of Life after Shopping. Talen began the act by taking up residence among the other sidewalk preachers on a street corner in Times Square in New York City as Mayor Rudolph Giuliani was transforming the area into a more tourist-friendly shopping space. Talen started out preaching about the impending "shopocalypse" across the street from the Disney store, which he saw as emblematic of the destruction of real public space in the United States and its colonization by ersatz

5.4. Reverend Billy and his choir on the sidewalk in front of a chain store. What Would Jesus Buy? *(2007)*

consumer culture. As the Reverend Billy character developed, he began recruiting others and designing incursions into the store itself. Talen also produced more traditional theatrical performances starring the character, developed a committed following and, eventually, a full choir, and now uses the persona and his congregation for actions directed against corporations like Walmart, Starbucks, and the Disney store, as well as in campaigns to rescue community gardens and other public landmarks in New York. They also conduct workshops, lectures, gospel concerts, live videocasts, public confessions, and revivals, and they are the subject of a documentary (produced by Morgan Spurlock) about consumerism, globalization, and the commercialization of Christmas called *What Would Jesus Buy?* (2007). In all, Talen preaches the gospel of less consumption, accompanied by enthusiastic "Amens" and "Hallelujahs" from his flock.

The retail actions are frequently structured as a form of invisible theater. For instance, in one early Disney store incursion, he coordinated what he calls a "Cell Phone Opera."[77] A group of other actor-volunteers accompanied him into the store, each with a predetermined backstory about why he or she was there and what toy he or she was planning on purchasing. Each participant, however, was to have a change of heart about the purchase, seeming to call someone else on a cell phone to have an argument about the issue. Within the store, then, individual conversations began to overlap with one another, growing in volume as participants shouted, "I will not buy this for Danny! I'll tell you why! I won't get this sweatshop tchotchke," and "This is not Pooka's idea of New York! This is not New York! Minnie Mouse with a torch."[78] As the store's security guards began to catch on, Talen revealed his reverend's costume and began to preach about the evils of consumerism. While he was being hustled out of the store by the police, the other participants then hid tape recorders among the merchandise that played statements made by sweatshop workers about the Disney company.

Actions such as these are designed to catch the attention of others in the store and to, at first, appear plausibly spontaneous, drawing bystanders into the unfolding scene (and buying the group time before their eventual eviction). Similar to the Yes Men, Talen aims to entice those around him into thinking about their everyday habits and trusted brand names politically and to generate collective anger, explaining, "Victoria's Secret is still not associated with clear-cutting virgin forests. Starbucks still insists it has nothing to do with employing 7 year olds. These companies have far more exposure from their famous ads than from the damning research that watchdog groups have on their websites. So then with these Devils, education becomes more important."[79] And he has chosen an ironic character through which to engage his audience, an over-the-top preacher who seems to have stepped out of a television screen. Because he is an unreal, semi-comedic character, it is somehow more permissible for him to rant and rave in public. Much like Moore's and Spurlock's on-screen personas, Reverend Billy allows Talen to take his convictions to almost grotesque extremes, both amusing and inspiring those around him. As he puts it, he is the "politicized fool."[80] And it is the fool who can most easily make us look at our world with fresh eyes.

IRONIC AUTHENTICITY

Without a doubt, the performative power of Reverend Billy makes what Talen has to say compelling. In his writing (he has authored two books, slipping in and out of character), he comes across as, well, preachy. Like Kalle Lasn's, his diatribes seem didactic and overwrought. In live performance as Reverend Billy, however, he is saved from many of these excesses through the distance that his ironic character affords him, an element that is difficult to translate into writing. This form of embodied irony is the key to the character's power, allowing him to tailor his act to the particular situation at hand and to respond to the momentary reactions of his audience. As Reverend Billy, Talen manages to be both playful and serious at the same time. In fact, Talen's preacher persona nicely throws the use of activist irony into relief. Though it could appear at first glance that he is simply mocking evangelist preachers and religiosity in general, this is far from the case. All of the journalists and commentators who have profiled Reverend Billy remark on the real passion he summons forth in his flock. A parodic send-up of a preacher such as one would find on *Saturday Night Live* would never attract the dedicated followers that Talen has.

Like the parodic news hosts, Reverend Billy is both not a preacher and not not a preacher. As Jonathan Kalb describes it:

> Flooding the halls he performs in with an astonishing torrent of righteous words about the spell of consumer narcosis, he ends up offering hundreds of hard-core artsy skeptics (often in their twenties) their first chance ever to shout "Hallelujah!" and engage in Pentecostal call-and-response. In so doing, they find themselves possessed of a precious community that is not accessed via flickering screens, as well as a delightful channel for various inchoate angers that he has done them the service of naming. Just as a placebo is sometimes more effective than medicine, a phony preacher is sometimes more comforting and inspiring than a real one.[81]

Reverend Billy preaches with genuine emotion and conviction, momentarily co-opting the real power that the preacher figure exerts, allowing everyone else to also get caught up in his fervor, but still maintaining a safely ironic gap. In the *What Would Jesus Buy?* documentary, there is a striking scene in which Billy performs what appears to be an impromptu baptism in a Staples store parking lot; Billy, his choir, and the baby's father become genuinely, strangely, touchingly engrossed in imbuing the baby with their hopes for a less commercialized future. Similarly, Talen recounts a revival he held to save Edgar Allan Poe's house from demolition: "[T]he impromptu sermon was working. I was repeating a single phrase five times and a congregation of ironists was shouting 'Amen' back, a knowing response that contained both parody and the hope that we would soon transcend it."[82] Here, the irony is not simply in the service of ridicule or a snarky superiority; rather, there is a more complicated form

5.5. Reverend Billy conducting an impromptu baptism in a strip mall parking lot. What Would Jesus Buy? *(2007)*

of play involved, one that is deeply dependent on a discursive community willing to participate in creating the ironic reality together.

The popularity of the Reverend Billy character provides an excellent case study for contemplating audiences' attraction to modes of communication like irony, parody, and satire. There is no doubt that all of the groups profiled here are politically left of center. As noted in the introductory chapter, there is almost certainly an issue of taste publics at play. On Reverend Billy's home turf of New York, in particular, there is a preponderance of young, hip liberals who tend to be wary of traditional systems of morality, but who would likely feel relatively at home with a savvy, self-referential, ironic sense of humor. A figure like Reverend Billy perfectly plays into this sensibility. As he describes it, the group does not believe in a continuous God:

> I myself am a straight white male, and history shows that I'm the last person to trust with a continuous, enthroned God. After a month of the same God I'd start shouting at the neighbors. After six months my tank's in your front yard. So we went around sampling gods. It took a while, but finally we found the god-goddess of an Egyptian Gnostic sect who believed in a new god every day. They said, "I wake up and know that today I will duet with the mystery, and we will make God together." Yes, the portable, renewable Supreme Being. Sounds much safer.[83]

Reverend Billy's church offers the chance to pick and choose the elements of religion that one likes (perhaps qualities like community, spirituality, and a higher truth), while remaining distrustful of organized religion and power. As the reverend proclaims, they strive to "Put the odd back in God!"[84] And this irreverent reverence is then funneled into political actions, drawing on the energy of creative, do-it-yourself activism, providing the strength and inspiration of a like-minded community, or counterpublic, while forgoing rigid dogma. For a generation predisposed to read the world with a detached criticality and self-reflexivity, it is the perfect combination of passion and purpose tempered with a knowing wink.

Conversely, irony as a mode of political discourse is certainly not appreciated by everyone. More often than not, it seems to polarize the audience, potentially frustrating or even enraging those who do not appreciate the joke, those outside of the discursive community. For example, during a piece on Billionaires for Bush on National Public Radio, a reporter interviewed bystanders at a Bush fundraiser that had attracted protesters, including the Billionaires. One onlooker responded to a question about the group by saying, "I think they're making a mockery out of it and it's a joke, and it's pretty embarrassing. It's confusing to children and it's confusing to a couple of adults here as well. And I have more respect for the people over there who are saying what they happen to feel. They dress normally. They don't have to come in costume and have a gimmick."[85] This woman professed greater respect for the regular protesters who were not portraying characters, as they were saying what they meant, and she was hitting on one of the major pitfalls of ironic discourse: it is predicated on indirection, potentially frustrating its audience through a perceived dishonesty or inauthenticity. Those who are unwilling to meet these groups halfway in reading their performance ironically typically dismiss them as nonsensical or see them as actively offensive.

Additionally, as Larry Bogad points out about an Australian drag performer cum political candidate (Simon Hunt as Pauline Pantsdown) who parodied a serious prime ministerial candidate (Pauline Hanson), while the performer did do serious damage to the politician's campaign, possibly contributing to her loss of the election, Hunt also likely activated her supporters, "polarizing the North, stereotypically constructed as white, rural, and homophobic, against the stereotype of the urbane, queer-friendly, cosmopolitan South."[86] Bogad goes on to say, "[S]uch is the risk with any political cartoon, an art form that is by definition unfair."[87] Likewise, groups such as Billionaires for Bush actively mobilize stereotypes of the wealthy and politically powerful as greedy and uncaring, while quite likely fueling stereotypes of liberals as effete, inauthentic intellectual snobs. Indeed, as discussed in chapter 2, the use of irony can feed a form of in-group elitism. It is important to note, however, that the irony itself does not create divisions; rather, it plays on existing differences of temperament and belief in the attempt to bring those beliefs to the surface.

It is highly unlikely that any of these groups believe that they will be able to transform the opinions of many committed conservatives. Instead, they play to those who already follow their logic and who appreciate their ironically arched eyebrow. In other words, they rely on the existence of discursive communities. Reverend Billy, for instance, understands his potential congregants well and provides them with a welcome focal point for their existing sensibilities, beliefs, and yearnings, so that they are willing to engage both the said and unsaid meanings of his performances. Hutcheon argues against the idea that irony actively creates in-groups. Rather, she explains, "*it is discursive communities that are simultaneously inclusive and exclusive—not ironies.*"[88] Though I am in agreement that discursive communities precede the deployment of irony, I believe she ignores the issue of creating solidarities, neglecting the work that having one's assumptions confirmed by others does in building the feeling of community. Or, perhaps, this is simply where the concept of discursive communities diverges from that of publics and counterpublics. The mere existence of shared sensibilities does not a counterpublic make. It seems clear that activist groups that draw on irony do so at least partially to bring observers' attention to their shared understandings, fueling the sense of community in opposition. In other words, they work to transform existing discursive communities into actively politicized ones, relying on the co-participatory workings of irony to spur people into viewing themselves as a community with collective power. Here, too, is where the techniques of invisible theater are aimed, ideally functioning to make individual bystanders feel as if they are part of a group with shared beliefs and goals, to make them aware of all those others with whom they share opinions, and to feel empowered by that strength in numbers.

This speaks to the performative element of counterpublics that Warner lays out, or what he more frequently refers to as their poetic function, in that each individual text or performance strives to bring into being a public that not only shares its worldview but will continue to circulate its discourse. The activist groups profiled here attempt to turn shared understanding into sustained circulation and communication. Since we all live in many different discursive communities at once, the trick for activists, I would argue, is to privilege the importance of one particular community in one particular moment in time. When there are multiple competing demands on one's attention and allegiances, it is crucial that activists be able to make one's connections to a particular community of interest seem especially tangible and pressing, thereby ensuring the continued circulation of that community's discourse. Rather than seeing this as preaching to the converted, it might make more sense to think of it as reconverting the converted. As the Yes Men put it in referring to the aims of their second documentary, "[W]e do preach to the choir. It's like cheerleading. One of the functions of the film is to say, 'All is not lost. All we have to do is get active. All we have to do is get out of our seats and do something.'"[89]

This community-enhancing ability, aided by an existing cultural predilection and a media system hungry for anything with entertainment value, makes irony a particularly attractive mode for contemporary activists, leading many to seize on it as a potentially forceful "weapon of the weak."[90] Unlike the entertainers profiled in earlier chapters, these groups are markedly less powerful, with no ready platform from which to broadcast. Their use of irony is what Michel de Certeau would refer to as a "tactic."[91] He differentiates between "strategies," which are employed by power structures that have a place from which to generate relations with an external group, and "tactics," which, conversely, do not have a base from which to operate. Instead, "a tactic insinuates itself into the other's place, fragmentarily, without taking it over in its entirety."[92] Along these lines, Reverend Billy stages confusingly unstraightforward incursions into the regulated, corporate space of a Starbucks cafe, while Billionaires for Bush ironically applaud the Republican Party at its own events, and the Yes Men insinuate themselves into spaces reserved for legitimate power. Just as de Certeau uses the metaphor of walking in the city, the walker constantly subverting, in tiny ways, the rigidly structured spaces of the city, all of the activist groups profiled here speak in terms of taking back public space or public airwaves. The billboard-altering culture jammers battle the colonization of public space by corporate speech, Reverend Billy rages against the destruction of neighborhood communities, the Yes Men hijack information flows, and Reclaim the Streets temporarily seizes common spaces for radical play. Each draws on relatively accessible technologies—documentary film, parody websites, internet networking, and viral replication—exploiting loopholes in the technologies (like a Google search's inability to tell a parody site from an authentic one) and wresting them from their more corporate usages. Each subverts the seriousness of the dominant order, ironically reading against the grain and turning the humorless status quo into a lark.

None of the groups is aiming for outright revolution with these actions, and the concrete effect of any given prank or happening is often difficult to see. It is for this reason that many commentators dismiss them as being of little consequence. As one reviewer remarks of the Yes Men's first documentary, "[W]hatever Bonanno and Bichlbaum are up to, and it looks like enormous fun, it doesn't strike me as particularly effective satire," concluding that the WTO has stopped responding to their attacks, likely because "the WTO, and George W. Bush's corporate America generally, finds it rather easy to rise above such childish pranks, perceiving in them no threat to their values whatsoever."[93] But the ironic practitioners themselves would not argue that playful activism, pranking, and identity nabbing are enough in and of themselves to produce mass change, nor would they assume that, once the WTO has been publicly embarrassed, we can hang up the towel and go home. Rather, they are one piece of the activist puzzle. All of the groups chronicled here work closely with or have even developed out of more traditional organizations like United for a Fair Economy, Greenpeace, anti-sweatshop groups, and fair trade campaigns, and would readily affirm the importance of those organizations. However, where the ironic methods excel is in engaging an audience, attracting attention, and rallying support, all of which are integral in building political momentum.

It should also be noted that the building of community, even one in opposition to outside groups, is not incompatible with pushing the perspective of that community into the wider political imaginary. While these groups do very likely appeal most to those who already share some of their assumptions, they also attract media attention to the issues they care about, and they help to influence the terms of discussion. So, whether or not one was particularly interested in Dow Chemical's liability in the Bhopal explosion, one was far more likely to even hear about it in the wake of the Yes Men's BBC hoax. Like the filmmakers profiled in chapter 4, these groups are working to shift public discourse, to affect the way we conceptualize particular institutions and policies, and to inspire others to become politically engaged. Earnestness alone is perhaps no longer up to those tasks. Ironically, maybe, it is the mode of discourse most associated with detachment and obfuscation that is driving a new form of political energy and will.

SIX

Moving beyond Critique

Though they are distinctly different genres, parodic news shows, satiric documentaries, and ironic activist groups are all manifestations of similar impulses. There is no question that the three genres are linked to larger cultural trends, of which both viewers and practitioners are cognizant. As one reviewer for the first Yes Men documentary put it in reference to the film's potential appeal, "[T]his is the era of Bush-Kerry, *Jackass: The Movie,* The Corporation, *Super Size Me,* the *Onion* and of course Michael Moore (who even makes a cameo appearance in *The Yes Men*), which is to say an era in which things once considered commercial anathema—like politics, documentaries, and anti-corporate dissent—are bankable."[1] The popularity of each serves to fuel the momentum of all. It is not a coincidence that Andrew Boyd of Billionaires for Bush explicitly links the sensibility of his group with that of *The Daily Show* and Michael Moore, arguing that each incorporates an "ironic sensibility, which is a deep current in youth culture,"[2] nor that Mike Bonanno of ®™ark and the Yes Men argues that, like Michael Moore's, his work is built on communicating information that is otherwise not found in the American press.[3]

The three genres share a cluster of characteristics, the first being a generalized political dissent, as the critic quoted above points to. More specifically, they share a desire to make an end run around the standard conduits of political information and around the standard formulas within the mainstream media. While the parodic news shows critique the substance and tenor of the debates carried on mainstream news programming, a group like the Yes Men mimics the performance of power and expertise in order to draw critical attention to its core. All attempt to reframe the terms of discussion and/or to temporarily hijack the discussion out of the hands of authority. All irreverently question taken-for-granted attributions of rationality and where that rationality resides, claiming alternative forms of expertise. They aim not just to dissent but to shift the topics and terms of the debate, often attempting to undermine the power of the dominant narrative.

In addition to this desire to reframe political narratives, all share a pointedly comedic and improvisational mode. This involves a heightened sense of irony; highlighting contradictions, inconsistencies, and absurdities; mining them for their humor; and even highlighting their own flaws and fakeries. This mode also involves an emphasis on impromptu encounters between individuals. The dynamic, first-person frame not only sets these genres apart from many traditional forms of satire but also allows them to actively impact the world of political deliberation. The performers interact with public officials, draw real political issues into their own satiric frames, and usurp traditional authority. They are always potentially threatening to their targets in that their parodic send-ups, satiric attacks, and ironic impersonations run the risk of becoming definitively real—of actually tripping up, revealing, or sabotaging. As performative satire, these forms have the potential to bring into being precisely that which they name or enact.

That is not to say that the people and groups surveyed here are always equally successful in achieving their goals, that they necessarily share exactly the same goals, or that they all have an analogous effect. As Richard Schechner explains about all forms of performance, including ritual and theater, each individual example involves some combination of both efficacy and entertainment. The two qualities, he writes, "are not so much opposed to each other; rather they form the poles of a continuum,"[4] and no performance is entirely lacking in one or the other. Accordingly, these particular examples embody differing combinations of efficacy and entertainment. The parodic news shows, for example, must position themselves primarily as entertainment, attracting significant numbers of viewers for their networks and advertisers. They do certainly, as I have argued, contain political material, serving as spaces for critique of the inadequacies of contemporary political discourse, but they do not necessarily involve an active politics nor an organized call to action. Yet, due to their high profile and topical immediacy, they sometimes end up having a larger impact on the political discussion than do many of the other examples.

The documentaries are also objects of mass entertainment designed for market consumption, though they have a more developed mandate to educate, to inspire, and, most important, to create a sustained sense of community in opposition. Finally, the activist groups have political efficacy as their primary goal, but they employ entertaining techniques as a means of attracting notice and maintaining enthusiasm since they are by far the most marginal of the case studies. Since they do not have steady media amplification at their disposal, they seek to momentarily capture the attention of existing sympathetic communities and, in so doing, to turn these discursive communities into actively politicized ones.

Regardless of their respective mixes of efficacy and entertainment, however, these genres and their practitioners have all succeeded to differing degrees in becoming pop culture phenomena, striking resonant chords for numerous fans. Each is able to function as a cultural reference point, becoming the medium through which particular issues are identified and pushed into wider discussion. In the process, they provide audience members with the satisfaction of hearing their own perspectives articulated in a public forum, while functioning as a shared reference for identification.

As widely circulated cultural texts, these entertainers and activists attract strong affective communities, or counterpublics, around them. While much of the sentiment expressed in these genres clearly preexists many of the particular texts themselves, the texts serve to heighten the feeling of community in opposition and to fuel the continued circulation of discourse around the issues in question. Indeed, as I have argued, this community-building function is one of the most significant aspects of their overall effect. I have conceptualized this element of rallying the troops and encouraging community in opposition in terms of building counterpublics, communities of discussion and opinion that are somehow opposed to the dominant. And, indeed, it seems that the ironic mode is particularly adept in this regard. The remaining issue is whether this counterpublic creation can move from simple opposition to a more fleshed-out platform for concrete change.

One of the most damning criticisms leveled at ironic, parodic, and satiric modes of critique is that they are parasitically linked with the society they are critiquing, meaning that these modes are always locked in a negative bind, criticizing but not helping to produce a positive vision for the future. Along these lines, Christine Harold argues that appropriation artists and pranksters, while providing some satisfaction, are always acting in reaction to corporations and brands, meaning they are "not up to the task of providing new material, new ways of responding to or amplifying the legal substrates that make brands and markets work in the first place,"[5] though they can help to call our attention to these substrates. Indeed, much of the time, parody and satire focus on what is wrong with the current situation, but they can sometimes do little toward articulating what an alternative might look like. This would seem to be a serious limitation, particularly for explicitly political material. However, as I have argued throughout much of this book, the highly politicized and engaged forms of satire chronicled here tend to gesture beyond the problematic present, often even providing concrete suggestions for alternatives. As discussed, the parodic news hosts frequently use their interview segments, in particular, as a form of inquiry into what alternatives might look like, actively searching for solutions to problems while modeling some of the qualities they would like to see in journalism. And the documentarians do often provide their audiences with suggestions for what could be done differently. Granted, they do not always succeed in this regard; *Fahrenheit 9/11*, for example, spends a lot of time tracing the links between enormous foreign political contributions and government policy, but it has few suggestions for reforming the system beyond voting George W. Bush out of office, even though he was clearly not the first to be influenced by these factors. However, elsewhere, Moore does offer a number of international examples (from countries like Canada, France, and Cuba) as illustrations of better solutions to a variety of problems. Most important, he attempts to rally his fans to demand change.

As far as activist groups are concerned, it is admittedly more common for them to mount a critique of the way things currently are or, in ironic mode, to poke fun at the flaws of policies, but some of the playful contemporary groups are also experimenting with ways of moving beyond negative critique alone. Most spectacularly, in November 2008, only a few days after the presidential election, a number of diverse activist groups, including the Yes Men, United for Peace & Justice, Code Pink, the Anti-Advertising Agency, Improv Everywhere, and others, came together in a massive collaboration, printing and distributing tens of thousands of copies of a fake edition of the *New York Times*. Rather than critique the state of the news media or a particular topical story, the activists created a vision of the world that they hoped to see in the not-too-distant future. The paper was a spot-on reproduction of the layout of the *Times,* which might have fooled most readers at first glance, but closer examination revealed that the date of publication was listed as July 4, 2009, roughly eight months in the future, and the slogan on the masthead was not "All the News That's Fit to Print" but "All the News We Hope to Print." The content was indeed aspirational. The top headline blared "Iraq War Ends," and the story explained that U.S. troops were all coming home while the United Nations was moving in to perform peacekeeping duties and to aid in rebuilding the country. Other stories included Congress passing a "maximum wage law," the treasury announcing a "true cost" tax plan which would tax items that are damaging to the environment, and impending national health care. Everything in the 14-page paper conjured an image of what the country could look like, given a progressive tilt in priorities. Even the advertisements were designed as a form of wishful thinking. A full-page fake ad for KBR, for instance, explained that, though it had supported military operations in Iraq in the quest for its resources, it would now celebrate the outbreak of peace, as it is a "solutions company" that will work toward planning municipal roads, power grids, schools, and hospitals. An advertisement for ExxonMobil declared that the company was committed to meeting the new congressional guidelines for "socially, economically, & environmentally responsible energy" and that it had learned that peace, not just war, can be lucrative.

The scale of the action was impressive, involving the production and printing of thousands of copies of the newspaper, the coordination of hundreds of volunteers handing out copies at subway stations, the creation of an accompanying fake *New York Times* website, and the release of a coordinated series of press releases. It also required the collaboration of a wide variety of existing groups and the amassing of funds in the form of small online donations solicited through the Yes Men's email list (without giving away exactly what they were raising money for). Beyond the logistical triumphs, though, the stunt also represented a significant shift in focus for many of the ironic and parodic activist groups involved. No longer loudly protesting the policies and tone of the Bush administration, as these groups had for eight years, this action was focused on creating a vision for what the upcoming Obama era *should* look like (a deliberately

6.1. The Yes Men attract attention after distributing thousands of copies of a fake edition of the *New York Times* filled with stories they and other activists would like to see making news under the Obama administration. The Yes Men Fix the World *(2009)*

idealized one). As one of the participants explained in a press release, she thought of it as a reminder that they needed to push harder than ever, since "we've got to make sure Obama and all the other Democrats do what we elected them to do. After eight or maybe twenty-eight years of hell, we need to start imagining heaven."[6] Another contributor explained, "It's about what's possible, if we think big and act collectively."[7]

This approach is what Jenkins and Duncombe have referred to as "critical utopianism,"[8] which is what happens when satiric, parodic, and ironic activists imagine a world that almost cannot be. Using the Yes Men's Dow Chemical stunt as an example, the authors explain that the group creates a glimpse of a world in which Dow would actually appear on the BBC and take moral and legal responsibility for its corporate actions, ideally leading viewers to ask the questions, "Why is it so crazy that a corporation would do this? Why is this something that has to be a prank?" The intent is to ultimately pose the larger question of "What if?" Contemplating the "what if?" should then spur people to consider alternatives and to start thinking about what actually needs changing. As Jenkins puts it, "[W]hen we imagine alternatives, we go back to the world we live in and ideally we also begin to think of the steps that will get us from the undesirable present to the much more desired future."[9] While

6.2. The Yes Men share a moment of optimism after the distribution of the fake *New York Times* edition, which incites readers to imagine alternatives to the status quo. The Yes Men Fix the World *(2009)*

the activists involved in the *New York Times* hoax likely did not believe that all of their policy predictions would come to pass in just a few months of a new administration, they were setting up the "what if?" by asking people to imagine alternatives to the present and to inspire them to work toward some of the objectives. One of the articles in the paper, in fact, gives a pointed account of the mass popular pressure that had supposedly resulted in the recent progressive tilt, explaining that a recent (fictional) study reported that there had been "a three-fold increase in the incidence of letters, phone calls, faxes, and email received by congressional offices, 88 percent of which were from people who identified themselves as new members of particular activist organizations."[10] The message is clear: some of this is possible if more of us get involved.

This stunt is particularly notable for its attempt to draw on the power of counterpublics, not just to get everyone angry about the present (which is certainly important in itself, as I have argued), but to further spur them to work toward particular alternatives. I am closing with this anecdote because it is a particularly good example of ironic critique that manages to move beyond criticism toward articulating a vision of what the future might look like. This is another instance of irony used in the service of entirely earnest ends, in this case very concrete ends. And, importantly, as some activists' opening salvo in the new era of the Obama presidency, an era that had been predicted to quash parody and irony, this stunt is both parodic *and* entirely sincere, hopeful, and engaged.

Regardless of technique, all of these examples of irony, satire, and parody are intended as methods of intruding into the public conversation. Rather than engendering cynicism, as their critics charge, they are a calculated shot across the bow of the cynically manufactured elements of public debate. The fact that these hybrid, highly political, and satiric genres are sparking so much interest, innovation, and enthusiasm is particularly significant, especially when seen against the background of what is reported as continued widespread political apathy and disinterest. In an era when political discourse is so often overproduced, stage-managed, and predictably choreographed, these examples of performative satire, parody, and irony offer a way of satisfyingly breaking through the existing script. That these modes are providing a sense of connection and purpose to many in a way that organized politics has often struggled to do should be significant to all those interested in political communication and in the circulation of cultural and political narratives.

NOTES

1. INTRODUCTION

1. Dentith, *Parody,* 185.
2. Newman, "Irony Is Dead," 1.
3. Warner, "The Mass Public and the Mass Subject," 396.
4. Young, *Justice and the Politics of Difference,* 109.
5. Griffen, *Satire,* 137.
6. Bloom and Bloom, *Satire's Persuasive Voice,* 23.
7. Hutcheon, *Irony's Edge,* 29.
8. Schutz, *Political Humor,* 9.
9. See Feinberg, *Introduction to Satire;* and Schutz, *Political Humor.*
10. Feinberg, *Introduction to Satire,* 5.
11. Ibid., 7.
12. Hutcheon, *Irony's Edge,* 30.
13. See Bloom and Bloom, *Satire's Persuasive Voice;* and Griffen, *Satire.*
14. Bloom and Bloom, *Satire's Persuasive Voice,* 21.
15. Griffen, *Satire,* 153.
16. Bloom and Bloom, *Satire's Persuasive Voice,* 16.
17. Feinberg, *Introduction to Satire,* 256.
18. Habermas, *Structural Transformation,* 27.
19. Ibid., 28.
20. Ibid., 161.
21. Ibid., 171.
22. Fraser, "Rethinking the Public Sphere," 116.
23. Ibid., 120.
24. Ibid., 123.
25. Warner, *Publics and Counterpublics,* 16.
26. Ibid., 114.
27. Fraser, "Sex, Lies, and the Public Sphere," 612.
28. Williams, *Sociology of Culture,* 204.
29. Robbins, *Phantom Public Sphere,* xii.
30. Gitlin, *The Whole World Is Watching.*
31. Gray, *Watching with the Simpsons,* 95.
32. McAfee, "Two Feminisms," 146.

33. Gray, *Watching with the Simpsons,* 169.
34. Hall, "Notes on Deconstructing 'the Popular,'" 192.
35. Fiske, *Media Matters,* 4.
36. Burbank, "Ladies against Women," 25.
37. Bogad, *Electoral Guerrilla Theatre,* 4.

2. IRONIC AUTHENTICITY

1. Jenkins and Duncombe, "Politics in the Age of YouTube."
2. Jenkins, *Convergence Culture,* 2.
3. Hutcheon, *Irony's Edge,* 11.
4. Purdy, *For Common Things,* xii.
5. Ibid.
6. Ibid., 15.
7. Hirschorn and Purdy, "The State of Irony."
8. Poniewozik, "Stop This Horrible Scourge!"
9. Purdy, *For Common Things,* 23.
10. Hirschorn and Purdy, "The State of Irony."
11. Rosenblatt, "Age of Irony Comes to an End," 79.
12. Ibid.
13. Beers, "Irony Is Dead!"
14. Ibid.
15. Kirkpatrick, "A Nation Challenged."
16. Warner, "Tyranny of the Dichotomy."
17. Ibid.
18. Ibid.
19. Boler and Gournelos, "Editor's Introduction."
20. Ibid.
21. Poniewozik, "Dave Eggers' Mystery Box."
22. McGrath, "No Kidding: Does Irony Illuminate or Corrupt?"
23. "Sarah Silverman and the Great Schlep."
24. Ibid.
25. Ibid.
26. Ibid.
27. Itzkoff, "Message to Your Grandma," C1.
28. "Sarah Silverman and the Great Schlep."
29. "Gossip Girl Stars: Talk to Your Parents about McCain."
30. Ibid.
31. Ibid.
32. "Obama's Loss Traced to Non-Voter."
33. Ibid.
34. Ibid.
35. Ibid.
36. Ibid.
37. Ibid.
38. Hutcheon, *Irony's Edge,* 2.
39. Bourdieu, *Distinction,* 234.

40. Gray, *Watching with the Simpsons,* 31.
41. Purdy, *For Common Things,* 10.

3. TRUTHINESS AND CONSEQUENCES IN PARODIC NEWS

1. Altman, *Film/Genre.*
2. Mittell, *Genre and Television,* 5.
3. Scannell, "Britain: Public Service Broadcasting," 28.
4. Fiddy, "That Was the Week That Was," 2310.
5. Koch, *Inside "Seven Days,"* 39.
6. Fiddy, "That Was the Week That Was," 2310.
7. Kercher, *Revel with a Cause,* 359.
8. "Guide to Comedy: *That Was the Week That Was.*"
9. Kercher, *Revel with a Cause,* 368.
10. Ibid., 388.
11. Koch, *Inside "Seven Days,"* 38.
12. Ibid., 36.
13. Ibid., 31.
14. Nash, *Prime Time at Ten,* 60.
15. Gilsdorf, "This Hour Has Seven Days," 2317.
16. Nash, *Prime Time at Ten,* 248.
17. Jenkins, "Rowan and Martin's Laugh-In," 1967.
18. *Rowan and Martin's Laugh-In* (NBC, Feb. 5, 1968).
19. Cader, *"Saturday Night Live,"* 13.
20. Ibid., 192.
21. Jones, "With All Due Respect," 43.
22. Gray, Jones, and Thompson, "Using One of Its Lifelines."
23. Spigel, "Introduction," 2.
24. Sconce, "What If?" 96.
25. Spigel, "Entertainment Wars," 256.
26. Collins, "Canada: Nation-Building Threatened?" 200.
27. Tinic, "Speaking 'Truth' to Power?" 169.
28. Caldwell, "Convergence Television," 49.
29. St. John, "The Week That Wasn't," 1.
30. Davis, *Stages of Emergency,* 85–86.
31. *The Colbert Report* (Comedy Central, Nov. 2006).
32. *Now with Bill Moyers* (PBS, July 11, 2003).
33. *The Daily Show* (Comedy Central, Mar. 21, 2005).
34. McKain, "Not Necessarily Not the News," 420.
35. *This Hour Has 22 Minutes* (CBC, Mar. 21, 2005).
36. Brioux, "Give Us Doris," 4.
37. Nuttall-Smith, "Wit of the Water Cooler," D9.
38. Monchuk, "Satire Gives Mercer Far More than 22 Minutes of Fame," D1.
39. *The Daily Show* (Comedy Central, Sept. 3, 2004).
40. *The Daily Show* (Comedy Central, Oct. 20, 2008).
41. O'Neill, "This Hour Has 22 Puerile Minutes," 2.
42. Tinic, "Speaking 'Truth' to Power?" 169.

43. Berland, "Writing on the Border," 145.
44. *The Daily Show with Jon Stewart: Indecision 2004* (DVD, Paramount, 2005).
45. Baym, *From Cronkite to Colbert,* 116.
46. *The Daily Show* (Comedy Central, Aug. 25, 2005).
47. Taylor, "Public Discourse from the Cheap Seats," A6.
48. *The Rick Mercer Report* (CBC, Oct. 10, 2006).
49. *The Daily Show* (Comedy Central, June 21, 2004).
50. *This Hour Has 22 Minutes* (CBC, Nov. 19, 2004).
51. Haas, "MPs Demean Their Office," A13.
52. In *Make Room for TV,* Spigel discusses the ways in which television was expected to link public and private worlds in the postwar United States, rendering real engagements with the outside world almost unnecessary.
53. Feuer, "The Concept of Live Television," 14.
54. Ibid.
55. Bourdon, "Live Television Is Still Alive," 185.
56. "Conversation with Stephen Colbert," *The Charlie Rose Show* (PBS, Dec. 8, 2006).
57. Hutcheon, *A Theory of Parody,* 2.
58. Baym, "*The Daily Show,*" 267.
59. "Jon Stewart Discusses Politics and Comedy," *Fresh Air.*
60. *The Daily Show* (Comedy Central, Dec. 7, 2006).
61. Thompson, "Faking News Alert!" 1E.
62. Jones, *Entertaining Politics: New Political Television and Civic Culture,* 93.
63. Riley, "The Unofficial Opposition," C12.
64. Cobb, "*This Hour* Has the Politicians," B7.
65. Howard, "Shot in the Arm for Our Forces," A19.
66. Ibid.
67. "Au Canada," *NewsHour* (PBS, Dec. 1, 2004).
68. Barker, "Look Out, Jon Stewart," 1D.
69. Garofoli, "Young Voters Turning to Fake Anchor," A1.
70. Smith, "On the Other Side of the Desk," E1.
71. Boler and Turpin, *"The Daily Show" and "Crossfire,"* 388.
72. *The Daily Show* (Comedy Central, Mar. 12, 2009).
73. Gold, "Funny? Maybe until He's Interviewing You," A1.
74. "Stephen Colbert's *The Colbert Report* Skewers TV's Political Talking Heads."
75. "Merriam-Webster's Words of the Year: 2006."
76. "White House Correspondents' Association Dinner" (C-SPAN, Apr. 29, 2006).
77. Ibid.
78. Gallagher, "Queen Bee," 72.
79. "Over the Shark You Go, Rick."
80. Graham, "Stewart Gains Popularity," E1.
81. Baym, "The Jester No More."
82. "Cable and Internet Loom Large."
83. Peterson, *Strange Bedfellows,* 40.
84. Boucher, "Television and Radio: Stewart, Comedy Central Sign Deal," E1.
85. de Moraes, "Seriously: Kerry on Comedy Central," C1.
86. "O'Reilly Discusses *The Daily Show.*"

87. Young, "Daily Show Viewers Knowledgeable."

88. "Bill O'Reilly Calls Viewers of *The Daily Show* with Jon Stewart a Bunch of 'Stoned Slackers.'"

89. Glynn, *Tabloid Culture,* 233.

90. Mittell, *Genre and Television,* 178.

91. Schechner, *Between Theater and Anthropology,* 6.

92. Hart and Hartelius, "The Political Sins of Jon Stewart," 263.

93. Baumgartner and Morris, "*The Daily Show* Effect," 352.

94. Ibid., 353.

95. Ibid., 341.

96. Ibid., 359.

97. Ibid., 345.

98. Baym, "*The Daily Show,*" 263.

99. Ibid.

100. Ibid.

101. Peterson, *Strange Bedfellows,* 145.

102. *The Colbert Report* (Comedy Central, Jan. 8, 2007).

103. Morris and Baumgartner, "*The Daily Show* and Attitudes toward the News Media," 329.

104. Young, "*The Daily Show* as the New Journalism," 242.

105. Baym, *From Cronkite to Colbert,* 118.

106. *The Colbert Report* (Comedy Central, Jan. 11, 2007).

107. Morreale, "Jon Stewart and *The Daily Show,*" 118.

108. *The Daily Show* (Comedy Central, Jan. 10, 2007).

109. Hariman, "In Defense of Jon Stewart," 276.

110. Gray, *Watching with the Simpsons,* 155.

111. Ibid.

112. Jones, *Entertaining Politics: Satiric Television and Political Engagement,* 225.

113. Carter, "Comedy Central Tries to Gauge Passion."

114. McKain, "Not Necessarily Not the News," 427.

115. Hartley, "From Republic of Letters to the Television Republic?" 411.

4. HEROES AND VILLAINS

1. Caro, "Moving Pictures," 1.

2. Corner, *The Art of Record,* 169–70.

3. Bruzzi, *New Documentary,* 4.

4. Ibid.

5. Fine, "Readers Write," 8A.

6. "Republican Launches 'Buy-Back' of Moore Film," R12.

7. Nolley, "*Fahrenheit 9/11,*" 15.

8. Toplin, *Michael Moore's "Fahrenheit 9/11,"* 7.

9. Ibid., 65.

10. Nolley, "*Fahrenheit 9/11,*" 15.

11. Toplin, *Michael Moore's "Fahrenheit 9/11,"* 9.

12. Jones, "A Cultural Approach to the Study of Mediated Citizenship," 369.

13. Brownstein, "Preview," D1.

14. Nichols, *Introduction to Documentary,* 34.
15. Ellis, *The Documentary Idea,* 59.
16. Aitkin, *The Documentary Film Movement,* 3.
17. Corner, *The Art of Record,* 13.
18. Ibid.
19. Grant, *Voyages of Discovery,* 12; Mamber, *Cinema Verité,* 2.
20. Grant, *Voyages of Discovery,* 32.
21. Corner, *The Art of Record,* 159.
22. Nichols, "The Voice of Documentary," 49.
23. Ibid.
24. Bruzzi, *New Documentary,* 24.
25. Williams, "Mirrors without Memory," 15.
26. Arthur, "Jargons of Authenticity," 127.
27. Brecht, *Brecht on Theatre,* 195.
28. Ibid., 100.
29. Handke, "Theater-in-the-Street and Theater-in-Theaters," 9.
30. Cohen-Cruz, "General Introduction," 1.
31. Schechner, *The Future of Ritual,* 45–93.
32. Ibid., 88.
33. Scott, "When All Those Big Macs Bite Back," 18.
34. Scott, "Now Playing: Eisner and Me," 16.
35. Howell, "Arch Enemy," D1.
36. Schechner, *The Future of Ritual,* 87.
37. Orvell, "Documentary Film and the Power of Interrogation," 17.
38. Speier, *Force and Folly,* 197.
39. Bakhtin, *The Dialogic Imagination,* 402.
40. Ibid., 163.
41. "Morgan Spurlock Discusses His Documentary *Super Size Me.*"
42. "Most Fascinating People of 2004."
43. MacFarquhar, "The Populist," 133.
44. Scott, "Now Playing: Eisner and Me," 16.
45. Feinberg, *Introduction to Satire,* 256.
46. Ibid., 12.
47. Schutz, *Political Humor,* 78.
48. Fraser, "Rethinking the Public Sphere," 124.
49. Warner, *Publics and Counterpublics,* 122.
50. Ibid.
51. Moore, "People's Choice Awards Nominates *Fahrenheit 9/11* as 'Favorite Film of the Year.'"
52. Moore, "In the Clearing Stands a Boxer."
53. "Most Fascinating People of 2004."
54. Nestruck, "Like a 90-Minute Participation Spot," B3.
55. Ghities, "The Liberal Hawk," 8.
56. Fierman, "The Passion of Michael Moore," 35.
57. Parker, "American Cynicism Becomes Terrorist Tool," 21.
58. Lacayo and Stein, "Winners and Losers," 82.
59. Clarke, "The End of an Era?"

60. Mattson, "The Perils of Michael Moore," 77.
61. Ibid.
62. Bloom and Bloom, *Satire's Persuasive Voice,* 20.
63. Ibid.
64. Burbank, "Ladies against Women," 25.
65. Hall, *Stuart Hall: Critical Dialogues,* 144.
66. Asen and Brouwer, "Reconfigurations of the Public Sphere," 25.
67. Toplin, *Michael Moore's "Fahrenheit 9/11,"* 135.
68. Marmor, Okma, and Rojas, "What It Is, What It Does and What It Might Do," 50.
69. Muñoz, *Dis-Identifications,* 7.
70. Ibid., 11.
71. Ibid., 31.
72. Gitlin, *The Whole World Is Watching,* 283.
73. Doxtader, "In the Name of Reconciliation," 65.
74. Klein, *No Logo,* 346.
75. Corner, "Documentary: The Transformation of a Social Aesthetic," 182.
76. Newfield, "An Interview with Michael Moore."
77. Ibid.
78. "Morgan Spurlock Discusses His Documentary *Super Size Me.*"
79. Downing, *Radical Media,* 28.

5. IRONY IN ACTIVISM

1. Gray, *Watching with the Simpsons,* 158–59.

2. This is an idea also explored, in a slightly different vein, by Tim Miller and David Román in their essay "Preaching to the Converted." In response to the critique frequently used to dismiss much queer community theater as *merely* preaching to the converted, they argue for the importance of shared events, occasions, and rituals in a community still marginalized within the larger culture, adding further that no community is ever as monolithic as the phrase "the converted" seems to infer.

3. Hutcheon, *Irony's Edge,* 59.
4. Ibid., 11.
5. Ibid., 12.
6. Ibid., 18.
7. Duncombe, *Cultural Resistance Reader,* 333.
8. Goddard, "'Something to Vote for,'" 44.
9. Debord, *Society of the Spectacle,* par. 12.
10. Jappe, *Guy Debord,* 58.
11. Ibid., 96.
12. Getty, "Books: Never Mind the Boulevards," 11.
13. Hoffman, *Best of Abbie Hoffman,* 99.
14. *Revolution for the Hell of It* is the title of Hoffman's first book, written in 1968.
15. Hoffman, *Best of Abbie Hoffman,* 17.
16. Ibid., 25.
17. Ibid., 52.
18. Rubin, *Do It!* 108.
19. Sawyer, "An ACT UP Founder 'Acts Up,'" 90.

20. Shepard, "Introductory Notes on the Trail from ACT UP to the WTO," 13.
21. Reed, *Art of Protest,* 193.
22. Ibid., 179.
23. Orenstein, "Agitational Performance," 145.
24. Boyd, "Truth Is a Virus," 369–78.
25. "The Province APEC Wrap Page 1"; "Guerrilla Media Offers the Province Some Editorial Direction on APEC."
26. Shepard and Hayduk, "Urban Protest and Community Building in the Era of Globalization," 1.
27. Reed, *Art of Protest,* 269.
28. Boyd, "Irony, Meme Warfare, and the Extreme Costume Ball," 249.
29. Klein, "The Vision Thing," 267.
30. Shepard and Hayduk, "Public versus Private Spaces," 201.
31. Jordan, "The Art of Necessity," 347.
32. Boyd, "Irony, Meme Warfare, and the Extreme Costume Ball," 247.
33. Reed, *Art of Protest,* 255.
34. Boyd, "Irony, Meme Warfare, and the Extreme Costume Ball," 249.
35. Dery, "Culture Jamming."
36. Ibid.
37. Klein, *No Logo,* 284.
38. Napier and Thomas, "The BLF Manifesto."
39. Klein, *No Logo,* 284.
40. Orenstein, "Agitational Performance," 144.
41. Goldman, "Debra Goldman's Consumer Republic."
42. Ibid.
43. Lasn, *Culture Jam,* xi.
44. Ibid., xvi.
45. Ibid., 135–36.
46. Harold, *Ourspace,* 57.
47. Ibid.
48. Guerrilla Girls, "Do Women Have to Be Naked to Get into the Met Museum?"
49. Guerrilla Girls, "The Advantages of Being a Woman Artist."
50. Guerrilla Girls, "The Trent L'ottscar Billboard."
51. Duncombe, *Dream,* 9.
52. Boyd, "Truth Is a Virus," 371.
53. Billionaires for Bush, "Do-It-Yourself Manual," 28.
54. Billionaires for Bush, "Recent Events."
55. Burbank, "Ladies against Women," 26.
56. Billionaires for Bush, "Do-It-Yourself Manual," 19.
57. Boyd, "Irony, Meme Warfare, and the Extreme Costume Ball," 369.
58. Ibid., 370.
59. Ibid., 373.
60. Duncombe, "Stepping Off the Sidewalk," 228.
61. Kershaw, *Politics of Performance,* 81.
62. Orenstein, "Agitational Performance," 149.
63. Bichlbaum, Bonanno, and Spunkmeyer, *The Yes Men,* 16.
64. Ibid., 39.

65. Ibid., 59.
66. Yes Men, "Identity Correction."
67. Myerson, "Art of Confusion," 30.
68. "The Yes Men," *Time Out New York,* 71.
69. Yes Men, "FAQ."
70. Hutcheon, *Irony's Edge,* 16.
71. Baudrillard, *Simulations,* 4.
72. Ibid., 25.
73. Yes Men, "FAQ."
74. Harold, *Ourspace,* 107.
75. Baudrillard, *For a Critique of the Political Economy of the Sign,* 173.
76. Boal, *Theatre of the Oppressed,* 141.
77. Talen, *What Should I Do if Reverend Billy Is in My Store?* 171.
78. Ibid., 73–75.
79. Talen, "Who's Your Devil?"
80. Dee, "Reverend Billy's Unholy War," 22.
81. Kalb, "The Gospel According to Billy," 163–64.
82. Talen, *What Should I Do if Reverend Billy Is in My Store?* 103.
83. Ibid., 82.
84. Talen, "Statement of Belief."
85. "Group of Anti-Bush Protesters Who Disguise Themselves as Billionaire Supporters of the President."
86. Bogad, *Electoral Guerrilla Theatre,* 198.
87. Ibid.
88. Hutcheon, *Irony's Edge,* 97.
89. Hartlaub, "Yes Man Invites You to Help 'Fix the World.'"
90. Scott, *Domination and the Arts of Resistance.*
91. de Certeau, *The Practice of Everyday Life,* xix.
92. Ibid.
93. Aspden, "Prank Outsiders, the Yes Men," 38.

6. MOVING BEYOND CRITIQUE

1. Pevere, "Yes Men: Droll Pranksters," D8.
2. Slack, "Billionaires for Bush? Well, Yes and No," A16.
3. Zion, "Affirmative Action Men," 14.
4. Schechner, *Performance Theory,* 120.
5. Harold, *Ourspace,* 160.
6. New York Times Special Edition Writers, "Newspaper Blankets U.S. Cities."
7. New York Times Special Edition Writers, "Hundreds Claim Credit for *New York Times* Spoof."
8. Jenkins and Duncombe, "Politics in the Age of YouTube."
9. Ibid.
10. Fielden, "Popular Pressure Ushers Recent Progressive Tilt," A1.

BIBLIOGRAPHY

Aitkin, Ian. *The Documentary Film Movement: An Anthology.* Edinburgh: Edinburgh University Press, 1998.

Altman, Rick. *Film/Genre.* London: British Film Institute, 1999.

Arthur, Paul. "Jargons of Authenticity." In *Theorizing Documentary,* ed. Michael Renov. New York: Routledge, 1993.

Asen, Robert, and Daniel C. Brouwer. "Reconfigurations of the Public Sphere." In *Counterpublics and the State,* ed. Robert Asen and Daniel C. Brouwer. Albany: State University of New York Press, 2001.

Aspden, Peter. "Prank Outsiders, the Yes Men, a Pair of Impudent Anti-Globalisation Satirists, Could Teach Self-Regarding 'Subversive' Artists a Trick or Two when It Comes to Upending Our Expectations." *Financial Times,* May 28, 2005.

"Au Canada." PBS *NewsHour,* Dec. 1, 2004.

Bakhtin, M. M. *The Dialogic Imagination.* Trans. Caryl Emerson and Michael Holquist. Ed. Michael Holquist. Austin: University of Texas Press, 1982.

Barker, Olivia. "Look Out, Jon Stewart." *USA Today,* Nov. 2, 2004.

Baudrillard, Jean. *For a Critique of the Political Economy of the Sign.* Trans. Charles Levin. St. Louis, Mo.: Telos, 1981.

———. *Simulations.* Trans. Paul Foss, Paul Patton, and Philip Beitchman. New York: Semiotext(e), 1983.

Baumgartner, Jody, and Jonathan S. Morris. "*The Daily Show* Effect: Candidate Evaluations, Efficacy, and American Youth." *American Politics Research* 34 (2006): 341–65.

Baym, Geoffrey. "*The Daily Show:* Discursive Integration and the Reinvention of Political Journalism." *Political Communication* 22 (2005): 259–76.

———. *From Cronkite to Colbert: The Evolution of Broadcast News.* Boulder, Colo.: Paradigm, 2010.

———. "The Jester No More: Jon Stewart, *The Daily Show,* and Campaign '08." Paper presented at International Communication Association conference, Chicago, 2009.

Beers, David. "Irony Is Dead! Long Live Irony!" *Salon* (2001), http://archive.salon.com/mwt/feature/2001/09/25/irony_lives/index.html.

Berland, Jody. "Writing on the Border." *CR: The New Centennial Review* 1.2 (2001): 139–69.

Bichlbaum, Andy, Mike Bonanno, and Bob Spunkmeyer. *The Yes Men: The True Story of the End of the World Trade Organization.* New York: Disinformation, 2004.

"Bill O'Reilly Calls Viewers of *The Daily Show* with Jon Stewart a Bunch of 'Stoned Slackers' and 'Dopey Kids' during Interview with Jon Stewart on 'The O'Reilly Factor.'" *PR Newswire* (2004), http://www.prnewswire.com/cgi-bin/stories.pl?ACCT=109&STORY=/www/story/09-30-2004/0002262661&EDATE=.

Billionaires for Bush. "Do-It-Yourself Manual." *Billionaires for Bush,* www.billionairesforbush.com/diy_v2_contents.php.

———. "Recent Events." *Billionaires for Bush,* www.billionairesforbush.com/events.php.

Bloom, Edward, and Lillian Bloom. *Satire's Persuasive Voice.* Ithaca, N.Y.: Cornell University Press, 1979.

Boal, Augusto. *Theatre of the Oppressed.* Trans. Charles A. McBride and Maria-Odilia Leal McBride. New York: Theatre Communications Group, 1985.

Bogad, L. M. *Electoral Guerrilla Theatre: Radical Ridicule and Social Movements.* New York: Routledge, 2005.

Boler, Megan, and Ted Gournelos. "Editor's Introduction." *Electronic Journal of Communication* 18.2–4 (2008), http://www.cios.org/www/ejc/v18n24toc.htm#introduction.

Boler, Megan, and Stephen Turpin. *"The Daily Show" and "Crossfire": Satire and Sincerity as Truth to Power.* Cambridge, Mass.: MIT Press, 2008.

Boucher, Geoff. "Television and Radio: Stewart, Comedy Central Sign Deal." *Los Angeles Times,* Feb. 16, 2005.

Bourdieu, Pierre. *Distinction: A Social Critique of the Judgement of Taste.* Trans. Richard Nice. Cambridge, Mass.: Harvard University Press, 1984.

Bourdon, Jérôme. "Live Television Is Still Alive: On Television as an Unfulfilled Promise." In *The Television Studies Reader,* ed. Robert C. Allen and Annette Hill. New York: Routledge, 2004.

Boyd, Andrew. "Irony, Meme Warfare, and the Extreme Costume Ball." In *From ACT UP to the WTO: Urban Protest and Community Building in the Era of Globalization,* ed. Benjamin Shepard and Ronald Hayduk. London: Verso, 2002.

———. "Truth Is a Virus: Meme Warfare and the Billionaires for Bush (or Gore)." In *Cultural Resistance Reader,* ed. Stephen Duncombe. London: Verso, 2002.

Brecht, Bertolt. *Brecht on Theatre: The Development of an Aesthetic.* Trans. and ed. John Willett. London: Eyre Methuen, 1964.

Brioux, Bill. "Give Us Doris." *Toronto Sun,* Nov. 21, 2000.

Brownstein, Bill. "Preview." *Gazette,* Nov. 17, 2006.

Bruzzi, Stella. *New Documentary: A Critical Introduction.* London: Routledge, 2000.

Burbank, Carol Elizabeth. "Ladies against Women: Theatre Activism, Parody, and the Public Construction of Citizenship in U.S. Feminism's Second Wave." Ph.D. diss., Northwestern University, 1998.

"Cable and Internet Loom Large in Fragmented Political News Universe." *Pew Research Center,* http://people-press.org/reports/display.php3?ReportID=200.

Cader, Michael. *"Saturday Night Live": The First Twenty Years.* Boston: Houghton Mifflin, 1994.

Caldwell, John. "Convergence Television: Aggregating Form and Repurposing Content in the Culture of Conglomeration." In *Television after TV: Essays on a Medium in*

Transition, ed. Lynn Spigel and Jan Olsson. Durham, N.C.: Duke University Press, 2004.

Caro, Mark. "Moving Pictures." *Chicago Tribune*, June 20, 2004.

Carter, Bill. "Comedy Central Tries to Gauge Passion of Its Viewers." *New York Times*, Aug. 25, 2009.

Clarke, Jason. "The End of an Era?" *MooreLies* (Nov. 3, 2004), http://moorelies.com/topics/fahrenheit-911.

Cobb, Chris. "*This Hour* Has the Politicians." *Toronto Star*, Dec. 8, 1996.

Cohen-Cruz, Jan. "General Introduction." In *Radical Street Performance: An International Anthology*, ed. Jan Cohen-Cruz. New York: Routledge, 1998.

Collins, Richard. "Canada: Nation-Building Threatened by the US-Dominated Media?" In *The Politics of Broadcasting*, ed. Raymond Kuhn. New York: St. Martin's, 1985.

"Conversation with Stephen Colbert." *The Charlie Rose Show*, PBS, Dec. 8, 2006.

Corner, John. *The Art of Record: A Critical Introduction to Documentary*. Manchester, England: Manchester University Press, 1996.

———. "Documentary: The Transformation of a Social Aesthetic." In *Television and Common Knowledge*, ed. Jostein Gripsrud. New York: Routledge, 1999.

Davis, Tracy. *Stages of Emergency: Cold War Nuclear Civil Defense*. Durham, N.C.: Duke University Press, 2007.

Debord, Guy. *Society of the Spectacle*. Trans. Black & Red. Detroit: Black & Red, 1970.

de Certeau, Michel. *The Practice of Everyday Life*. Trans. Steven Rendall. Berkeley: University of California Press, 1984.

Dee, Jonathan. "Reverend Billy's Unholy War." *New York Times*, Aug. 22, 2004.

de Moraes, Lisa. "Seriously: Kerry on Comedy Central." *Washington Post*, Aug. 24, 2004.

Dentith, Simon. *Parody*. New York: Routledge, 2000.

Dery, Mark. "Culture Jamming: Hacking, Slashing and Sniping in the Empire of Signs." 2004. www.markdery.com.

Downing, John. *Radical Media: Rebellious Communication and Social Movements*. Thousand Oaks, Calif.: Sage, 2001.

Doxtader, Erik. "In the Name of Reconciliation: The Faith and Works of Counterpublicity." In *Counterpublics and the State*, ed. Robert Asen and Daniel C. Brouwer. Albany: State University of New York Press, 2001.

Duncombe, Stephen, ed. *Cultural Resistance Reader*. London: Verso, 2002.

———. *Dream: Re-Imagining Progressive Politics in an Age of Fantasy*. New York: New Press, 2007.

———. "Stepping Off the Sidewalk: Reclaim the Streets/NYC." In *From ACT UP to the WTO: Urban Protest and Community Building in the Era of Globalization*, ed. Benjamin Shepard and Ronald Hayduk. London: Verso, 2002.

Eggers, Dave. *A Heartbreaking Work of Staggering Genius*. New York: Vintage, 2001.

Ellis, Jack. *The Documentary Idea: A Critical History of English-Language Documentary Film and Video*. Englewood Cliffs, N.J.: Prentice-Hall, 1989.

Feinberg, Leonard. *Introduction to Satire*. Ames: University of Iowa Press, 1967.

Feuer, Jane. "The Concept of Live Television: Ontology as Ideology." In *Television: Critical Approaches: An Anthology*, ed. Ann Kaplan. Frederick, Md.: University Publications of America, 1983.

Fiddy, Dick. "That Was the Week That Was." In *Museum of Broadcast Communications Encyclopedia of Television,* ed. Horace Newcomb. New York: Fitzroy Dearborn, 2004.

Fielden, Samuel. "Popular Pressure Ushers Recent Progressive Tilt." *New York Times Special Edition,* Nov. 12, 2008.

Fierman, Daniel. "The Passion of Michael Moore." *Entertainment Weekly,* July 9, 2004.

Fine, Avrum. "Readers Write." *Atlanta Journal-Constitution,* June 29, 2004.

Fiske, John. *Media Matters: Everyday Culture and Political Change.* Minneapolis: University of Minnesota Press, 1996.

Fraser, Nancy. "Rethinking the Public Sphere: A Contribution to the Critique of Actually Existing Democracy." In *Habermas and the Public Sphere,* ed. Craig Calhoun. Cambridge, Mass.: MIT Press, 1992.

———. "Sex, Lies, and the Public Sphere: Some Reflections on the Confirmation of Clarence Thomas." *Critical Inquiry* 18.3 (Spring 1992): 595–612.

Gallagher, Aileen. "Queen Bee." *Bust Magazine,* Dec. 2005.

Garofoli, Joe. "Young Voters Turning to Fake Anchor for Insight." *San Francisco Chronicle,* Oct. 21, 2004.

Getty, Hulton. "Books: Never Mind the Boulevards." *Independent,* July 14, 2001.

Ghities, Frida. "The Liberal Hawk Can Still Find It Hard to Back Bush." *Chicago Tribune,* Oct. 17, 2004.

Gilsdorf, William O. "This Hour Has Seven Days." In *Museum of Broadcast Communications Encyclopedia of Television,* ed. Horace Newcomb. New York: Fitzroy Dearborn, 2004.

Gitlin, Todd. *The Whole World Is Watching: Mass Media in the Making & Unmaking of the New Left.* Berkeley: University of California Press, 1980.

Glynn, Kevin. *Tabloid Culture: Trash, Taste, Popular Power and the Transformation of American TV.* Durham, N.C.: Duke University Press, 2000.

Goddard, Leslie. "'Something to Vote for': Theatricalism in the U.S. Women's Suffrage Movement." Ph.D. diss., Northwestern University, 2001.

Gold, Matea. "Funny? Maybe until He's Interviewing You." *Los Angeles Times,* Mar. 14, 2009.

Goldman, Debra. "Debra Goldman's Consumer Republic." *Adweek,* Nov. 22, 1999.

"Gossip Girl Stars: Talk to Your Parents about McCain." 2008. http://www.mccainfree whitehouse.org.

Graham, Renee. "Stewart Gains Popularity, but Is He Losing His Edge?" *Boston Globe,* Aug. 31, 2004.

Grant, Barry Keith. *Voyages of Discovery: The Cinema of Frederick Wiseman.* Urbana: University of Illinois Press, 1992.

Gray, Jonathan. *Watching with the Simpsons: Television, Parody, and Intertextuality.* London: Routledge, 2006.

Gray, Jonathan, Jeffrey P. Jones, and Ethan Thompson. "Using One of Its Lifelines: Does Politics Save *Saturday Night Live* from Oblivion?" *FlowTV* (2009), http://flowtv .org/?p=2911#.

Griffen, Dustin. *Satire.* Lexington: University Press of Kentucky, 1994.

"Group of Anti-Bush Protesters Who Disguise Themselves as Billionaire Supporters of the President." *Day to Day,* National Public Radio, Mar. 12, 2004.

Guerrilla Girls. "The Advantages of Being a Woman Artist." *Guerrilla Girls* (1988), www.guerrillagirls.com/posters/advantages.shtml.

———. "Do Women Have to Be Naked to Get into the Met Museum?" *Guerrilla Girls* (1989), www.guerrillagirls.com/posters/getnaked.shtml.

———. "The Trent L'ottscar Billboard." *Guerrilla Girls* (2003), www.guerrillagirls .com/posters/trent.shtml.

"Guerrilla Media Offers the Province Some Editorial Direction on APEC." 1997. http:// www.guerrillamedia.8m.com/news_archive/press_releases/nr_prov_1997.htm.

"Guide to Comedy: *That Was the Week That Was.*" *British Broadcasting Corporation,* http://www.bbc.co.uk/comedy/guide/articles/t/thatwastheweekth_7776280 .shtml.

Haas, Corrie. "MPs Demean Their Office Acting like Village Idiots." *Ottawa Citizen,* Feb. 29, 2000.

Habermas, Jürgen. *The Structural Transformation of the Public Sphere: An Inquiry into a Category of Bourgeois Society.* Trans. Thomas Burger and Frederick Lawrence. Cambridge, Mass.: MIT Press, 1989.

Hall, Stuart. "Notes on Deconstructing 'the Popular.'" In *Cultural Resistance Reader,* ed. Stephen Duncombe, 185–92. London: Verso, 2002.

———. *Stuart Hall: Critical Dialogues in Cultural Studies.* Ed. David Morley and Kuan-Hsing Chen. New York: Routledge, 1996.

Handke, Peter. "Theater-in-the-Street and Theater-in-Theaters." In *Radical Street Performance: An International Anthology,* ed. Jan Cohen-Cruz. New York: Routledge, 1998.

Hariman, Robert. "In Defense of Jon Stewart." *Critical Studies in Media Communication* 24.3 (2007): 273–77.

Harold, Christine. *Ourspace: Resisting the Corporate Control of Culture.* Minneapolis: University of Minnesota Press, 2007.

Hart, Roderick P., and Johanna Hartelius. "The Political Sins of Jon Stewart." *Critical Studies in Media Communication* 24.3 (2007): 263–72.

Hartlaub, Peter. "Yes Man Invites You to Help 'Fix the World.'" *San Francisco Chronicle,* Oct. 25, 2009.

Hartley, John. "From Republic of Letters to the Television Republic? Citizen Readers in the Era of Broadcast Television." In *Television after TV: Essays on a Medium in Transition,* ed. Lynn Spigel and Jan Olsson. Durham, N.C.: Duke University Press, 2004.

Hirschorn, Michael, and Jedediah Purdy. "The State of Irony." *Slate* (1999), http://www .slate.com/id/35152/entry/35165.

Hoffman, Abbie. *The Best of Abbie Hoffman.* Ed. Daniel Simon. New York: Four Walls Eight Windows, 1989.

Howard, Robert. "Shot in the Arm for Our Forces." *Hamilton Spectator,* Feb. 24, 2005.

Howell, Peter. "Arch Enemy." *Toronto Star,* Apr. 23, 2004.

Hutcheon, Linda. *Irony's Edge: The Theory and Politics of Irony.* London: Routledge, 1994.

———. *A Theory of Parody: The Teachings of the Twentieth Century Art Forms.* New York: Methuen, 1985.

Itzkoff, Dave. "Message to Your Grandma: Vote Obama." *New York Times,* Oct. 7, 2008.

Jappe, Anselm. *Guy Debord*. Trans. Donald Nicholson-Smith. Berkeley: University of California Press, 1999.

Jenkins, Henry. *Convergence Culture: Where Old and New Media Collide*. New York: New York University Press, 2006.

———. "Rowan and Martin's Laugh-In." In *Museum of Broadcast Communications Encyclopedia of Television*, ed. Horace Newcomb. New York: Fitzroy Dearborn, 2004.

Jenkins, Henry, and Stephen Duncombe. "Politics in the Age of YouTube." *Electronic Journal of Communication* 18.2–4 (2008), http://www.cios.org/www/ejc/EJCPUBLIC/018/2/01848.html.

Jensen, Robert. "Stupid White Movie: What Michael Moore Misses about Empire." *Counterpunch* (July 5, 2004), http://www.counterpunch.org/jensen07052004.html.

"Jon Stewart Discusses Politics and Comedy." *Fresh Air*, National Public Radio, WHYY, Philadelphia, Sept. 30, 2004.

Jones, Jeffrey P. "A Cultural Approach to the Study of Mediated Citizenship." *Social Semiotics* 16.2 (June 2006): 365–88.

———. *Entertaining Politics: New Political Television and Civic Culture*. Lanham, Md.: Rowman and Littlefield, 2005.

———. *Entertaining Politics: Satiric Television and Political Engagement*, 2nd ed. Lanham, Md.: Rowman and Littlefield, 2010.

———. "With All Due Respect: Satirizing Presidents from *Saturday Night Live* to Lil' Bush." In *Satire TV: Politics and Comedy in the Post-Network Era*, ed. Jonathan Gray, Jeffrey P. Jones, and Ethan Thompson. New York: New York University Press, 2009.

Jordan, John. "The Art of Necessity: The Subversive Imagination of Anti-Road Protest and Reclaim the Streets." In *Cultural Resistance Reader*, ed. Stephen Duncombe. London: Verso, 2002.

Kalb, Jonathan. "The Gospel According to Billy." *Theater* 31.3 (2001): 161–67.

Kercher, Stephen E. *Revel with a Cause: Liberal Satire in Postwar America*. Chicago: University of Chicago Press, 2006.

Kershaw, Baz. *The Politics of Performance: Radical Theatre as Cultural Intervention*. New York: Routledge, 1992.

Kirkpatrick, David D. "A Nation Challenged: The Commentators: Pronouncements on Irony Draw a Line in the Sand." *New York Times*, Sept. 24, 2001.

Klein, Naomi. *No Logo: No Space No Choice No Jobs*. New York: Picador, 2002.

———. "The Vision Thing: Were the DC and Seattle Protests Unfocused, or Are Critics Missing the Point?" In *From ACT UP to the WTO: Urban Protest and Community Building in the Era of Globalization*, ed. Benjamin Shepard and Ronald Hayduk. London: Verso, 2002.

Koch, Eric. *Inside "Seven Days": The Show That Shook the Nation*. Scarborough, Ont.: Prentice-Hall/Newcastle, 1986.

Lacayo, Richard, and Joel Stein. "Winners and Losers." *Time*, Nov. 15, 2004.

Lasn, Kalle. *Culture Jam: How to Reverse America's Suicidal Consumer Binge—and Why We Must*. New York: HarperCollins, 1999.

MacFarquhar, Larissa. "The Populist: Michael Moore Can Make You Cry." *New Yorker*, Feb. 16, 2004.

Mamber, Stephen. *Cinema Verité in America*. Cambridge, Mass.: MIT Press, 1974.

Marmor, Theodore R., Kieke G. H. Okma, and Joseph R. Rojas. "What It Is, What It Does and What It Might Do: A Review of Michael Moore's *Sicko*." *American Journal of Bioethics* 7.10 (2007): 49–51.

Mattson, Kevin. "The Perils of Michael Moore." *Dissent* 50.2 (Spring 2003): 75–80.

McAfee, Noëlle. "Two Feminisms." *Journal of Speculative Philosophy* 19.2 (2005): 140–49.

McGrath, Charles. "No Kidding: Does Irony Illuminate or Corrupt?" *New York Times*, Aug. 5 2000, http://query.nytimes.com/gst/fullpage.html?res=9D07E2DC153CF936A3575BC0A9669C8B63&sec=&spon=&pagewanted=print.

McKain, Aaron. "Not Necessarily Not the News: Gatekeeping, Remediation, and *The Daily Show*." *Journal of American Culture* 28 (2005): 415–30.

"Merriam-Webster's Words of the Year: 2006." *Merriam-Webster's*, http://www.m-w.com/info/06words.htm.

Miller, Tim, and David Román. "Preaching to the Converted." *Theatre Journal* 47.2 (May 1995): 169–88.

Mittell, Jason. *Genre and Television: From Cop Shows to Cartoons in American Culture*. New York: Routledge, 2004.

Monchuk, Judy. "Satire Gives Mercer Far More than 22 Minutes of Fame: Comedian Honoured at Banff Festival." *Montreal Gazette*, June 9, 2003.

Moore, Michael. *Downsize This: Random Threats from an Unarmed American*. New York: Crown, 1996.

———. *Dude, Where's My Country?* New York: Warner, 2003.

———. "In the Clearing Stands a Boxer . . . A Letter from Michael Moore." Michael Moore email list (Jan. 8, 2005), http://www.michaelmoore.com/words/mikes-letter/in-the-clearing-stands-a-boxer-a-letter-from-michael-moore.

———. "People's Choice Awards Nominates *Fahrenheit 9/11* as 'Favorite Film of the Year.'" Michael Moore email list (Dec. 8, 2004), in author's possession.

———. *Stupid White Men*. New York: Regan, 2001.

"Morgan Spurlock Discusses His Documentary *Super Size Me*." *All Things Considered*, National Public Radio, WBEZ, Chicago, May 6, 2004.

Morreale, Joanne. "Jon Stewart and *The Daily Show:* I Thought You Were Going to Be Funny!" In *Satire TV: Politics and Comedy in the Post-Network Era*, ed. Jonathan Gray, Jeffrey P. Jones, and Ethan Thompson. New York: New York University Press, 2009.

Morris, Jonathan S., and Jody C. Baumgartner. "*The Daily Show* and Attitudes toward the News Media." In *Laughing Matters*, ed. Jody C. Baumgartner and Jonathan S. Morris. New York: Routledge, 2008.

"Most Fascinating People of 2004." *The Barbara Walters Special*, ABC, Dec. 8, 2004.

Muñoz, José. *Dis-Identifications: Queers of Color and the Performance of Politics*. Minneapolis: University of Minnesota Press, 1999.

Myerson, Sylvie. "Art of Confusion: An Interview with RTMark's Frank Guerrero." *In These Times* (Apr. 1, 2002), http://www.inthesetimes.com/issue/26/09/culture3.shtml.

Napier, Jack, and John Thomas. "The BLF Manifesto." *BLF*, www.billboardliberation.com/manifesto.html.

Nash, Knowlton. *Prime Time at Ten: Behind-the-Camera Battles of Canadian TV Journalism*. Toronto: McClelland and Stewart, 1987.

Nestruck, Kelly J. "Like a 90-Minute Participaction [*sic*] Spot." *National Post,* May 7, 2004.

Newfield, Jack. "An Interview with Michael Moore." *Tikkun* 13.6 (1998): 25–29.

Newman, Andy. "Irony Is Dead. Again. Yeah, Right." *New York Times,* Nov. 23, 2008.

New York Times Special Edition Writers. "Hundreds Claim Credit for *New York Times* Spoof." *New York Times,* Nov. 12, 2008.

———. "Newspaper Blankets U.S. Cities, Proclaims End to War." *New York Times,* Nov. 12, 2008.

Nichols, Bill. *Introduction to Documentary*. Bloomington: Indiana University Press, 2001.

———. "The Voice of Documentary." In *New Challenges for Documentary,* ed. Alan Rosenthal. Berkeley: University of California Press, 1988.

Nolley, Ken. "*Fahrenheit 9/11:* Documentary, Truth-Telling and Politics." *Film and History: An Interdisciplinary Journal of Film and Television Studies* 35.2 (2005): 12–16.

Now with Bill Moyers. PBS, July 11, 2003.

Nuttall-Smith, Chris. "Wit of the Water Cooler." *Montreal Gazette,* Nov. 1, 2003.

"Obama's Loss Traced to Non-Voter." *CNNBC Video,* http://www.cnnbcvideo.com/?combined=Amber%20Day&first=Amber&name_id=32749&last=Day&id=14590–577450-bYQdWrx&nid=cYI.GrbSBFdsQM73_4g8SDMyNzQ5.

O'Neill, Terry. "This Hour Has 22 Puerile Minutes." *Alberta Report,* Apr. 1, 2002.

"O'Reilly Discusses *The Daily Show*." *The O'Reilly Factor,* Fox, Sept. 17, 2004.

Orenstein, Claudia. "Agitational Performance, Now and Then." *Theater* 31.3 (2001): 139–51.

Orvell, Miles. "Documentary Film and the Power of Interrogation: *American Dream & Roger and Me*." *Film Quarterly* 48.2 (1994–1995): 10–18.

"Over the Shark You Go, Rick." *Toronto Star,* Feb. 8, 2005.

Parker, Kathleen. "American Cynicism Becomes Terrorist Tool." *Chicago Tribune,* Aug. 4, 2004.

Peterson, Russell L. *Strange Bedfellows: How Late-Night Comedy Turns Democracy into a Joke*. New Brunswick, N.J.: Rutgers University Press, 2008.

Pevere, Geoff. "Yes Men: Droll Pranksters Playing the Corporate Game." *Toronto Star,* Oct. 1, 2004.

Poniewozik, James. "Dave Eggers' Mystery Box." *Time,* July 2, 2000.

———. "Stop This Horrible Scourge before It Destroys Us All!" *Fortune,* Oct. 11, 1999.

Purdy, Jedediah. *For Common Things: Irony, Trust, and Commitment in America Today*. New York: Knopf, 1999.

Reed, T. V. *The Art of Protest: Culture and Activism from the Civil Rights Movement to the Streets of Seattle*. Minneapolis: University of Minnesota Press, 2005.

"Republican Launches 'Buy-Back' of Moore Film." *Globe and Mail,* Sept. 18, 2004.

Riley, Susan. "The Unofficial Opposition: *This Hour* Troupers Are Prepared to Be the Voice of the Downtrodden—as Long as There's a Laugh in It." *Toronto Star,* Feb. 16, 1997.

Robbins, Bruce. *The Phantom Public Sphere*. Minneapolis: University of Minnesota Press, 1993.

Rosenblatt, Roger. "The Age of Irony Comes to an End." *Time,* Sept. 24, 2001.

Rowan and Martin's Laugh-In. NBC, Feb. 5, 1968.

Rubin, Jerry. *Do It! Scenarios of the Revolution.* New York: Ballantine, 1970.

St. John, Warren. "The Week That Wasn't." *New York Times,* Oct. 3, 2004.

"Sarah Silverman and the Great Schlep." *YouTube* (2008), http://www.youtube.com/watch?v=AgHHX9R4Qtk.

Sawyer, Eric. "An ACT UP Founder 'Acts Up' for Africa's Access to AIDS." In *From ACT UP to the WTO: Urban Protest and Community Building in the Era of Globalization,* ed. Benjamin Shepard and Ronald Hayduk. London: Verso, 2002.

Scannell, Paddy. "Britain: Public Service Broadcasting, from National Culture to Multiculturalism." In *Public Broadcasting for the 21st Century,* ed. Marc Raboy. Luton, England: University of Luton Press, 1996.

Schechner, Richard. *Between Theater and Anthropology.* Philadelphia: University of Pennsylvania Press, 1985.

———. *The Future of Ritual: Writings on Culture and Performance.* London: Routledge, 1993.

———. *Performance Theory.* London: Routledge, 1988.

Schutz, Charles E. *Political Humor: From Aristophanes to Sam Ervin.* Cranbury, N.J.: Associated University Presses, 1977.

Sconce, Jeffrey. "What If? Charting Television's New Textual Boundaries." In *Television after TV: Essays on a Medium in Transition,* ed. Lynn Spigel and Jan Olsson. Durham, N.C.: Duke University Press, 2004.

Scott, A. O. "Now Playing: Eisner and Me." *New York Times,* May 16, 2004.

———. "When All Those Big Macs Bite Back." *New York Times,* May 7, 2004.

Scott, James C. *Domination and the Arts of Resistance: Hidden Transcripts.* New Haven, Conn.: Yale University Press, 1990.

Shepard, Benjamin. "Introductory Notes on the Trail from ACT UP to the WTO." In *From ACT UP to the WTO: Urban Protest and Community Building in the Era of Globalization,* ed. Benjamin Shepard and Ronald Hayduk. London: Verso, 2002.

Shepard, Benjamin, and Ronald Hayduk. "Public versus Private Spaces, Battlegrounds, and Movements." In *From ACT UP to the WTO: Urban Protest and Community Building in the Era of Globalization,* ed. Benjamin Shepard and Ronald Hayduk. London: Verso, 2002.

———. "Urban Protest and Community Building in the Era of Globalization." In *From ACT UP to the WTO: Urban Protest and Community Building in the Era of Globalization,* ed. Benjamin Shepard and Ronald Hayduk. London: Verso, 2002.

Slack, Donovan. "Billionaires for Bush? Well, Yes and No." *Boston Globe,* Mar. 26, 2004.

Smith, Lynn. "On the Other Side of the Desk, Stewart Puts the Jokes Aside." *Los Angeles Times,* Oct. 18, 2004.

Speier, Hans. *Force and Folly: Essays on Foreign Affairs and the History of Ideas.* Cambridge, Mass.: MIT Press, 1969.

Spigel, Lynn. "Entertainment Wars: Television Culture after 9/11." *American Quarterly* 56.2 (2004): 235–70.

———. "Introduction." In *Television after TV: Essays on a Medium in Transition,* ed. Lynn Spigel and Jan Olsson. Durham, N.C.: Duke University Press, 2004.

———. *Make Room for TV: Television and the Family Ideal in Postwar America.* Chicago: University of Chicago Press, 1992.

Spurlock, Morgan. *Don't Eat This Book: Fast Food and the Supersizing of America.* New York: Penguin, 2005.
"Stephen Colbert's *The Colbert Report* Skewers TV's Political Talking Heads." *60 Minutes,* CBS, Apr. 30, 2006.
Talen, Bill. "Statement of Belief." *RevBilly,* www.revbilly.com/about_us.
———. *What Should I Do if Reverend Billy Is in My Store?* New York: New Press, 2003.
———. "Who's Your Devil?" *RevBilly,* www.revbilly.com/campaigns/interventions.php#devil.
Taylor, Louisa. "Public Discourse from the Cheap Seats." *Ottawa Citizen,* Apr. 9, 2006.
"The Province APEC Wrap Page 1." (1997). http://gmedia.tripod.com/apc_satx.htm.
Thompson, Kevin D. "Faking News Alert! Faking News Alert! On the Set of Jon Stewart's *Daily Show.*" *Palm Beach Post,* Oct. 29, 2004.
Tinic, Serra. "Speaking 'Truth' to Power? Television Satire, *Rick Mercer Report,* and the Politics of Place and Space." In *Satire TV: Politics and Comedy in the Post-Network Era,* ed. Jonathan Gray, Jeffrey Jones, and Ethan Thompson. New York: New York University Press, 2009.
Toplin, Robert Brent. *Michael Moore's "Fahrenheit 9/11": How One Film Divided a Nation.* Lawrence: University Press of Kansas, 2006.
Warner, Jamie. "Tyranny of the Dichotomy: Prophetic Dualism, Irony, and *The Onion.*" *Electronic Journal of Communication* 18.2–4 (2008), http://www.cios.org/www/ejc/EJCPUBLIC/018/2/01841.html.
Warner, Michael. "The Mass Public and the Mass Subject." In *Habermas and the Public Sphere,* ed. Craig Calhoun. Cambridge, Mass.: MIT Press, 1992.
———. *Publics and Counterpublics.* New York: Zone, 2002.
"White House Correspondents' Association Dinner." C-SPAN, Apr. 29, 2006.
Williams, Linda. "Mirrors without Memory: Truth, History and the New Documentary." *Film Quarterly* 46.2 (1992–1993): 9–21.
Williams, Raymond. *The Sociology of Culture.* Chicago: University of Chicago Press, 1995.
Yes Men. "FAQ." *The Yes Men,* www.theyesmen.org/faq.
———. "Identity Correction." *The Yes Men,* www.theyesmen.org.
"The Yes Men." *Time Out New York,* Feb. 16, 2005.
Young, Dannagal Goldthwaite. "*The Daily Show* as the New Journalism: In Their Own Words." In *Laughing Matters,* ed. Jody C. Baumgartner and Jonathan S. Morris. London: Routledge, 2008.
———. "*Daily Show* Viewers Knowledgeable about Presidential Campaign." *Annenberg Public Policy Center* (2004), http://www.annenbergpublicpolicycenter.org/naes/2004_03_late-night-knowledge-2_9-21_pr.pdf.
Young, Iris Marion. *Justice and the Politics of Difference.* Princeton, N.J.: Princeton University Press, 1990.
Zion, Lawrie. "Affirmative Action Men." *Australian,* July 6, 2005.

INDEX

Page numbers in italics indicate photographs.

AMBER DAY is Assistant Professor of Performance Studies in the English and Cultural Studies Department at Bryant University. Her research focuses on irony, satire, and political debate.